Book Typography

Ari Rafaeli

Book Typography

Oak Knoll Press

The British Library

2005

First published in 2005 by
Oak Knoll Press
310 Delaware Street, New Castle, Delaware, USA
www.oakknoll.com

and

The British Library
96 Euston Road, London NW1 2DB, UK

Library of Congress Cataloging-in-Publication Data
    Rafaeli, Ari.
      Book typography / Ari Rafaeli.
          p.   cm.
      Includes bibliographical references and index.
      ISBN 1-58456-157-2
      1. Graphic design (Typography). 2. Type and type-founding.
      3. Typesetting. 4. Book design. I. Title.
      Z246.R25 2005
      686.2'24—dc22   2004063582

British Library Cataloguing-in-Publication Data
A CIP Record for this book is available from The British Library

ISBN 1-58456-157-2 (Oak Knoll Press)
ISBN 0-7123-0693-5 (The British Library)

Designed and typeset by the author in 11-point Monotype Ehrhardt
Publishing Director: J. Lewis von Hoelle

Ari Rafaeli's web address is www.rafaeli.co.uk

Printed and bound in the United States of America on archival, acid-
free paper meeting the requirements of the American Standard for
Permanence of Paper for Printed Library Materials.

Contents

As a typographer, you are the servant of the author – colleague, if you like – but your job is to help the author to reach his public. You are not making works of art of your own; you are transmitting, with as much skill, grace and efficiency as may be required, the words of someone else.

RUARI M^cLEAN
The Thames and Hudson Manual of Typography

The work of the inside designer is an extension of the publisher's editorial function. Nothing in the layout of the page, or the chapter openings or the preliminary pages should be allowed to call attention to itself and so distract the reader from what the author has to say. The keynote of the typography should, therefore, be simplicity, legibility and common sense.

EDWARD YOUNG
from a speech given at the opening of the National Book League's Exhibition of British Book Production, 1967

Preface and acknowledgements

This book presents a personal view of modern book typography but it is also intended to instruct. I shall trust that the reader won't find it difficult to distinguish reference to universal principles from personal tastes which may none the less be instructive or useful also.

I do not agree with the opinion of some writers that the design of books is 'an arcane subject'. The student and the practitioner are interested in rational approaches to practical problems. This book is concerned with the kind of typography which requires, as Stanley Morison said in his *First Principles*, 'an obedience to convention which is almost absolute'. This is not to say that personal tastes should be deemed impermissible or thought to be necessarily disobedient to convention. In the production of a book there are at every turn choices of different treatments and variations of treatments to be considered and applied with adroitness, sensitivity and imagination. And the factor of taste, if it is the product of extensive study and practice, is as necessary to typography as it is to any other craft.

The focus of this book is on the design of literary texts but most of the principles and methods which are examined are applicable to other kinds of book and text typography. The chapter on style (punctuation, dashes, etc.) deals only with some of the more disputed problems. The final chapter is a survey of popular text types with remarks on the serviceability of the current digital versions of them. Hardly more than a cursory glance is taken of the types and, indeed, in the other chapters one has merely touched upon complicated and ramified matters.

'Points' and 'picas' are used according to their desktop publishing descriptions (12 points = 1 pica; 6 picas = 1 inch), and 'em' when used alone will refer to the body size of a type (e.g. 'an indent of two ems'). Dimensions are given height before width. 'Leading' is used in the modern sense to mean any kind of line-spacing in composed text.

This book was composed by means of QuarkXPress 4 on my four-years-old Macintosh iMac which uses an OS 9 operating system; pages 27 and 29 were composed in Adobe InDesign 3 (the most recent version of the application) by means of another iMac which uses the OS X operating system. One desires to be as up-to-date as possible, but one's circumstances did not allow for more up-to-date equipment or material than what were used. At the time of this book's publication the most recent version of QuarkXPress is version 6; there is no essential difference, however, in respect of parameters and methods between later versions of QuarkXPress and the version which was used and described in this book. The reader should therefore find the information and remarks pertaining to QuarkXPress applicable to the newer versions of the application and the OS X operating system.

My warmest thanks to Robin Nicholas (the Senior Luminary at Monotype, as Lawrence Wallis calls him) for his generous contribution of types;

to the Newberry Library in Chicago; St Bride Printing Library in London; Plantin-Moretus Museum in Antwerp; to Michael Harvey MBE; Richard Hendel; Zuzana Licko; Bob Hlavna, Dan Ryan and The Henderson Company in Chicago; R. Russell Maylone, curator of Special Collections at the Deering Library of Northwestern University at Evanston, Illinois. I am greatly indebted to Dennis Jarrett, Tom Asch, José Escobar, Ric Addy, Ric Graham, Bill Tarlin, and to my family, for their unstinted assistance, support and good advice.

Above all I am grateful to Mr John von Hoelle of the Oak Knoll Press for agreeing to publish this book of personal tastes and views and allowing me the greatest latitude for editorial control and direction of its design.

1 The school of close spacing

Good text typography is distinguished by close and even spacing of words and this is always to be preferred to loose or excessive word-space, even if it means numerous word-breaks in a paragraph or on a page. This is not a heretical idea but, as Geoffrey Dowding shows in *Finer Points in the Spacing and Arrangement of Type*, an 'established practice for over five hundred years':

> An examination of the best work of the most famous printers since the mid-fifteenth century seems to indicate that one belief was held commonly, and adhered to consistently, by them all: they believed, as all good printers nowadays believe, that when words are set for continuous reading they should always be *closely* spaced and not en or em quadded![1]

The first Penguins were published in 1935 and in a year over three million were sold. Owing to the great production volume the composition was always done by many printers scattered throughout the country (among them Cox & Wyman at Reading, Hunt, Barnard & Co. and Hazell, Watson & Viney at Aylesbury, Clays at Bungay, Suffolk, C. Nicholls & Co. at Manchester, the venerable R. & R. Clark of Edinburgh) and no consistent style existed before Jan Tschichold was put in charge of typography in 1947. Before Tschichold, by Gerald Cinamon's account, 'the design and production for the first 12 years varied from the shoddy to the ingenious.'[2] The Penguin Composition Rules (originally four pages, expanded to eight pages after Tschichold's tenure) were over time adopted by most of the British book printers and their influence continues to the present day. The first words read: 'All text composition should be as closely word-spaced as possible. As a rule the spacing should be about a middle space or the thickness of an "i" in the type size used.'[3]

We'll note here that while much of book typography produced at present is poor, the history of typography is chequered and the present situation is not the result of continuous or inexorable decline. But that is cold comfort, for unfortunately the basic tenet (the 'absolute principle', as Ruari McLean calls it) of close word-spacing is not very well observed today, even at the better houses, and slovenly composition with excessive word-space and the deplorable *rivers of white* which occur as a consequence is now quite common. So common that perhaps there's now a taste for it. The reason for this is a matter of much debate and of course there are the usual suspects: faults of technology, corporate cost-cutting (by outsourcing and other means), a change of ethos in the industry and the craft and in society, democratisation of printing arts brought about by desktop publishing, lack of traditional training and so lack of appreciation for standards of quality.

Standards of quality are seen to suffer during periods of technological transition and in the graphic arts industry the past fifty years have been a period of constant technological transition. And it is true that hyphenation routines have been faulty and parameters defining middle word-space,

Fig. 1 The perils of outsourcing. In the 1990s many of John Murray's books were typeset by Pure Tech India Ltd (now called Kolam Information Services Pvt Ltd), at Pondicherry, and though the publisher's costs may have been reduced, the quality of typography was severely diminished so that only a handful of divided words are found in *Ancient as the Hills* by James Lees-Milne (1997) but there's no shortage of word-space. It may have been that directions were given to hyphenate as little as possible to keep reading and correction costs down. The reference marks (which are doubled here – figures should have been used) are set in smaller point-sizes than the text and po-sitioned higher than the ascenders. Proper Bembo italic non-lining or 'old style' figures appear in the italic date-lines only after p. 119; until then they are Baskerville italic lining figures (in the first two entries on pp. 3–4), as can be seen here, and then they are Baskerville italic old-style figures, but once, on p. 115, just before they're cor-rectly set, they are *roman* Bembo old style! This oddity is all the odder because Bembo old-style figures are properly set in an earlier book of Lees-Milne's diaries of the same style, *A Mingled Measure* (1994), also produced by Pure Tech.

It is a challenge to read such a book (wor-thy as the writing is) but the good news seems to be that the publishers have now restored or much improved their standards. It was discovered by many publishers that the costs of correcting an outsourced job could make it more dear than if it were done at home. Typesetting has lately been done at Servis Filmsetting Ltd in Manchester. Reduced from 234 mm deep.

---

4   ANCIENT AS THE HILLS

faintest envy. Such honours mean very little to me, which sounds disingenuous, but truthfully isn't; also I *know* that Robin has done far more for the N. Trust than I ever did. I had my years of glory, a long time ago, twenty-five years or more, but did not sustain them. No, I am happy that Robin's services have been recognized. These are honest sentiments.

A. and I went to Leslie Hartley's[*] memorial service in Holy Trinity, Brompton. Congregation large, all old friends, most of them with one foot in the grave. The young seldom go to such services, and when they do their youth shines out like a good deed in a naughty world. We sang the first hymn, which had a phrase reminding us, the singers, how short a time we had to go. Not very tactful, I thought. Christabel Aberconway,[†] escorted by Ralph Dutton,[‡] sat beside me. She smelled of gin and talked throughout. Took one of my fingers and said loudly, 'Do you remember who I am?' Poor Norah Smallwood[§] felt faint and had to walk out, a long way down the nave all by herself. She sat under the tower with smelling salts and was taken home by Lennox and Freda.[¶]

Thursday, 11th January

Hugh Montgomery-Massingberd[**] lunched at Brooks's. Told me more news of the plans for Burke which he is fostering. Thinks that Weldon, the part owner of Bryant's index, may edit Burke's guide to country houses. Hugh definitely intends to tackle this formidable task, with the help of a committee of people like John Harris,[††] John Cornforth,[‡‡] me, etc. Is producing next month Burke's *Guide to the Royal Family* which won't interest me much. He

[*] L. P. Hartley, 1895–1972; novelist; author of *The Go-Between*, etc.
[†] Christabel, Lady Aberconway, widow of 2nd Baron (who d. 1953).
[‡] Ralph Dutton, FSA, 1898–1985; architectural historian and writer; s. cousin as 8th Baron Sherborne, 1982.
[§] Norah Smallwood, 1909–84; publisher; chairman of Chatto and Windus.
[¶] Lennox Berkeley, 1903–90; Kt 1974; composer; m. 1946 Freda Bernstein (b. 1923).
[**] Hugh Montgomery-Massingberd, b. 1946; genealogist, writer, and Obituary Editor of the *Daily Telegraph* 1986–94.
[††] Architectural historian; b. 1931.
[‡‡] Architectural historian, and writer, notably for *Country Life*.

variously called 'normal', 'desired', or 'optimum' space, have been unsatisfactory.* In 1991 Lawrence Wallis took a particularly poor view of 'optimum space'.

Loose word spacing is a modern malaise afflicting much composition and emanates principally from computer line justification algorithms targeting on a so-called 'optimum' space, instead of on a thoughtfully-established minimum space appropriate to the typeface in use. ... Opening up the text to a wider optimum space induces an ugly and discomforting gappiness which deprives a page of colour and cohesion. The Seybold organisation in the U.S.A. has been vocal and prominent in encouraging software developers to incorporate an optimum space in line justification algorithms and to the detriment of fine composition. Optimum, as a description, is a scandalous misrepresentation for a wider than necessary average inter-word space.[4]

But one wonders if poor hyphenation routines weren't a greater problem. In any event, the width of the 'optimum' space which was found in desktop page-layout applications in 1991, such as QuarkXPress, was relatively easy for the user to adjust (or specify) – as it is now. Indeed that was the idea. The 'optimum' space can be rendered identical to the 'thoughtfully-established minimum space' if you desire, and even if it is wider than the minimum it can be adjusted in such a way that it will not induce any gappiness – indeed to the thickness of an 'i'.

If truth be told, the normal or 'middle' word-space of both the Monotype metal-cast typesetters and the Monophoto filmsetter was a little on the wide side also and actually very near the width of the QuarkXPress word-space when adjusted to 100 per cent.† An adjusted optimum space of 80 per cent was used for the text of this book.

All text composition should be as closely word-spaced as possible.
Optimum word-space 110 per cent (QuarkXPress default)

All text composition should be as closely word-spaced as possible.
Optimum word-space 100 per cent

All text composition should be as closely word-spaced as possible.
Optimum word-space 80 per cent

A greater mischief perhaps was that the Quark defaults allowed for (or caused) automatic adjustments of character-space (see fig. 3 on page 13). Adjustment of character-space – increasing or decreasing – by various methods to mitigate the excessive word-space which occurs when an inappropriate measure is used, or when hyphenation is inadequately applied, is an expedient which has been practised since the early 1960s when second-generation filmsetting made it possible, but it has never been done to good effect. There seems lately to be a trend in this direction notwithstanding and automatic modification of character-space and also of character widths (to reduce hyphenation and render closer word-space) are featured in one of the newer but already very popular applications ('poised to take publishing into the new millennium'[5]): Adobe InDesign (introduced in 1998).

* Called 'normal' in later versions of the Corel and Xerox Ventura page-layout applications (user-modifiable h&j's did not exist in earlier versions), 'desired' in Aldus (later Adobe) PageMaker and InDesign, and 'optimum' in QuarkXPress.

† 4, 5, or 6 units of an 18-unit em (a lower-case i had a width of 5 units); a facility for 3-unit space was available only as a special attachment.

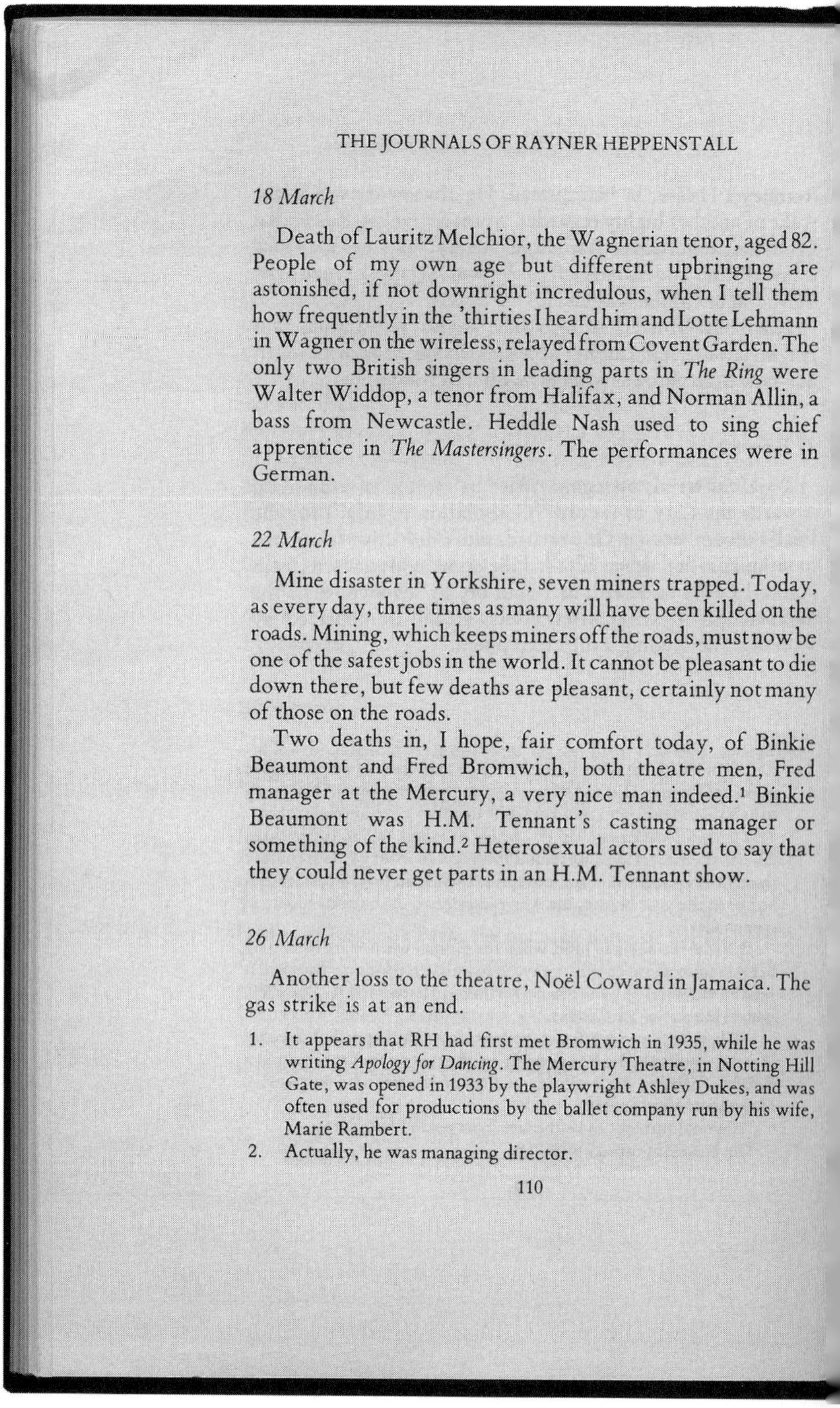

Fig. 2 In slovenly typesetting a collateral damage is done by the great contrasts which occur between lines with excessive word-space and lines with normal word-space. In the caption to fig. 1 I impute the poor state of recent book typography to outsourcing but shoddy work can just as easily be produced at home, as can be seen in Rayner Heppenstall's journals, *The Master Eccentric*, published by Allison & Busby in 1986, typeset at All Print Services, Bromley. The main text, set in 11/13 Bembo, has suffered letter-spacing (or 'positive tracking') and, as in the example of fig. 1, hyphenation is nearly non-existent and so great splodges of word-space are found in every page. Note also the tightly-spaced headline, folio set smaller than text (the size of the footnotes), the entry dates drifting above the entries, the want of non-lining figures, f-ligatures, the curious treatment of footnotes set with reverse indents, full figures and unnecessary mutton. The whiting-out (spacing of paragraphs) which has got to be done in any diary is here however done rather sloppily with the entry for 26 March too close to the footnotes. It would seem that desktop publishing was not the cause of the 'modern malaise' as this job was produced long before desktop publishing applications existed and there are many such examples. Reduced from 234 mm deep.

THE JOURNALS OF RAYNER HEPPENSTALL

18 March

Death of Lauritz Melchior, the Wagnerian tenor, aged 82. People of my own age but different upbringing are astonished, if not downright incredulous, when I tell them how frequently in the 'thirties I heard him and Lotte Lehmann in Wagner on the wireless, relayed from Covent Garden. The only two British singers in leading parts in *The Ring* were Walter Widdop, a tenor from Halifax, and Norman Allin, a bass from Newcastle. Heddle Nash used to sing chief apprentice in *The Mastersingers*. The performances were in German.

22 March

Mine disaster in Yorkshire, seven miners trapped. Today, as every day, three times as many will have been killed on the roads. Mining, which keeps miners off the roads, must now be one of the safest jobs in the world. It cannot be pleasant to die down there, but few deaths are pleasant, certainly not many of those on the roads.

Two deaths in, I hope, fair comfort today, of Binkie Beaumont and Fred Bromwich, both theatre men, Fred manager at the Mercury, a very nice man indeed.[1] Binkie Beaumont was H.M. Tennant's casting manager or something of the kind.[2] Heterosexual actors used to say that they could never get parts in an H.M. Tennant show.

26 March

Another loss to the theatre, Noël Coward in Jamaica. The gas strike is at an end.

1. It appears that RH had first met Bromwich in 1935, while he was writing *Apology for Dancing*. The Mercury Theatre, in Notting Hill Gate, was opened in 1933 by the playwright Ashley Dukes, and was often used for productions by the ballet company run by his wife, Marie Rambert.
2. Actually, he was managing director.

110

Word-division

Perhaps the idea of modifying character-space and design of characters would have less currency if a better approach to word-division were taken. It may want some undoing of certain cherished prejudices. Of the matter of specifying a minimum number of letters of a divided word to follow a hyphen, a user's guide for InDesign counsels: 'Some people don't mind if the "ly" in "truly" sits all by itself on a line. You care about type, so you set this to at least three.'[6] And this seems to have become an *idée reçue*.

InDesign provides two devices for control of hyphenation which are not featured in other applications: (1) the Paragraph Composer which, according to the company's literature, 'considers the implications of breakpoints across an entire paragraph' and *evaluates* 'the downstream implications of a line break' and so adjusts 'earlier lines in a paragraph to eliminate unattractive spacing later on' in order to render 'more even spacing and fewer hyphens – desirable goals in any publishing context',[7] and (2) a 'Hyphen-

Fig. 3 'Edit Hyphenation & Justification' dialog box for QuarkXPress version 4, showing the default settings. In the box under 'Name:' the user labels his/her customised parameters. When 'Break Capitalized Words' is unticked it is not possible to divide any word which is capitalised. Automatic modification of character-spacing by 4% is allowed.

Fig. 4 (*a*) The Hyphenation dialog box for Adobe InDesign version 3, showing default settings. If indeed 'words longer than 5 letters' is the default (as it appears to be on the particular application I've used) that is well (longer than four would be better), but other examples in Adobe's own literature show the number as set at seven. Note the 'Hyphenation Penalty Slider' and the choice of 'Better Spacing' or 'Fewer Hyphens'. (*b*) The Justification dialog box with 'Glyph Scaling' for automatic condensing or expanding of letter-forms (horizontal scaling). The default settings in both programs (Quark and InDesign) concern us because they *suggest* to the user a desirable standard of style.

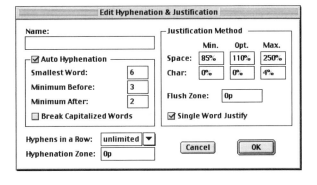

(*a*)

(*b*)

ation Penalty Slider', which 'recalculates the hyphenation for the paragraph',[8] 'so you can strike a balance between even text spacing and minimal hyphenation; if you select the Preview option, you can see the results interactively'[9] (fig. 4), because 'when even spacing is achieved by an over-reliance on hyphenation, the resulting "ladders" or stacked hyphens are equally undesirable'.

This sentence appears not in the original Penguin Rules but in the expanded Rules of 1972: 'An effort should, however, be made to avoid more than two successive hyphens and hyphens at the end of pages, particularly recto pages.'[10] This is obviously a right and proper principle which accords with every book printer's principles, but unfortunately it is nowadays often invoked at the expense of proper spacing.

One of the illustrations in Geoffrey Dowding's *Finer Points* is a detail of the 42-line Bible of Gutenberg, printed in Mainz, *c.* 1455. In this particular detail there are seven hyphens in succession. On page 15 he writes:

> It is a most unfortunate fact that many apprentice compositors are still being taught that to have more than two successive break lines, i.e. lines ending with a divided word, is bad practice. This kind of training encourages the easy, slovenly solution: it is infinitely preferable to have a number of break lines succeeding each other than to have openly spaced lines.

The school of close spacing demands firm adherence to its principles; it does not allow for ambivalence, diffidence, indecision; it views with suspicion the sliding of Hyphenation Penalty Sliders.* If it's a choice between an 'awkward' but permissible break (at *ly*, *er*, *ed* (if pronounced as a syllable)) and a conspicuous increase of word-space in a given line, it is better to break.†

'And in ease of reading we tend to gain more by the close spacing of words than we lose in the momentary pauses occasioned at the ends of lines by word-division: one pauses at the end of each line in any case.' (Geoffrey Dowding, *Finer Points*, p. 14.)

There are two principles of word-division: the etymological (or rootbased) and the phonetic (or syllabic), the latter long-established in the US and now widely adopted in Britain (though it's been vigorously resisted especially in the old groves of Academe). An example: etymologically: *omnipo-tent*; phonetically: *om-nip-o-tent*.

There are, depending who you ask, 350 to 480 million speakers of English in the world at present but not as many who are are well-versed in etymology; when the majority of people read, however, they are cognisant of the

---

* But in favour of the idea we may refer to this passage from Ronald McIntosh's *Hyphenation*: 'Some years ago, when the old technology still ruled, a famous dictionary was set by this dedicated breed of workers. In the printed product only four or five hyphens showed on a double-column page. When the same text had to be reprocessed by a powerful computer, every page displayed as many as 20 or 30 hyphens. The new method could not match the quality of the old because of the limitations of the computer program, which had not been instructed how to "cut and try again" for a better result. Happily, automatic justification is now getting better all the time.'

† In QuarkXPress it is often possible to bring an 'ly' up (if it's not followed by a punctuation) by placing the cursor just before the offending word and keying 'command–hyphen'.

The deplorable *ly*-break is sanctioned on p. 58 of *The Editor's Manual of Penguin House Style* (1973): 'Do not leave behind or take over a syllable of less than three letters except such common prefixes and suffixes as: a- de- re- in- un- -ly (not -es -ed -er)'. I have yet to leave behind a solitary *a*, but I'll suffer no qualms if I must take down *er* or *ed* and even *es*.

sounds of the words they're reading. When a word is judiciously divided by the phonetic method the end-part is foretokened by the fore-part. The phonetic method naturally deals in inconsistencies (*photo-graph, photog-raphy, psycho-path, psychol-ogy* – the short *o* in photography, biography, etc., is an *ectasis*, a lengthened syllable: one says pho-*toh*-graphy, bi-*oh*-graphy,* but the only way to indicate this (phonetically) is to break after the *g*) and it is disdained mainly for this reason, but the etymological method seems to have similar shortcomings. Ronald McIntosh, the co-inventor† of an algorithmic program for hyphenation of 'forty to fifty languages depending on how you count language' called Hyphenologist, wrote an excellent book (*Hyphenation*, 1990) and of the etymological method he says: 'There are so many cases of uncertainty and unhelpfulness generated by the etymological method that one must question both the validity and the utility of this approach. It assumes more knowledge in the reader than can reasonably be expected.'[11]

In some houses both the etymological and phonetic approaches are taken (or neither is shunned). *Hart's Rules*, on page 14: 'divide according to etymology, where this is obvious: atmo-sphere, bio-graphy, tele-phone, transport, un-equal. Otherwise divide according to *The Oxford Spelling Dictionary*.'[12]

The etymologico-phonetic approach which has been advocated also at Cambridge and Penguin, and which is still advocated in the thoroughly revised and modernised *Hart's Rules*, now called *The Oxford Guide to Style*, will not mean fewer inconsistencies – the etymological proponents' main complaint about the strictly phonetic approach. We should note here that the phonetic method, this 'frowned on'‡ American infiltration into British practice,[13] has been employed in the UK for decades. Cox & Wyman, in *Types at Your Service* in 1962, recommended a strictly phonetic method (interesting that their house style then was different to Penguin's, their main client), as did Cowells in 1952 and Mackays in 1959.

Long before the etymological principle of word-division or the American phonetic method of hyphenation prevailed, words were divided at the printer's (the compositor's or proof-reader's) discretion. In *Hyphenation* Ronald McIntosh observes:

As recently as ten years ago there was still at work a legion of grizzled compositors, journeymen who answered to the Imperial Father of the Chapel in their trade union devotions, and to the pernickety proof-readers and editors for their spelling, their adherence to house style, and their word-breaks. They were the inheritors of the once jealously guarded know-how of the art of printing, which had changed remarkably little since Gutenberg, and they served as a discreet but vital interface between the author and his readers.

Following the custom of their craft, sometimes also described as their commonsense, the comps placed the hyphens where they seemed necessary and where they looked right.

And that is more to the point. The method by which the best typography can be achieved is the one which should be used.

* Or a variation of this pronounciation. In any case, the o is the stressed syllable.
† With David Fawthrop. Ronald McIntosh was also the co-inventor (with Peter Purdy) of the Linotron 505, the first widely-used CRT typesetter, manufactured 1967–73 by Linotype-Paul.
‡ Judith Butcher, *Copy-Editing*, 2nd edn (Cambridge, 1989), p. 64.

Beyond the problem of inconsistencies or 'cases of uncertainty and un-helpfulness' in either approach lies the problem of 'bad breaks' which are computer-generated. If the phonetic is more reader-friendly than the etymological it is not necessarily more computer-friendly and such breaks as 'Be-mbo' will occur even with advanced versions of Quark.

'The break-hyphen, both British and American, is not so robust as it once was, partly because of its propagation by untutored computers in the early days of electronic composition. These produced word-breaks by the million, but since they relied on elementary, even simplistic, algorithms they very often generated "idiot breaks" '(McIntosh). This might have been the reason for the execrably unhyphenated texts shown in figures 1 and 2.

The version of QuarkXPress which is used for this book has however seldom wanted its hyphenation corrected ('Be-mbo' was one of the few anomalies) and InDesign seems also to have a reliable hyphenation routine. The user of modern programs can choose American or British (RP) routines and spelling dictionaries with confidence to divide such words as 'pro-gress' or 'prog-ress', 'con-troversy' or 'controv-ersy', and Anthony Po-well, Co-lin Pow-ell. These are brighter days.*

Even when a hyphenation routine to ensure close word-spacing is maintained there are now and again some disobliging words† or words attached to abbreviations, numbers, dates. It's bad form to take down *ble* or *que*, and proper names should never be broken between first and middle initials, nor between forename and initial, nor should VIII be separated from Henry (though any single name, forename, surname, compound surname, should be broken when the situation warrants). It is never pleasant to have to separate a title (Dr, Mr, Sir, Prof.) from its holder or the initials of orders, affixes, etc. (C.H., O.B.E., M.D.), or Jnr, Jr, but when it must be done it won't do to be squeamish. It is also never nice to bring a.m. or p.m. down to a new line, and it's even more vexing to leave p. or pp. (or fig., vol., etc.) at the end of a line. And what of dimensions or dates? Whoever desires to produce good typography will deal with such details carefully, rather than invoke simplistic and ineffectual rules which forbid the *-ly* etc.

Some points even finer

In his *Finer Points* Geoffrey Dowding also advocates, as Eric Gill did, for the use of an ampersand to replace 'and' in any line of a text where it can effect better spacing of the line. He cites these words from Gill's *An Essay on Typography* :

The absurd rule that the ampersand (&) should only be used in 'business titles' must be rescinded, & there are many other contractions which a sane typographer should encourage.[14]

* The Hyphenologist program is ' "data driven" from rule bases that are specially developed for each language taking into account "custom and practice". We find however that "custom and practice", dictionaries and published methods are substantially different from each other, and often internally inconsistent. Hyphenologist does not therefore reproduce any specific system of hyphenation.'

† Disobliging typographically: internet addresses, unspaced proprietary names (HarperCollins, InDesign).

The ampersand may be used or not used in resettings and it would not be necessary to use the symbol when quoting from printed texts in which it is used: it is a typographical element, such as a double eff, rather than a textual one.

Geoffrey Dowding shows a detail of a page of Francesco Colonna's *Hypnerotomachia Poliphili*, printed by Aldus Manutius at Venice in 1499, containing a great number of ampersands which 'despite the frequency of their occurrence . . . do not obtrude themselves'.[15] Indeed a very good case is made for the use of ampersands 'in a sensible & logical way' but it is so much at variance with the practices and tastes of the present day and also of Dowding's day that it doesn't look like ever gaining acceptance. It was obviously not very easy to follow this practice even in hand-composition but, save for a special function such as InDesign would offer, the job would be scarcely less difficult nowadays.

On pages 32–3 of *Finer Points*, Dowding says that 'The indention of the first lines of paragraphs often produces an ugly serration of the left-hand edges of pages or text columns especially when the matter consists of very short paragraphs, e.g. in conversational passages.' He suggests therefore that 'well-designed paragraph marks, either set flush or overhanging the text, should be considered as an alternative means of marking the beginnings of paragraphs.' Gill used such paragraph marks in his *Essay*; they are not used in *Finer Points* (which featured for didactic reasons a 'traditional method of setting') but are used to good effect in Dowding's second book for the Primers for Students of Typography series, *Factors in the Choice of Type Faces* (fig. 5), which is also set ragged-right (or with fixed word-space), as Gill's book is.

Readers of our first volume [*Finer Points in the Spacing and Arrangement of Type*] may remember that ragged-edged setting was advocated for work in narrow measures, and also, on occasion, for work in normal measures – as a means of securing a high standard of composition from an indifferent printer. In this book the pages have been set with an uneven right-hand edge for three reasons. First, to achieve with maximum economy what the best printers of the past insisted on, and those of the present still insist on – closely word-spaced lines of text matter; and second, to obtain this spacing consistently on a normal Monotype keyboard, that is, without special keyboard attachments. And lastly, to give students an opportunity of comparing the traditional method of setting text pages, as in *Finer Points*, with those set with an uneven right-hand edge.[16]

A ragged-right setting would look well in a book with a type area exceeding customary depth and the only reason this book is not set ragged-right is to show our h&j's in action.

Geoffrey Dowding's *Factors* provides us with a superb example of Monotype Imprint. He uses stemless paragraph marks from Monotype Lutetia in the manner of Caxton. It is a pity that special paragraph marks are seldom found in the character-sets of digital types – even the unique paragraph marks of Octavian have been replaced with the common-or-garden kind, alas! It is interesting that the paragraph marks in *Factors* are never used for 'running-in' the paragraphs and are only occasionally used in this manner in Eric Gill's *Essay*.

For the right edge (as well as left edge), Geoffrey Dowding also advocates

FACTORS IN THE CHOICE OF TYPE FACES

forced to distort their italics and make them weak and characterless.'¹ ²

abcdefghijklmnopqrstuvwxyz

abcdefghijklmnopqrstuvwxyz

abcdefghijklmnopqrstuvwxyz

abcdefghijklmnopqrstuvwxyz

fafefhfifkflfmfnfofpfrfsftfufyfaffeffiffoffuff fi fl,'.IfOfOff

abcdefghijklmnopqrstuvwxyzfffifl

Both lines of 24pt italic above are named Caslon Old Face. The first is the Linotype and the other the founder's (Stephenson Blake's) rendering of this classic face. Compare them for kerning and slope. The 12pt lines are recuttings of a 17th century face called Janson and show, in order, Linotype's Ordinary Fount of the italic, their Special No 5 Janson double-letter italic and Special No 5 double-letter italic logotypes. Last, for comparison, appears Stempel Janson italic for hand-composition. Even a brief appraisal suffices to establish the superiority of the non-slug faces.

(b) Duplexed matrices: 'Two characters on one matrix is a basic and valuable feature of the Linotype system. The extension of this principle to 18 and 24pt sizes allows the Linotype user still further advantages, because he can cast two large display founts from a single fount contained in a single magazine. This means twice the service from fount and magazine as well as the conserving of storage space. The layout man,

¹ D.C.McMurtrie. *The Ludlow System of Slugline Composition.* See bibliography, p 118.
² 'The principal difficulty in designing a non-kerning italic lies in the ascending and descending sorts and particularly in the letters *f* and *j* . . . Whereas the slope of the italic main-strokes in the kerning type will be found frequently to be as much as 1 in 3, it is necessary to reduce it to about 1 in 5 in designing a non-kerning fount, and 1 in 4 is generally the maximum slope permissible. With this the *f* requires to be considerably distorted and shows excess of side-wall and consequent space between it & the adjacent characters.' Legros and Grant. *Typographical Printing-Surfaces.* See bibliography, p 117.

96

The Method of Composition—Linotype

with an eye to practical considerations, will be quick to take advantage of these display founts . . .'¹

⟨'A basic . . . . . feature of the Linotype system'—not only for display but for the composition or text sizes also! For example, the 12 point alphabets of Granjon roman and italic upper- and lower-case shown below are duplexed.

ABCDEFGHIJKLMNOPQRSTUVWXYZ

ABCDEFGHIJKLMNOPQRSTUVWXYZ

abcdefghijklmnopqrstuvwxyz

abcdefghijklmnopqrstuvwxyz

This means that the italic alphabet is of exactly the same set-width as the roman—a principle which strikes at the very roots of good letter design. Italic handwriting, though not necessarily sloping, was normally a rapidly written & therefore somewhat compressed hand (it is difficult, if not impossible, to write a round hand quickly). It was this *natural* lateral condensation—the space saving quality of italic writing—that commended it to Aldus. Griffo preserved this feature in the first italic type—and in this the most knowledgeable of the designers & founders of italic types have followed him up to the present day.²

⟨Conversely, in the founding of jobbing types, the thickening & general modification which a normal weight (or basic) roman undergoes in its transformation to a bold face usually makes it *wider* than the type from which it derived. But when a roman face is duplexed with its bold the latter is of the same set-width as the roman.

⟨Thus in some of these duplexed founts, roman, italic and bold are all of the same set-width!

¹ *Linotype Matrix.* No 18.
² There are, of course, composition sizes of bold jobbing faces, in which the italic *is* wider than the accompanying roman.

97   H

Fig. 5 Geoffrey Dowding's *Factors in the Choice of Type Faces* (Wace, 1957), set ragged-right in 10/12 Monotype Imprint and 'printed on Wiggins Teape Dover Opaque Offset Snow White paper D/Medium 70lb' by Benham & Co. Ltd at Colchester. Paragraph marks from Lutetia, ampersand (on p. 97), no points after No (for number) and p (for page) and no space between 24 and pt; 'contained' is broken at the *ed* (p. 96), the inverted comma (open quote) in note no. 2 on p. 96 overhanging to avoid 'untidy' indention (as prescribed in pages 21–2 of *Finer Points*). It is a first-rate job of design and composition. It is also a very good example of this excellent Monotype face, the digital form of which is regrettably unserviceable. Reduced from 187 mm deep.

for hanging punctuation and this is something which Adobe InDesign advocates and offers as an 'option' they call Optical Margin Alignment. It is described in their literature with their special terms – 'frame' and 'story', meaning text area and total continuous text of a document.

When selected, it can adjust the position of characters at either end of a line in order to make the margins of a text frame appear more even; while the effect is most pronounced for punctuation marks, such as quotes and hyphens, the positions of other characters are subtly adjusted as well. The amount that characters adjacent to the frame edge move depends on the point size you enter in the Optical Margin Alignment field of the Story palette; the value you enter provides a target baseline point size to use when adjusting characters at the margins of frames in the story. Because this attribute applies to an entire story, you'll get the best results if the value you enter matches the point size of your body text.[17]

Unfortunately, in this and nearly every other of its features, InDesign tends to be over-zealous and the option causes disconcerting misalignments (or undesirable adjustments) when 'the positions of other characters are subtly adjusted as well'. Although one can specify the degree to which the hanging occurs (partially or fully outside the measure), one cannot specify for which characters or which edge (e.g. only the punctuation on the right edge and not the letter A on the left).

Character-spacing (1)

Successful marketing of filmsetting to printers in the 1950s and 1960s was owed in large part to the pains taken to make the product resemble as closely as possible the metal technology it proposed to replace.* This was true not only for the designs of the letter-forms of types but also for the side-spaces or side-bearings peculiar to a type which determine fitting† or character-space and thus the 'colour' of composed text. Some significant discrepancies occurred none the less when the designs of metal types were adopted for filmsetting types and usually the spacing of certain letter combinations of the latter was greater than the former: in filmsetting types a single type design and character-space was often used for all sizes of setting and so an 'optimum' spacing (not too close for small sizes) was needed.‡ The design and character-space of the digital versions of Linotype and Monotype faces usually followed the filmsetting types with only occasional and mostly negligible deviations.

Digital types (or 'fonts')§ are supplied with pre-programmed values for side-bearings, and also for special character combinations known as 'kern pairs', and these values are called 'metrics'. All the characters of a font must have values for side-bearings whether or not kerning (or 'pair-kerning') values are additionally specified. Generally the character-spacing of a digital type is determined by the side-bearings values but in many cases the characters are fitted with rather rough-wrought side-bearings and the manufacturer will then modify the spacing of certain character-combinations by

* By 'metal' I mean machine-cast types (Monotype or Linotype), not foundry types.

† Also called letter-fit. Character-space is also called intercharacter-space, letter-space; side-bearings are also called side-walls.

‡ Monotype produced proportional designs for display or text sizes for many of their 'Monophoto' faces.

§ Character-sets of any size of a particular type.

specifying kern pairs.* When the type is used with an application that 'supports kerning' (QuarkXPress, InDesign) the kern pairs will, by default or by operator's action, override the side-bearings values. This is known as automatic kerning; when automatic kerning is not applied the spacing is determined entirely by the side-bearings values.

The character-spacing of the type used for the main text of this book† was adjusted, using a program called Macromedia Fontographer, to render it more like the original metal version. The machine-cast type which I used as a model‡ is considerably better than the digital version as supplied for having a closer character-spacing generally (the digital version's kern pairs notwithstanding), but it has not got the tucked-in points and commas and other closed-up character combinations which are often seen in digital types and are effected by pair-kerning. The unclosed-up spaces in such combinations as Fa, Te, Vo, y., etc., of metal types were owed to the verticality of side-bearings; to bring the characters closer together they'd have to be kerned (in the method used for metal types) and that would have rendered them vulnerable to breaking, or special sorts (logotypes) would have to be made, but it is questionable whether or not they should have ever been altered.

It is of course now possible to specially adjust every conceivable combination of characters but it was also possible to do that in pre-digital filmset-

---

* This is often done in order to provide *optimum* spacing when the type is used at small point-sizes.

† A PostScript version of Monotype Ehrhardt set in 11-point.

‡ From the manufacturer's specimens.

Fig. 6 (*a*) Some lines of text from the third volume of Sir John Rothenstein's autobiography, *Time's Thievish Progress* (Cassell, 1970), set in machine-cast 11/12 Monotype Ehrhardt and printed by Ebenezer Baylis & Sons Ltd (The Trinity Press). (*b*) The lines set by myself using QuarkXPress and the PostScript version of Monotype Ehrhardt with character-spaces adjusted in Fontographer to emulate those of the metal version; (*c*) with the character-spacing as supplied. In both *b* and *c* the headline is tracked with 20 Quark units; the em-rule was condensed 10 per cent to match the rule in *a*.

(*a*)

STUDIOS AND PRIVATE FACES—II   103

however remotely, to that of certain of the abstract expressionists. The resemblance was accidental and superficial—but it momentarily obscured the fact that the artist was as solitary a figure among his contemporaries as he had ever been, and it impelled many who had ignored or discounted his work to scrutinize it with close attention.

(*b*)

STUDIOS AND PRIVATE FACES—II   103

however remotely, to that of certain of the abstract expressionists. The resemblance was accidental and superficial—but it momentarily obscured the fact that the artist was as solitary a figure among his contemporaries as he had ever been, and it impelled many who had ignored or discounted his work to scrutinize it with close attention.

(*c*)

STUDIOS AND PRIVATE FACES—II   103

however remotely, to that of certain of the abstract expressionists. The resemblance was accidental and superficial—but it momentarily obscured the fact that the artist was as solitary a figure among his contemporaries as he had ever been, and it impelled many who had ignored or discounted his work to scrutinize it with close attention.

ting technology and in the 1960s David Kindersley advocated for a complete reworking of the character-spacing derived from metal types:

> Photo-printing has brought us an entirely new set of circumstances. No hard and fast barrier need exist between letters. Letter-spacing can once again reign. Each space can be the direct expression of each character.[18]

'Each letter should appear to be exactly in the centre (i.e. in a passive position) between its two neighbours. To me this is the only criterion.'[19] I rather believe this theory is better applied to new designs than to types derived directly from earlier versions. Not everyone, moreover, believes as Kindersley did, that the machine-cast metal types were so fraught with error. In *Letters of Credit* Walter Tracy writes:

> And there is the London typesetter who was heard to say, 'Before the introduction of the adjustable spacing program filmsetting looked like metal setting' – as if the printing of the past, from Aldus and Estienne to the Elzevirs and on to Whittingham, Rudge of Mount Vernon, the Doves Press, Nonesuch and Curwen, to omit many, lacked a desirable but unattainable improvement.[20]

Many of the digital versions of formerly metal book faces feature such closed-up character combinations as mentioned above; there seems now to be quite a preference for them; they are considered to be correct and desirable; allegedly it is the 'cheaper' or inferior digital types which do not feature them. This view accords with Kindersley's:

> Art schools used to teach 'students' that their compositions should either pass beyond the frame or be kept well within, but never finish just touching the frame. I think this is a valid statement. In the same way a letter should ideally override its neighbour if the square law dictates. However, there are purists who speak of letters as sacred. They say no letter should violate another by lapping over it. To meet this somewhat dreary concept, true spacing must at that point be abandoned.[21]

But let us consider Walter Tracy's remarks about the '"kerning" routine' used in electronic or digital typography, 'which allows a letter to intrude into the "air space" of another':

> Too often the program reduces the space between the letters by too much, diminishing the identity of the letters and causing a clot of congestion. One reason for this may lie with a precedent – the logotypes To, Tr, Ye and so on which Linotype used to make for some of their book types.[22]

Such 'logotypes' were produced in great variety because of the slug-casting Linotype's inability to cast single kerned letters. They were mainly combinations of the f and a following letter but the technique was applied to some other letters in doubtful need of closing up. Walter Tracy refers to Bruce Rogers's view that 'the cutting of such letters as V, W, to make them set closer than their natural width is usually very much overdone.'

> The new logotypes cut for this purpose are equally faulty in this respect. The resulting effect is more noticeable and more objectionable than the natural setting of the type would be. Anything that strikes the eye as strange or unusual in a line of type is to be avoided.[23]

The 'natural setting' of a letter is defined by its side-bearings which are vertical as plumb-lines. Each letter or character of a roman type in its natural relation to an adjacent letter implies the existence of a straight line between them. If an r is tucked under a T, or a comma under a P or an F, an embarrassing problem is created: the natural spaces between T and i, F and l, P and h, now seem unnaturally excessive.* This should be enough to put paid to the cult of closing-up but the sad fact is that their name is Legion and the side-bearings preservationists are few.

Character-spacing (2)

While the f and J (and often the j) of a digital font are sometimes called 'vestigial' kerns, owing to placement of their side-bearings, the term now usually applies to the adjustment of font metrics as we've described and also (usually as *kerning* or *kerned*) to any decreasing of space between any two characters which is done in the process of composition, thus affecting the setting rather than the type (or the 'font'). The word is also often used for the practice of increasing space, hence 'negative' and 'positive' kerns. This species of character-spacing existed in the phototypesetting technology of the early 1970s and, owing especially to the fashion of extra-tight letter-spacing done on the drawing-table with Letraset, it proved immensely popular in commercial typography. It was practised with great zeal by advertising typesetters, not only with display type set large but (by some over-zealous folk) also to smarten-up the apostrophes, dashes, brackets or even the spaces between certain letters (v and e for example and other such combinations as were mentioned earlier) of 11-point text.

The practice is different to *tracking* (or 'range kerning') which is usually to increase or decrease the character-spacing of groups of letters, lines of text or entire texts. Words set in capitals (e.g. running heads) are thus treated to increase the letter-spacing (typically 20 units of a 200-unit em in QuarkX-Press), but otherwise the practice should not be applied to the texts of books. Nor for that matter should most letter-pairs ever be kerned or spaced in the manner described above. There are however certain anomalous combinations which occur in digital type which, if the type itself is not modified, will want added space in the setting, such as between round brackets and the letters J and f and between roman brackets and italic letters where the characters may even overlap. Also the space between letters and colons, semicolons, question and exclamation marks is usually too little in most digital types; they're given 20 Quark units in this book.†

* We should note that the italics letters d, g, j, i, y, and often A, T, V, W, have traditionally been kerned.

† 'Colons, semicolons, quotation, exclamation, and interrogation marks should be separated by an extra hair space from the words they adjoin; this also applies to the spacing between parentheses and the first and terminal letters enclosed when these letters are lower-case ascenders or descenders or capitals with upright stems, e.g. (liberated) not (liberated).' (Oliver Simon, *Introduction to Typography* (Faber and Faber, 1945), p. 30.)

'Colons and semi-colons are often carelessly spaced also. Only a hairspace is necessary *before* them, that is, between them and the words they follow, and this can be omitted if the letter preceding the colon or semi-colon happens to be f, k, r, t, v, w, x, y, or z.' (Geoffrey Dowding, *Finer Points in the Spacing and Arrangement of Type*, p. 20.) Rather curiously he does not say anything about question or exclamation marks.

See also Walter Tracy, *Letters of Credit* (Gordon Fraser, 1986), pp. 76–7, and Bruce Rogers, *Paragraphs on Printing* (New York, William E. Rudge's Sons, 1943; reprinted New York, Dover, 1979), p. 94: 'Colons and semicolons have traditionally been set apart from the word they follow, whether in capitals or lower case. In old books they are frequently centered in the space between the words where they occur. Exclamation and interrogation points should if possible be set off with thin spaces because they often form disagreeable and confusing combinations with the last letter of the word, such as ff!, ll! f?, etc.'

A variation on the theme of the three methods of character-spacing we've described is InDesign's Optical Kerning, of which they say:

> By calculating the area between two adjacent character shapes, the ideal spacing between two characters is determined based on their optical appearance. Because the approach is visually based, different point sizes or font changes are easily accommodated. Automatic optical kerning is essentially on-the-fly, and it makes short work of what can be a time-consuming manual process.[24]

The Adobe Corporation call it 'a major innovation in desktop typography' but the idea of it is not new; it has many forebears (among them the *hz*-program described below).[25] It would seem an agreeable answer to the problems created by optimum character-space but let us take note of the first part of the last sentence. *Automatic optical kerning is essentially on-the-fly.* This means that character-space is adjusted not just according to typeface and point-size (so that, for example, every combination of e and v of a particular type set in 11-point would be treated the same) but that it is also variable in the way that word-space is variable. The optical kerning option functions then in much the same way as tracking (if tracking were automatic) or a variable character-spacing value (other than 0%) in the justification routine – though less crudely, purportedly. 'Ideal spacing' is thus the spacing of a *particular* setting (particular line, paragraph, etc.) rather than that which was determined by a type's designer. And so it is unsuitable.* We want to confine variable spacing to word-space. There really seems no alternative to producing special designs for common text sizes along with appropriate character-space.

InDesign also has a Metrics Kerning option, which alternatively renders character-spacing to the type's pre-programmed values; it is essentially the same thing as 'auto kern' in QuarkXPress except that it can be applied selectively to any part of a composed job – one size of one typeface, for example – rather than affecting all of a job.

> Using the pair kerning metrics in a font offers an alternative, font-based solution to the problem of automating kerning. As part of their design, most typefaces include a table of kern pairs, which contain instructions for adjusting the space between two characters. Some fonts include robust kern pair tables; if you specify those fonts, InDesign uses all of the kern pair metrics in the font.[26]

If 'robust kern pair tables'[27] means such tuckings-in as are viewed dimly by the side-bearings preservationists, a type such as the Monotype Ehrhardt used in this book, with untucked-in commas, points, etc., would accordingly want the optical kerning option while a type such as Adobe Minion

---

* 'The design job – as any reasonable designer knows – includes an anticipation of the thing in use: this has to be built into the drawings or the computer program.

'At least as important as the printing process for this view of a typeface is the typographic treatment of the text: how long is the measure, how much space between the words and between lines. All this affects our perception of the typeface, though these factors lie outside the sphere over which the typeface designer can have any influence. But there is one area of space that the designer of a typeface may dispute with those in charge of the composition of letters, and which has a vital effect on the appearance of the typeface: *between the letters.* One can state without much fear of contradiction – certainly not from any typeface designer – that the space around the letter, between one letter and the next, is an essential factor in defining the appearance of those letterforms.' (Robin Kinross, 'What is a Typeface?' *Baseline*, no. 7 (1986), p. 17.)

wouldn't require it.* But it would seem likely that the user of the new-millennium InDesign would also use a twenty-first century type with a robust kern pair table and so should have little need the 'major innovation' of optical kerning. The user's guide isn't clear on this point.

There is also in the InDesign repertory the Glyph Scaling option for automatic modification of character widths.

The Word Spacing and Letter Spacing options allow you to control how much the text composition engines can deviate from the spacing designed into the font. The Glyph Scaling option works a little differently: rather than changing the spacing for a line of text, glyph scaling subtly adjusts the widths of the letters to lengthen or shorten a line of justified text. You can fine-tune the behavior of the composition engines by adjusting these values in the Justification dialog box.[28]

I am confused by 'lengthen or shorten a line of justified text' but obviously one would expect the option to cause a distortion of each character of an affected line of justified text and perhaps the characters of the preceding or following lines to also suffer distortions, though differently, as widening or condensing will occur according to the amount of word-space which wants either reducing or increasing. Only the *slightest* distortions, of course.

This is the idea that informs the hz-program conceived by Hermann Zapf (hz) for URW in 1988, and in his words:

it is partly based on a typographically acceptable expansion or condensing of letters, called scaling. Connected with this is a kerning program which calculates kerning values at 100 pairs per second. The kerning is not limited only to negative changes of space between two critical characters, but also allows in some cases positive kerning, which means the addition of space.[29]

It is regrettable that the venerable designer of some of the best types of the twentieth century should say that such a distortion of letter-forms is 'typographically acceptable'. It may be argued that the distortions, because they are ever so slight, won't be noticed† but that is not true: I can see them very well in Hermann Zapf's example (fig. 7).

This is all to do with a loathing of hyphens which has bedevilled typographers for many years.‡ Among them was Richard Clay IV in 1966 (as we learn from Andrew Bluhm, *Photosetting*, 1968):

Richard Clay (the Chaucer Press) Ltd. of Bungay, Essex [*sic*], a large book-printing house, became one of the first Linasec users in 1963; an account of the system based on $2\frac{1}{2}$ years' experience has been written by the company's chairman, Richard Clay. He emphasizes the importance of operator selection and training, and considers the possibility of eliminating word-breaks altogether (for books) through variations of set-width or letter-spacing on suitably equipped photosetting machines.[30]

But the Glyph Scaling option of InDesign, the hz-program, and all ideas of the kind are extravagant and extreme. The problem itself is not extreme and a satisfactory treatment of it is one which will not disturb or distort the

* But oddly the optical kerning option *opens up* such 'robust' kern pairs as 'r,' (see fig. 13).

† 'If the glyph scaling values you enter define a narrow enough range – say 98% for Minimum and 102% for Maximum – the differences in the letterforms will be noticeable only to the most attentive expert.' (Adobe Systems, 'In Depth: Text and Typography', p. 8.)

‡ The hz-program 'is a complete aesthetic program for micro-typography with a maximum of two consecutive hyphenated words. Good typography allows us up to three hyphenations.' (Hermann Zapf, 'About micro-typography and the hz-program', *Electronic Publishing*, vol. 6, no. 3 (September 1993), p. 288.)

Fig. 7 A 'regular setting' in the left column and 'composition using the URW *hz*-Program' in the right column with distortions of letters which Hermann Zapf has deemed to be 'typographically acceptable'. The typeface is Antiqua 2015, designed by Hermann Zapf and issued by URW in 1988. (From 'About micro typography and the *hz*-program', *Electronic Publishing*, vol. 6, no. 3 (September 1993), p. 287.)

What makes the Gutenberg Bible the unattainable masterpiece of the art of printing? The printing on a hand-press? Not really, because of today's standards, the inking was not of extraordinary quality. We could order hand-made rag paper also in our day. Maybe the secret of his beautiful pages is in the proportions of the columns on the paper. But this we are also able to copy. Therefore only the composition is to be considered.

How could Gutenberg get those even grey areas of his columns without disturbing or unsightly holes between words? His secret: the master achieved this perfection by using several characters of different width combined with many ligatures and abbreviations in his type case. He finally created 290 characters for the composition of the 42-line Bible. An enormous time consuming job to realize his idea of good typographic lines: the justified lines of even length, compared to the flush-left lines of the works of the famous mediaeval scribes.

But with Johannes Gutenberg's unusual ligatures and abbreviations, today we can't use this principle for contemporary composition. Now we can get help through the versatility of modern electronic software and formats to receive a perfect type area in our production, to get closer to Gutenberg's standards of quality: The *hz*-Program of URW.

What makes the Gutenberg Bible the unattainable masterpiece of the art of printing? The printing on a hand-press? Not really, because of today's standards, the inking was not of extraordinary quality. We could order hand-made rag paper also in our day. Maybe the secret of his beautiful pages is in the proportions of the columns on the paper. But this we are also able to copy. Therefore only the composition is to be considered.

How could Gutenberg get those even grey areas of his columns without disturbing or unsightly holes between words? His secret: the master achieved this perfection by using several characters of different width combined with many ligatures and abbreviations in his type case. He finally created 290 characters for the composition of the 42-line Bible. An enormous time consuming job to realize his idea of good typographic lines: the justified lines of even length, compared to the flush-left lines of the works of the famous mediaeval scribes.

But with Johannes Gutenberg's unusual ligatures and abbreviations, today we can't use this principle for contemporary composition. Now we can get help through the versatility of modern electronic software and formats to receive a perfect type area in our production, to get closer to Gutenberg's standards of quality: The *hz*-Program of URW.

type. In these pages, and in other careful jobs of typography where the simple principle of close word-spacing is observed, hyphenation is controlled by using numerous h&j's of incremental variation (trying first one and then another); the hyphenation which does occur is not excessive and it is, in accordance with our principles, an acceptable trade-off.

Size and design

The Monophoto filmsetters featured 'differently-proportioned sets of matrices': 'A' sets designed for 6 and 7 point and 'B' sets for 8 to 12 point. A 'C' set for 14 to 24 point was also produced for the Bembo series.[31] The designs were taken from the metal versions.* There are no such sets for most of the digital types currently produced and many of the best text types (Bas-

---

* But strangely and sadly the 'B' set for Imprint was derived from the designs for the smallest sizes (6 to 9 point) and as these designs were considerably different to the designs for the larger sizes the type was rendered unserviceable as a text type (the digital version suffered the same fate).

kerville, Garamond, Perpetua, Ehrhardt) are much too light, anaemic and spindly, for being designed to do double duty as text and display types.*This is a greater problem than the problem of optimum letter-fit and it is amazing that after so many years it is still not put to rights.

The 'A', 'B' and 'C' sets for Monophoto proved a good compromise in the circumstances but nowadays when production and use of type is quite more affordable there isn't any reason why appropriate designs taken from metal designs (e.g. 6–9, 10, 11, 12 point, and then display sizes) cannot or should not be produced. (The price of additional types would gladly be paid by serious typographers; there would be no difficulty in using them; an operator could select a particular size of a type easily as select roman, italic, bold-face.) Until this is done it hardly makes sense to alter character-pairs which were considered optimum for the range of sizes a single design would be set in.

The following is from Robin Kinross's article, 'What is a typeface?', in *Baseline*, 1986:

> Thus one may speak, as Harry Carter did, of an 'optical scale' in typeface design. The logic of this, as every punchcutter knew, and as every good software designer is trying to reassert, is that the letter-forms of a typeface must be adjusted for every size at which they are to be used. So again, the simple, single typeface comes into question. The best, most sophisticated typeface cannot be represented by a single set of drawings or images, but consists of modulations on some perhaps notional standard.[32]

In 1992 the Adobe Corporation issued a series of types called Multiple Masters and this was near as we had ever come to having digital types appropriate to size.[33] It was a clever and complicated idea whereby a typographer could choose different weights and different widths (condensings or extendings) of a type – if it was a Multiple Master – to achieve the effect which would obtain with a type specially designed for a particular size. But it missed the point; its failings were obvious: to condense or extend letter-forms is to distort them; the purpose-built metal types were made from special drawings for each size in which the shapes and slopes, twists and turns, curves and corners were uniquely treated.[34]

Adobe currently offer a new kind of type in their OpenType format which features 'opticals' (or 'optical variants') which are designs based on the principle of the purpose-built metal types and which can be used at any point-size but are intended and designated for 'Caption' (6–8 point), 'Text' (9–13 point), 'Subhead' (14–24 point) and 'Display' (25–72 point) – a variation of the Multiple Masters idea but with special character-spacing, heavier or lighter strokes and serifs (depending on which 'variant').[35] This is very good news indeed and any of the new types, such as Adobe's own Minion, should prove very satisfactory. The designs were approved if not actually done by the designer himself (in the case of Minion, Robert Slimbach) and thus there is no reason to question their quality or appropriateness, but it seems they are variations specified by algorithm and such an approach applied to types which are digital versions of metal designs will produce mutant forms the likes of which we have never seen.

* Not helped by current printing methods, paper, absence of 'ink squash' (ink spread).

Fig. 8 Two of Pascal's *Pensées* set in 11/13 Adobe Minion Pro *Caption* (*a*), *Text* (*b*), *Subhead* (*c*) and *Display* (*d*).

(*a*) 205-68. — Quand je considère la petite durée de ma vie, absorbée dans l'éternité précédent et suivant le petit espace que je remplis et même que je vois, abîmé dans l'infinie immensité des espaces que j'ignore et qui m'ignorent, je m'effraie et m'étonne de me voir ici plutôt que là, car il n'y a point de raison pourquoi ici plutôt que là, pourquoi à présent plutôt que lors. Qui m'y a mis ? Par l'ordre et la conduite de qui ce lieu et ce temps a-t-il été destiné à moi ? *Memoria hospitis unius diei praetereuntis.*
   206-201. — Le silence éternel de ces especes infinis m'effraie.

(*b*) 205-68. — Quand je considère la petite durée de ma vie, absorbée dans l'éternité précédent et suivant le petit espace que je remplis et même que je vois, abîmé dans l'infinie immensité des espaces que j'ignore et qui m'ignorent, je m'effraie et m'étonne de me voir ici plutôt que là, car il n'y a point de raison pourquoi ici plutôt que là, pourquoi à présent plutôt que lors. Qui m'y a mis ? Par l'ordre et la conduite de qui ce lieu et ce temps a-t-il été destiné à moi ? *Memoria hospitis unius diei praetereuntis.*
   206-201. — Le silence éternel de ces especes infinis m'effraie.

(*c*) 205-68. — Quand je considère la petite durée de ma vie, absorbée dans l'éternité précédent et suivant le petit espace que je remplis et même que je vois, abîmé dans l'infinie immensité des espaces que j'ignore et qui m'ignorent, je m'effraie et m'étonne de me voir ici plutôt que là, car il n'y a point de raison pourquoi ici plutôt que là, pourquoi à présent plutôt que lors. Qui m'y a mis ? Par l'ordre et la conduite de qui ce lieu et ce temps a-t-il été destiné à moi ? *Memoria hospitis unius diei praetereuntis.*
   206-201. — Le silence éternel de ces especes infinis m'effraie.

(*d*) 205-68. — Quand je considère la petite durée de ma vie, absorbée dans l'éternité précédent et suivant le petit espace que je remplis et même que je vois, abîmé dans l'infinie immensité des espaces que j'ignore et qui m'ignorent, je m'effraie et m'étonne de me voir ici plutôt que là, car il n'y a point de raison pourquoi ici plutôt que là, pourquoi à présent plutôt que lors. Qui m'y a mis ? Par l'ordre et la conduite de qui ce lieu et ce temps a-t-il été destiné à moi ? *Memoria hospitis unius diei praetereuntis.*
   206-201. — Le silence éternel de ces especes infinis m'effraie.

Quark and InDesign

The following examples are set 10/12 Sabon (Adobe) to a measure of 26 picas. The first (fig. 9) was produced by QuarkXPress 4 (as was the balance of this book), using the default h&j parameters shown in figure 3 on page 13; the second example (fig. 10) is set with the h&j's which are used in the text of this book generally. In both examples 'auto kern' is applied and the program's hyphenation exception dictionary is used as supplied.

The examples shown opposite (figures 11–13) were produced by Adobe InDesign. The default h&j parameters shown on page 13 (fig. 4) are used in the first example (fig. 11) with 'metrics kerning' applied, and also in the second (fig. 12) with 'optical kerning' applied; the third example (fig. 13) shows metrics kerning with adjusted word-space and word-division parameters. The program's hyphenation dictionary was used without modifications. The Paragraph Composer and Optical Margin Alignment were used for each setting but not the Hyphenation Penalty Slider.

Any type could have been used for this demonstration; Sabon (the type-face designed by Jan Tschichold and issued in 1967 by Stempel, Linotype and Monotype) is used here to go with the quotation which is from 'The Printer', an article written by the printer Elliott Viney for *Penguins Progress 1935–1960* (pp. 24–5).

Fig. 9 QuarkXPress default hyphenation settings: *smallest word* (which can be broken): 6 letters; *minimum* (number of letters of a word which must stand) *before* (it can be divided): 3; *minimum after*: 2; *hyphens in a row*: unlimited; the 'justification method': *minimum* word space: 85%; *optimum* word space: 110%; *maximum* word space: 250%; *minimum* character space: 0%; *optimum* character space: 0%; *maximum* character space: 4%. Capitalised words (such as Tschichold) cannot be divided.

At this low point Jan Tschichold was put in charge of Penguin production and many printers will remember what a stimulating, painful, almost alarming impact he had on composing rooms up and down the country. No detail of production was overlooked, but it was in the composing room that his influence was most strongly felt – meticulous and immensely detailed layouts were followed by revises without number and sometimes even by personal visits. He was particularly concerned with obtaining an improved arrangement of the printed page, using less space between words, with the layout of the title-page and other preliminary matter, and with other typographical details perhaps not apparent to the general reader but without which a visually satisfactory book cannot be produced. Of course, Tschichold is not alone in this; other publishers were fighting the same battle, but because of the large number of printers with whom Penguins dealt he had a great personal influence on this section of the trade.

Fig. 10 QuarkXPress with adjusted h&j settings: *smallest word*: 5 letters; *minimum before*: 2; *minimum after*: 2; *hyphens in a row*: unlimited; the 'justification method': *minimum* word space: 45%; *optimum* word space: 80%; *maximum* word space: 100%; *minimum* character space: 0%; *optimum* character space: 0%; *maximum* character space: 0%. Division of capitalised words is allowed.

At this low point Jan Tschichold was put in charge of Penguin production and many printers will remember what a stimulating, painful, almost alarming impact he had on composing rooms up and down the country. No detail of production was overlooked, but it was in the composing room that his influence was most strongly felt – meticulous and immensely detailed layouts were followed by revises without number and sometimes even by personal visits. He was particularly concerned with obtaining an improved arrangement of the printed page, using less space between words, with the layout of the title-page and other preliminary matter, and with other typographical details perhaps not apparent to the general reader but without which a visually satisfactory book cannot be produced. Of course, Tschichold is not alone in this; other publishers were fighting the same battle, but because of the large number of printers with whom Penguins dealt he had a great personal influence on this section of the trade.

Fig. 11 Adobe InDesign with 'metrics kerning' applied. The default hyphenation settings are:
Words Longer than: 5 letters
After First: 2 letters
Before Last: 2 letters
Hyphen Limit: 3
Hyphenate Capitalized Words.
The default justification settings are:
Word Spacing: 80% minimum; 100% desired; 133% maximum
Letter Spacing: 0%
Glyph Scaling: 100%.
Optical Margin Alignment is set to the point-size, as recommended, affecting undesirably the situation of the initial A.

Fig. 12 Adobe InDesign with 'optical kerning' applied. The default hyphenation and justification settings are used. The optical kerning option tends to increase the spacing of characters as it moves them rightways or leftways and so the user's guide recommends that after the 'kerning' is applied some negative tracking should be applied generally to compensate for this. The literature does not say how much tracking might be needed but –7 seems sufficient for this example. Note that the r and the comma in 'matter,' (in the tenth line) are now agreeably spaced.

Fig. 13 Adobe InDesign with metrics kerning and modified hyphenation and justification settings as follows:
Words Longer than: 4 letters
After First: 2 letters
Before Last: 2 letters
Hyphen Limit: unlimited
Hyphenate Capitalized Words.
Word Spacing: 50% minimum
80% desired
100% maximum
Letter Spacing: 0%
Glyph Scaling: 100%.

At this low point Jan Tschichold was put in charge of Penguin production and many printers will remember what a stimulating, painful, almost alarming impact he had on composing rooms up and down the country. No detail of production was overlooked, but it was in the composing room that his influence was most strongly felt – meticulous and immensely detailed layouts were followed by revises without number and sometimes even by personal visits. He was particularly concerned with obtaining an improved arrangement of the printed page, using less space between words, with the layout of the title-page and other preliminary matter, and with other typographical details perhaps not apparent to the general reader but without which a visually satisfactory book cannot be produced. Of course, Tschichold is not alone in this; other publishers were fighting the same battle, but because of the large number of printers with whom Penguins dealt he had a great personal influence on this section of the trade.

At this low point Jan Tschichold was put in charge of Penguin production and many printers will remember what a stimulating, painful, almost alarming impact he had on composing rooms up and down the country. No detail of production was overlooked, but it was in the composing room that his influence was most strongly felt – meticulous and immensely detailed layouts were followed by revises without number and sometimes even by personal visits. He was particularly concerned with obtaining an improved arrangement of the printed page, using less space between words, with the layout of the title-page and other preliminary matter, and with other typographical details perhaps not apparent to the general reader but without which a visually satisfactory book cannot be produced. Of course, Tschichold is not alone in this; other publishers were fighting the same battle, but because of the large number of printers with whom Penguins dealt he had a great personal influence on this section of the trade.

At this low point Jan Tschichold was put in charge of Penguin production and many printers will remember what a stimulating, painful, almost alarming impact he had on composing rooms up and down the country. No detail of production was overlooked, but it was in the composing room that his influence was most strongly felt – meticulous and immensely detailed layouts were followed by revises without number and sometimes even by personal visits. He was particularly concerned with obtaining an improved arrangement of the printed page, using less space between words, with the layout of the title-page and other preliminary matter, and with other typographical details perhaps not apparent to the general reader but without which a visually satisfactory book cannot be produced. Of course, Tschichold is not alone in this; other publishers were fighting the same battle, but because of the large number of printers with whom Penguins dealt he had a great personal influence on this section of the trade.

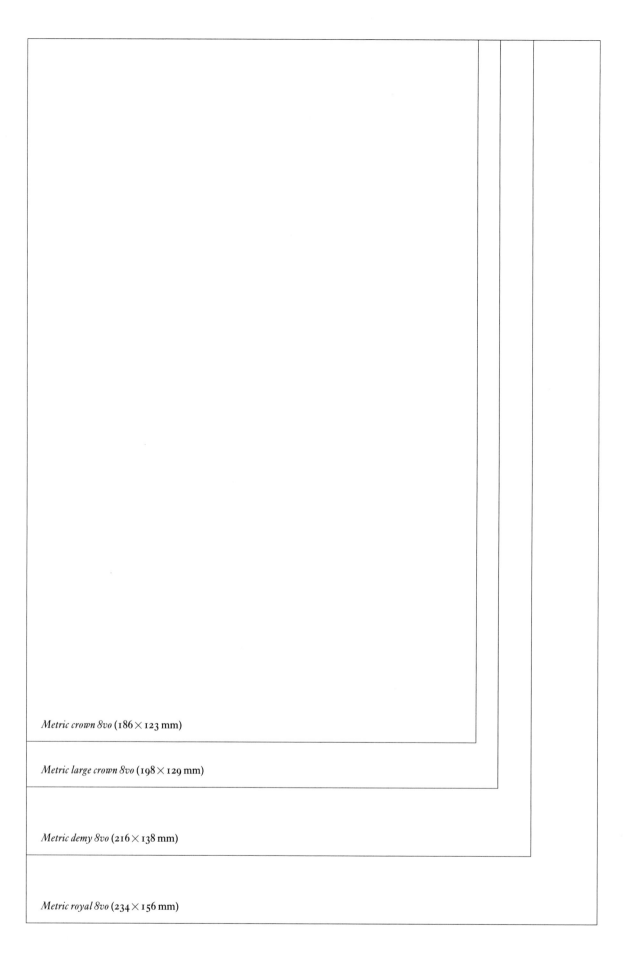

Metric crown 8vo (186 × 123 mm)

Metric large crown 8vo (198 × 129 mm)

Metric demy 8vo (216 × 138 mm)

Metric royal 8vo (234 × 156 mm)

Fig. 14 Trimmed metric octavo pages
(British Standard 1430: 1970)

The large crown and demy octavos are pleasing sizes: easily held in the hands, not too big for bedtime reading but not too small for 11-point type. For many years these were the most common sizes for books of text but, owing to marketing interests, the smaller sizes have been all but superseded by the metric royal octavo. It is also a pleasing size and its proportions are agreeable but it is often too large.* This appears to be the case also for American books: 9×6 inches now commonly used for books which in the past would probably have been produced in a size such as $8 \times 5\frac{3}{8}$ inches.

The choice of size is determined (when commercial or industrial interests allow) as much by aesthetics as by subject-matter or intended use and certainly there are many other formats besides the octavo which a designer can choose from. Many of them existing as stock sizes. One might use the word 'format' for 'size', though it may mean other things besides width and height.† The commonness of the octavo has inevitably proved a factor in the choice of wider or narrower formats when designers have been left to their own devices. According to Hugh Williamson (in *Methods of Book Design*):

Some typographers like their books a little narrower than usual, others prefer them squarer; there are even those who have the temerity to assert that one proportion of width to height is aesthetically correct and that all others are wrong. On the whole, leading designers who wish to produce a particularly attractive book seem to favour a slight narrowing of format from the standard proportions of octavo books.[1]

Are slightly narrower formats deemed particularly attractive (by leading designers) because the octavo is seen as overused? Or is the octavo indeed too wide? Certainly there are many exemplary books (by Aldus Manutius, by Bodoni, Doves Press) which are wide rather than narrow. Are slightly narrowed margins preferable to a slightly narrowed measure of the type area? Is it of any importance that the book will not lie flat when it is open? These are such questions as which importune the mind of a book designer.

When the page-size of a book is decided upon, the kind of type, point-size, leading and measure, and the disposition of the type area and illustrations will then determine the apportionment of the white space, the margins. That is one way to do it, though of course it can be done the other way round: margins dictating type area etc. A recent book, *About Face: Reviving the Rules of Typography* by David Jury – which is an excellent survey of

*There is also a trend for larger paperbacks and many of the hard-cover metric royal 8vos are produced in metric demy 8vo paperback versions. It seems the metric demy 8vo is now more commonly used for paperbacks than hard-covers.

† In the glossary to R. A. Hewitt's *Style for Print* 'format' is described as 'the size and shape of a page; the general appearance of a book, its layout, typography, paper, style of presentation, binding, etc.' Sir Francis Meynell: 'the feel of a book, its weight, shape, edges, the synthesis of sensitive things which is represented by that most insensitive word "format".' ('The Personal Element', *The Nonesuch Century* (Nonesuch, 1936), p. 40.)

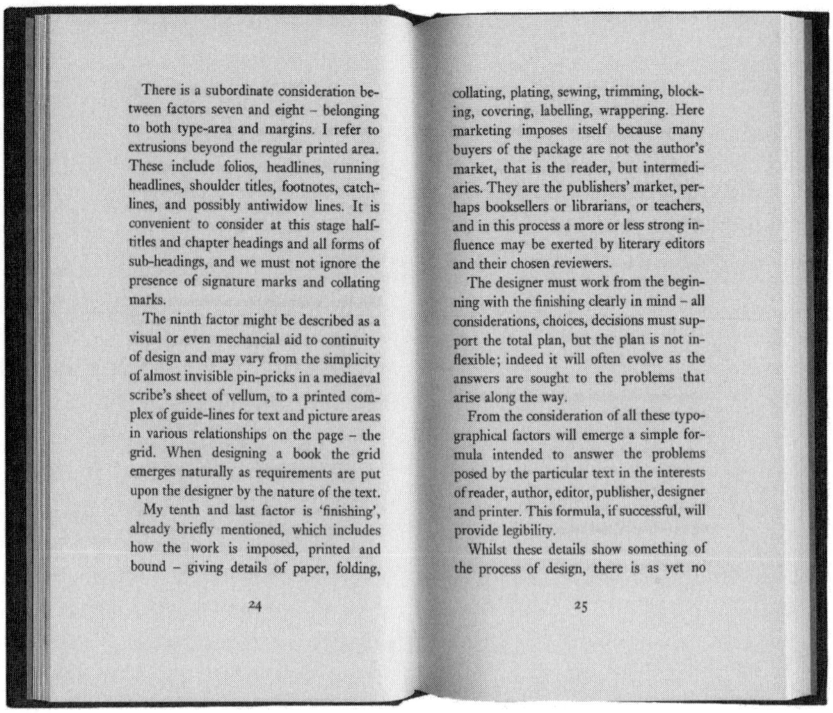

Fig. 15 *The Case for Legibility*, written and designed by John Ryder, set in Monotype Ehrhardt and printed by the Stellar Press, Hatfield, published by The Bodley Head in 1979. The format is rather too small and narrow and word-spacing inevitably suffers with justified 12-point type set in a 17-picas measure. Reduced from 190 mm deep.

traditions, technologies and practices of book and commercial typography, with detailed information given in short chapters and user-friendly sections, beautifully illustrated with examples of contemporary design as well as many antique books from the St Bride Printing Library, printed on heavy high-white paper in a 260 × 226 mm format – uses a soft or not-so-rigid Swiss style with 8/11 Univers 45 set left-ranged and unhyphenated in $14\frac{1}{2}$-pica columns in a three-column grid, abundant white space. It is readable and attractive but the type can have been larger without unduly compromising the design. Indeed it is overdesigned and the contents are made to dance to the tune of the form.

A book of continuous text, of the common-or-garden kind, even if formatted unusually narrowly or widely, will normally present little challenge to the designer in the matter of margins and disposition of type area. In art monographs there is often much more space to work with than content – if the content is typeset in anything like a readable type, point-size, measure. Gallery catalogues or art books should of course receive generous creative treatments but often they contain some sort of text and even if it is Post-Modernist rubbish it should not be treated in such a way as to make it unreadable (typographically). Shoddy (if not unreadable) and often uninspired typography, handled, it would seem, by interior decorators rather than typographers, is quite commonly found in art books, photographers' books especially.

Let us consider a job which isn't shoddy but which is none the less typographically wayward. The text of the Whitechapel Lucian Freud catalogue designed by Derek Birdsall in 1993 is set in 16-point (PostScript) Monotype Walbaum to a measure of 58 picas. It is inimical to our principles; it is scarcely readable but neither is it attractive.

That's not to say it is outlandish: it is rather tame, rather dull, even. Another design for Whitechapel, a four-page leaflet entitled *Georg Baselitz: Model for a Sculpture*, designed by Richard Hollis in 1980, also employs inordinately long measures, but unlike the Birdsall job, the type (Century Old Style) is close-leaded, left-ranged, unhyphenated, with double-em paragraph indents chopping up the edges; images and type are not given customary margins but are situated injudiciously close together; the effect is to appear clumsy while Birdsall's design is not clumsy in any respect. Hollis's design is terribly un-Swiss. It rather gives the impression of a preliminary 'comp' or work a few stages away from completion. Indeed that may have been the desired effect. It is illustrated on p. 170 of Robin Kinross's *Modern*

Fig. 16 A verso page from *About Face* by David Jury (Mies, Switzerland, Roto-Vision, 2002), designed by Vince Frost and Sonia Dyakova of London in the Swiss fashion but reminiscent of Sixties British design. Reduced from 260 mm deep.

Fig. 17 Derek Birdsall's design for *Lucian Freud : Recent Work* by Catherine Lampert (Whitechapel Art Gallery, 1993), with text set 16/24 Monotype Walbaum to a measure of 57¾ picas, printed greyishly on off-white coated paper. Derek Birdsall RDI was art director of the 1960s *Nova* magazine, designer of the first Pirelli calendar in 1964, the *Independent Magazine* in 1988, designer and co-author with Bruce Bernard of the immense *Lucian Freud* (Cape, 1996) with 290 colour reproductions, and Bruce Bernard's *12 Photographs of Francis Bacon* (Visual Arts, 1999). He often designs square books. In *Typographic*, no. 11 (1977), he said, 'where I've got a choice and where the books are illustrated, which almost all of my books are, I've found it almost impossible to beat the square format'. Reduced from 297 mm.

left to upper right in the bed frame, chair, thigh and those in the opposite direction on the pillow and lower leg, together with the figure's depth evoke a rectangular box and a departure.

Freud never uses figures for compositional reasons and it is often the sitters who suggest how they wish to lie down or sit. The blonde girl stretched out against the bank of rags in *Lying by the Rags* makes a stiff effect rather sarcophagi-like except that she almost levitates in space. Leigh's body see-sawed between the green-striped mattress and the pile of rags contains a sequence of triangles that pulls our vision towards his centre and then out along the silhouette, giving a profound sense of organic and inorganic. Curiously, such a sense of substance and proximity Freud can achieve in the etchings, at least those dating from 1985. The needle scratches the copper plate in discrete patterns, frequently as facsimile representations with spores for muscles and horsehair stuffing mimicking pubic hair, with the traceries of the etching needles relating to the painted images as the dried veins of a leaf do to the live version. Where the swelling convex forms, like those of shoulders and stomach, emerge they read as much more brilliantly white and solid than the paper of the background and the ideas correspond to the jolting effect of the sharp 'guillotined' line of the paper edge.

In the past Freud's response to still-life, his favourite plants, textiles and books, produced fanatic and melancholy detail that intimated a chosen isolation. It still comes into the inert material, although the backgrounds are less frequently entirely monochromatic, and are sometimes enriched with smeared or saturated impasto or doe-skin-like softness or pungent red cushioning. A wildflower-like display of painting wipings behind *Ib and her Husband* suggests this 'landscape' belongs to her and in the early stages of its execution the radiator resembled a fence (it is still a dark barrier) and ultimately it is her face that is heavenly. A deliberate change between works according to the people in them makes some surrounding areas read as more obviously pungent, in a sepulchral manner like those of Rembrandt or Manet, and others belong to anachronistically fussy surroundings, stippled like those wall surfaces of David. What Lawrence Gowing wrote of Vermeer applies: 'The space in which Vermeer's figures are disposed, so singular by comparison with other painters' versions of his themes, is like a magnetic field. It is formed exactly by the tensions which the figures set up. The design precisely contains them'.[25]

21

Typography and he says of it: 'the design approach is that of subtle and responsive rationality',[2] which is an interesting way of putting it.

It is interesting to compare such work to the Marlborough catalogues done in the Sixties by Gordon House, who was both a painter and a typographer. They show the influence of the Swiss style (though they don't seem quite as Swiss as David Jury's *About Face*); nearly all of them are set in Univers, and they are simple and accessible, if conservative – texts handled with a great regard for the reader. To be sure, the Swiss style was much overused (prodigious presence of Univers, Helvetica and other grots, if not always the three-column Swiss grid, in weekly magazines, government documents, annual reports, and of course Penguin covers), but I think that in the Marlborough catalogues it is the *subtleties* (which I do not find in the Richard Hollis design which Robin Kinross calls subtle), the handling of spaces between elements, the careful settings, the *sensitive things*, to use Sir Francis Meynell's words, which invest them with enduring quality.

Along these lines but of greater consequence was the work of Herbert Spencer, design consultant to Lund Humphries, founder and editor of *Typographica* (1949–67), editor and designer of the *Penrose Annual* (1964–73), who was one of a few designers who could contribute as much to commercial and business design or magazine work as to books. Among my favourite books are two designs which he did in 1971 for Lund Humphries: Roland Penrose's *Portrait of Picasso* and James Moran's *Stanley Morison*.

A great number of illustrated books are more like magazines than books. That is of course quite the desired effect in many cases and doubtless there is a point-of-sale advantage; books of an ephemeral nature* are quite popular. But even they might be designed in such a way as commercial design will enhance rather than obtrude into book design.

* By which I mean interest to the reader rather than shelf-life.

Fig. 18 *Francis Bacon: Recent Paintings* (Marlborough Fine Art, 1967). One of many catalogues designed for Marlborough Fine Arts in the Sixties by Gordon House. Set in Univers. Printed by Tillotsons. Michel Leiris's introduction is presented in French on grey cartridge paper and followed by an English translation (shown here) printed on the high-quality art paper which was used for the balance of the book. Reduced from 228 mm deep.

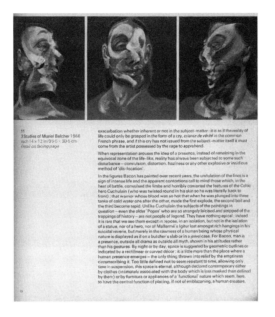

Fig. 19 *Portrait of Picasso* by Roland Penrose (Lund Humphries, 1971), designed by Herbert Spencer, Hansje Oorthuys, and Brian Coe. Text is set in unjustified and unhyphenated Monotype Plantin on art paper, captions and index in Monotype Grotesque 126, heads and folios in Grotesque 216. Uncluttered, uncrowded. This is the second edition; the first edition was set in Monotype Walbaum. Reduced from 247 mm.

Fig. 20 The 'companion' book to
J. Bronowski's BBC-TV series, *The Ascent
of Man* (BBC, 1973), printed by Sir Joseph
Causton & Sons Ltd, but no designer is
credited. That is a pity for it is a beautiful
book worthy of the author's magnificent
project – which to my mind remains the
best thing ever done in television. It is a
book which one wants to keep in one's per-
manent collection. The design was no easy
job : illustrations of every description had to
be incorporated into nearly every page – a
good deal of them traversing verso and recto
pages. In each case this was done expertly.
What impresses me most is the treatment of
running heads and captions which vary in
measure as the need occurs. But I find the
placement of folios in the outer margin
rather awkward. The folios in the original
setting of Eric Gill's *Essay on Typography*
are treated in this unconventional way also,
but here they're placed at the foot which I
think makes them a little more awkward. I
think the text would have benefited from an
unjustified setting as Joanna (Monophoto
Joanna on coated paper – too light!) does
not suffer excessiveness of word-space very
well at all. Reduced from 247 mm deep.

The Ascent of Man

science had been entirely concerned with exploring nature as she
is. But now the modern conception of transforming nature in
order to obtain power from her, and of changing one form of
power into another, had come up to the leading edge of science.
In particular, it grew clear that heat is a form of energy, and is
converted into other forms at a fixed rate of exchange. In 1824
Sadi Carnot, a French engineer, looking at steam engines, wrote
a treatise on what he called 'la puissance motrice du feu', in which
he founded, in essence, the science of thermodynamics – the
dynamics of heat. Energy had become a central concept in
science; and the main concern in science now was the unity of
nature, of which energy is the core.

And it was a main concern not only in science. You see it
equally in the arts, and the surprise is there. While this is going on,
what is going on in literature? The uprush of romantic poetry
round about the year 1800. How could the romantic poets be
interested in industry? Very simply: the new concept of nature
as the carrier of energy took them by storm. They loved the word
'storm' as a synonym for energy, in phrases like *Sturm und Drang*,
'storm and thrust'. The climax of Samuel Taylor Coleridge's
Rime of the Ancient Mariner is introduced by a storm that breaks the
deadly calm and releases life again.

> The upper air burst into life !
> And a hundred fire-flags sheen,
> To and fro they were hurried about !
> And to and fro, and in and out,
> The wan stars danced between.
>
> The loud wind never reached the ship,
> Yet now the ship moved on !
> Beneath the lightning and the Moon
> The dead men gave a groan.

A young German philosopher, Friedrich von Schelling, just at
this time in 1799, started a new form of philosophy which has
remained powerful in Germany, *Naturphilosophie* – philosophy of
nature. From him Coleridge brought it to England. The Lake
Poets had it from Coleridge, and the Wedgwoods, who were
friends of Coleridge's and indeed supported him with an
annuity. Poets and painters were suddenly captured by the idea

282

1 37
The new concept of nature
as the carrier of energy
took them by storm.
A pithead, about 1790.

Folios, headlines

There should be nothing fancy about headlines or folios. In American books they're often nowadays set incongruously and grotesquely in bold grots or overly letter-spaced lineals or scripts.* An otherwise well designed book, the excellent English translation of Guido Ceronetti's *Il Silenzio del corpo* (*The Silence of the Body*)† was unfortunately given such a treatment: running headlines – or rather *foot-lines* – carrying just the title of the book and omitting the folio on the verso pages, on the recto the folio alone, set in Snell Roundhand script centred beneath the text which is set soberly in Linotype Fairfield.

Let us consider Stanley Morison's advice that:

> No printer, in safeguarding himself from the charge of monotony in his composition, should admit, against his better judgement, any typographical distraction doing violence to logic and lucidity in the supposed interests of decoration.[3]

The foot-lines in *The Silence of the Body* are gimmicky and that is to be regretted, but they do a greater injury because they have the effect of unbalancing the page or turning it upside-down. The greater bottom margin of a page, following the traditional proportions of $1\frac{1}{2}$ for inner, 2 for top, 3 for outer, and 4 for foot, or a variation of that, *supports* the contents of the page, if illusively, but its ability to do so is greatly diminished when anything save a folio is placed in its area.

The headlines and the folios should be the same point-size as the text.‡ If they're smaller, even by a point, they often seem insubstantial or uncertain and uncomfortably so. If they're positioned judiciously there is no advantage in setting them smaller.

The inadvisability of placing folios too near or at the edge of the inner margin should be obvious. If the folio is placed with the headline it should be positioned against the outer margin either full-out or indented. Dropped folios are sometimes placed in the foot-margins of pages where a new chapter is started and the headline discontinued, but they're certainly not indispensable. If the folio is to be placed normally at the foot of the page it can be omitted from short pages. The folios of Eric Gill's *Essay on Typography* (in the original setting done at Pigotts in 1931, but not in the resettings) are placed in the outer margins about two ems from the text and aligned with the first line of the text. This placement works rather well; the folios don't call undue attention to themselves, but in the later resettings they are situated conventionally in the headlines. The folios in *The Ascent of Man* (fig. 20) are also positioned in the outer margin but aligned with the last line of the text and for that reason they look rather awkward.

Folios in italics or set inside square brackets can look well but even such a modest touch will have a pronounced effect. In the same respect headlines may be 'enlivened' (to use Oliver Simon's word) by rules, *single*, *double*, *total*, or *parallel*, though the practice is a bit antiquated.

---

* Though it must be said the Grotesque 216 folios look well in *Portrait of Picasso* (fig. 19).

† Guido Ceronetti, *The Silence of the Body*, translated by Michael Moore, New York, Farrar, Strauss and Giroux, 1993.

‡ Though the Snell Roundhand and Fairfield used in *The Silence of the Body* are set in the same point-size the former looks much larger than the latter; one wonders if the designer had desired that effect.

Headlines (or foot-lines) are often used when they're not needed (this is the case for *The Silence of the Body* where no chapters or sections exist). Usually the verso headline will carry the book's title and the recto will be a section or chapter headline or a page headline (indicating particular contents of a page).* For indexes, bibliographies, glossaries and other end-matter the book's title should be omitted and the section titles should be shown on both left and right pages. Authors' names should not be put in headlines unless in anthologies, symposia, etc.

In diaries, notebooks, letters (which are considered in greater detail below), the headline can be used – and indeed in many cases should be used – to guide the reader to the dates of entries or letters. The dates can be given on both verso and recto pages (omitting the book's title if necessary); they should in most cases give month as well as year, but this depends of course on the particular contents of the book. Looking through some books from my own collection, I find month and year in the headlines of Virginia Woolf's *Diary* (set in full caps, ranged left on verso, right on recto, folios centered in the foot margin); in Evelyn Waugh's *Diaries* the section (e.g. THE THIRTIES DIARY 1930–39) is on the verso page and the dates of entries for both verso and recto pages are displayed in the recto headline (e.g. 19–26 NOVEMBER 1930); in *Pages from the Goncourt Journal* the full date of the first entry (e.g. 7 APRIL 1857) is given on each page;† in Stephen Spender's *Journals 1939–1983* only the particular journal (e.g. Journal/1954–8) is given, but in Rayner Heppenstall's *Journals*, Frances Partridge's *Everything to Lose*, Woodrow Wyatt's *Journals*, only the year is given; the headlines, both verso and recto, in *Journal of a Man of Letters* (Paul Léautaud) carry only the book's title and so if one wants to know, for instance, in which year the entry for Sunday, March 5th, on page 85 was written, one must thumb through pages to find the page (page 75) where the year (1905) is given in a cross-head, for there's nothing otherwise to indicate. It is well to note Seán Jennett's view of running headlines:

> I can see no sense in the running headline, and in my opinion not even the plea of decoration can justify its use. . . . The truth, of course, is that it is a habit; many people, publishers and printers included, never *see* the headlines, and the running head is there because no one thought of omitting it. The only recommendation I have heard for it is that it serves as an advertisement, enabling your neighbour in train or bus to see what you are reading.[4]

One would need better eyes than I've got and a specially favourable vantage-point, I should think, to see by this method what one's neighbour is reading, but running headlines may prove useful if the book is to be photocopied.

* I am using Seán Jennett's term. 'Headlines are mainly of three different kinds: running headlines or title headlines; section headlines; and page headlines. The term "running head" is in common use; the others I have had to invent because there is no satisfactory nomenclature. "Page headline" or "page heading" too often mean simply headline.' (*The Making of Books*, 4th edn (Faber, 1967), p. 293.)

† In this book – *The Goncourt Journal* – the conventional form of referring to the first new entry is followed. If one is accustomed to it, this form is seldom very discommodious. Hugh Williamson takes a different view. 'A section headline in some books is likely to refer not to the section immediately adjacent to the headline but to a section title some way down the page, an old custom but not a particularly good one.' (*Methods of Book Design*, 3rd edn (Yale, 1983), p. 164.)

Quoted matter or extracts

When quoted matter is broken off from the main text and set in the same point-size, it shouldn't be necessary to indent it on left and right sides but only on the left (and only by an em). The first line should not be additionally indented. The quotation may be offset by line-space (or half- or quarter-line-space) above and below, but some designers may consider this undesirable for 'destroying that even tone of colour which connoisseurs of good bookwork regard as eminently desirable' (R. A. Hewitt).* Unless one desires a specially ugly effect, the practice, suggested by Hugh Williamson in *Methods of Book Design*, of distinguishing extracts by setting them solid when the text is otherwise set with leading should be shunned. The extracts in this book are set one size smaller than text and usually a quarter-line-space ($3\frac{1}{4}$ points), but sometimes more or less to adjust the depth of text, is inserted between quote and text. The line-spacing is also reduced by one point but this is not a proportional reduction and so the quote is slightly more leaded than the text. The first line of the quote is indented by 11 points as one agrees with R. A. Hewitt's view: 'Where more than one size of type appears on a page the indention should be the same number of points in each case. This obviates the irregular appearance given to the page by varying indentions.' In many books, however, the quoted matter when set smaller is not indented but set full-out. When poetry is quoted it should, if not too lengthy, be set in the same point-size as text and – especially if just a stanza – centrally positioned by the longest line. This is a conventional style which is appropriate for books with conventionally centred heads, folios, etc., but in a book with a predominately left-orientated design it may be well to apply only the normal paragraph indent. Seán Jennett favours neither setting quotations in smaller sizes nor indenting them. Of the one he says it 'destroys the unity of the page by imposing upon it a colour of a different kind from that of the text' and has the effect of 'belittling'† the author who's quoted; of the other he says 'The result is a ragged page that cannot but look uncomfortable'. He suggests a third way.

I prefer to set quotations in the text type, exactly as an ordinary paragraph of the text, but quoted at the beginning and end, as they should be, to show that they are quotations. Set in this way they do not stand out from the page or disturb its even tenor, and there is no doubt for the reader that what he is reading is a quotation. If this is not considered sufficient distinction a half-line of space may be left before and after the quotation.[5]

But certain connoisseurs won't be satisfied with the half-line and one questions whether one point smaller indeed belittles an author or whether the alternative is so injurious (or uncomfortable) to the tenor of the page.

When quotations accompany chapter openings as epigraphs they may be set smaller than the extracts; the indentions or positioning should be consistent or harmonious with the style of the other elements. Quotation marks

---

* *Style for Print* (Blandford, 1957), p. 37.

† *The Making of Books*, p. 280. I have put 'belittling' in quotes but the sentence is: 'Presumably the writer does not mean to belittle the author from whom he quotes, but that is what he is doing; usually he quotes from him in order to enhance his own point, and if that is the case it is surely better that the authority should speak in a normal voice rather than in a repressed whisper.'

aren't needed. The author of the quoted lines may be set in small capitals the same size as the quote; the book, play, poem, etc., may be given if necessary but a footnote or endnote should be used for anything more than that. An English translation may be put directly below in square brackets or as a footnote. If the quote and author fit in one line an en rule or em rule preceding author's name may look well. There are innumerable possible treatments.

A book is not a tin of beans. – SIR ALLEN LANE

La véritable éloquence consiste à dire tout ce qu'il faut, et à ne dire que ce qu'il faut.
La Rochefoucauld*

These are typical treatments for a centred, symmetrical page. A leftwardly-orientated or asymmetrical book may prove a more difficult exercise. An unjustified setting, a right indent, might be employed.

> In all permanent forms of typography, whether publicly or
> privately printed, the typographer's only purpose is to express,
> not himself, but his author.
>   Stanley Morison, *First Principles of Typography*

A doubtful practice in which short quotations from other authorities to reinforce a point made in the text are placed in the outer margin as sidenotes is found in a recent book, *On Book Design*, by Richard Hendel.† They are set in a 7-point sans-serif type alongside a text set in 11-point Garamond in a more or less conventional fashion.

Diaries, letters

I've kept, or have tried to keep, a diary since 1989. In 1994 it became a typographical undertaking as well, and eventually I would write the pages up directly into Quark documents as I found it a much more user-friendly application than Microsoft Word, and though the diaries (or Journals as I call them) remain unpublished there are now two volumes of approximately 350 pages each which are designed for Metric Royal 8vo pages (set in 11/13 Monotype Plantin to a measure of 27 pica ems, by 40 lines (or 43 picas) in depth) the proofs of which are output from an HP 2300 on A4 paper. In the process I've made a few revisions to style – though there are a few rather unusual styles I devised early in the day which I'm obliged to stick with (or for which I have developed a certain fondness). Among them is a style for quoting and citing other authors' works whereby the name and book, publisher, date and page are put in round brackets just under the block of quote and indented an additional em. I have learnt much, however, about the special problems and niceties of diaries and the composition of them, having become rather keen, in the process of writing one, on reading published diaries. There are as many approaches as there are printed volumes, but such

---

* ['True eloquence consists in saying all that is required and only what is required.' (*Maxims*, trans. Leonard Tancock (Penguin, 1959), p. 70.)] A footnote is usually preferable to placing the translation directly beneath the quotation. Square brackets are often used to distinguish translations (given by an editor) from an author's own footnotes.

† Mr Hendel calls them 'sidebars'. His remarkable book is considered in greater detail in the next chapter.

Fig. 21 A page from the second volume of my unpublished Journals, set in 11/13 Monotype Plantin in a 27-picas measure. Entries, set full-out with dates in italics followed by one mutton, are normally separated by one line (13 points) of white; paragraphs within entries (which are always indented) are separated when the occasion necessitates by half a line; but there is a great deal of adjustment either to move lines of text to following pages or to keep lines together. Extracts are indented by one em on the right. The design is conventional while allowing as much as possible for peculiarities (short lines, lists, etc.) which occur in private diaries. Reduced from 234 mm deep.

London grime. My own taste rather favours the yellow or golden or orangey-brown 'patination' such as is found on ancient marbles and the black grime as well. The important point is made (by Ian Jenkins, p. 30) that 'some part of the outrage expressed at the 1930s cleaning had to do with the fact that people had become used to seeing the sculptures in their dirty state.'

Predictably a good deal of ignorance or wilful distortion (about patination, about their care) has figured in the political campaign for the sculptures' return to Greece. Tiresome Christopher Hitchens writing another sloppy, irresponsible book; Tariq Ali, John Fowles, Martin Amis, Salman Rushdie, Sir Sean Connery, Joanna Lumley, Dame Judi Dench, Vanessa Redgrave, Bill Clinton, all getting into the act. But that is another matter.

Francis King also remarks on Roger Hinks's habit of polishing his diaries.

All through his time in Athens, Hinks laboured at his journal. He wrote it, he re-wrote it, and he re-wrote it yet again. 'But, Roger, a diary should be spontaneous!' I once protested. 'Oh, I hate spontaneity! When people are being spontaneous, they say and do such silly things!' he retorted. I think that he genuinely believed that he was producing something on par with the Goncourt Journals. But when, under the title *The Gymnasium of the Mind*, a selection was published, it caused little stir. Perhaps a more generous and less discreet selection may eventually bring him the posthumous fame which he so clearly expected.

(*Yesterday Came Suddenly*, p. 129)

None the less the book is filled with marvellous stuff (like the passage I quoted 15th February) despite its alleged want of spontaneity. Certainly the selection should have been more generous and less discreet and it's a pity it isn't. As regards his re-writing, Lees-Milne was right, of course, when he said 'It's terribly important not to fudge diaries' (*Spectator*, 14th September 1996, p. 20). I'm afraid I've done some polishing, tidying, titivation in these pages. And still I say such *silly things*! If it makes any difference, I have usually done this within a day of writing up the entry.

23rd March   On 11th–15th December 2001, I complained in these pages about books with 'deckle-edge pages, as lately seem to be the

things as headlines, footnotes, endnotes, spacing of paragraphs, will call for special attention and involve a bit more work than is usually involved in other kinds of books. Bruce Rogers wrote: 'Uneven leading or extra leading between paragraphs may sometimes be necessary in a reference or other special kind of book, but for ordinary text it throws lines out of register, interrupts the continuity of text, and offends the eye.'[6] In nearly every entry of my own Journals the paragraphs are separated by a half-line (6½ points). This does rather offend the eye and I regret I started doing this (from the very first entry) because it means much travail in the matter of maintaining the depths of each page, adjusting and re-adjusting again (or *whiting-out*, to use the old compositor's term). But I cannot change it because these spaces reflect my train of thought or lack of it, my second thoughts or afterthoughts or interrupted thought process etc. In other words, this is an essential aspect of my diary-writing and to close up the paragraphs would greatly change the nature of my reflections etc. (one is glad therefore of not having to deal with a publisher or designer who would direct such a style despite one's wishes). Also there are many widows, unbreakable elements (such as the citation style), etc. But such problems are encountered in nearly every diary. And handled, of course, slightly differently in this one or that one.

In some diaries etc. the pages are allowed to fall short when a date-line or subheading awkwardly occurs at the last line but this remedy should be applied only when other ways of adjustment are impossible. I do not agree with the practice of 'vertical justification' of a page, such as is possible in Quark and InDesign, to fill the text area. This is no more acceptable than altering the letter-space of a line. If one doesn't want a short page, there's nothing for it but the arduous business of counting up the total points of the extra line-space between paragraphs and either reducing or adding space evenly. This often has to be done for hundreds of pages and any changing, editorial or otherwise, may oblige the compositor to redistribute the lines or space again over a number of pages. There might be quoted passages or other matter which will not be well disposed to breaking and in such cases there may be no alternative but to countenance an abnormally short page.

When dates with day, month and year are put into the headlines, especially if ordinal endings (*rd, st, th*) are used,* capitals and lower-case roman or italics might look better than small capitals. The small caps, if used, should in most cases be letter-spaced. If this is done, the letters may look well but not the figures.†

If chapters are incorporated into pages rather than started on new pages (as may be advised for a book with short chapters), the space above the chapter heading and between heading and text should be apportioned in such a way as to maintain the page depth (e.g. a line and a half and a half-line).

Footnotes, endnotes

In my diaries and in this book I have used both footnotes and endnotes, the former indicated with symbols, the latter with superior figures, and though it may not be an ideal practice it is not scorned by any of the authorities and it is a convenient and manageable method for me. In this book the footnotes are mainly for comments, exposition or second thoughts which can't be nicely worked into the text (owing perhaps in some cases to the author's lack of skill) but which are deemed important enough to be taken note of immediately; the endnotes are for citing the sources of extracts

* These endings are not advocated by Oxford, Cambridge, nor in the *Rules of Printed English* by Herbert Rees, but they are not so wayward and if a diarist uses them consistently they should not be changed.

† 'If letter-spaced capitals are used for the headline, the figures of the page number may be similarly spaced; ranging figures benefit more from letter-spacing than do hanging figures.' (Hugh Williamson, *Methods of Book Design* (1966), p. 143.)

(i.e. references), or to contain much larger notes than the pages can reasonably accommodate or such notes as are not immediately essential but might be interesting to the reader who doesn't mind the exercise. Occasionally the source of a quote is given in a footnote and occasionally something is consigned to the endnotes which perhaps should have been situated in a footnote. That is not a fault of the system but editorial error.

There are as many styles, variations, nuances, for footnotes as there are for headlines or folios or chapter heads. The preferred or most common academic style favours figures rather than symbols and there are obvious advantages to this. However, it is a matter, as with all other details, of the kind of book and what particular treatment will prove most suitable, practical, serviceable, attractive, or least distracting.

It is well to consider the uses and applications of footnotes or endnotes as well as the typographical style of them. Both footnotes and endnotes may prove an inconvenience to the reader. As P. G. Burbidge advises, the author 'in the recording of the sources of innumerable small quotations . . . should consider whether . . . he is not disturbing his reader to a point at which the advantage of precision is not offset by the difficulty of adhering to the line of thought.'* That distraction may or may not be a good reason for using endnotes in preference to footnotes (if the note or reference can't be omitted). The reader may be more inclined to ignore the endnote if he/she wishes (reckoning that the information given there is not worth the trouble of leaving and returning to the text) but the note-indicator (whether symbol or superior figure or 'see note 250') would be in the text notwithstanding and if it is the note itself and not the indicator which causes the interruption I should think a greater inconvenience would be caused by the endnote.

The note-indicator (or notifier, or 'cue' as it's called in *The Oxford Guide to Style*) should follow the full-stop of a sentence or be situated 'after a break in the sense'.† There are occasions when it must be placed within a sentence to make any sense, and of course more than one footnote, endnote, may occur in the same sentence. A notifier should follow a punctuation mark. There are, however, two schools of thought on this matter. In Herbert Rees's *Rules of Printed English*, which I find the most detailed and well-reasoned account of the subject, the conditions for placement are specified (in his rules 331–2) as follows:

> The superior figure or mark should normally be set outside an adjacent mark of punctuation or quotation mark:
>
> It was his last work;[3] three weeks later he was dead.
>
> [3] The final chapter was completed on 24 July.

> But a superior referring exclusively to a word or phrase immediately preceding it should be set thus:
>
> It was a matter of *sauve qui peut*[*]; we all bolted.
>
> [*] every man for himself

In the books I've examined, all of which were printed in the UK within the past fifty years (my own books, so not an exhaustive study), the notifier is placed, in both conditions described above, *after* the mark of punctuation in nearly all of them. Indeed I've found only one book in which the notifiers are placed as in Rees's second example: *The Noël Coward Diaries* (Weiden-

---

* *Notes and References* (Cambridge, 1952), p. 4.   † ibid. p. 5.

feld & Nicolson, 1982). But the notifiers (superior figures) in this book are in *every* instance placed before the punctuation marks.

The distinction of categories as specified by Rees is not always immediately clear and it may be preferable – typographically at least – to have a consistent treatment of the notifier placement. At any event, placement of the notifier, whether symbol or figure, before a mark of punctuation creates a gap which is even more irritating, even gappier, than that which is created when a notifier follows punctuation.*

It is interesting that the asterisk in Rees's second example precedes a *semi-colon*: might the example look less natural if it were a comma? Rees's second condition is not advocated in Burbidge's *Notes and References*, nor in *Hart's Rules*, nor G.V. Carey's *Punctuation*.

Other interesting differences exist among the authorities. Herbert Rees advises (in his rule 347) that 'Notes simply giving a reference to a book title, author, publisher, date of publication, volume and page, require no full point. Nor do notes giving only an explanatory phrase or reference.' But this is not done in most books. If the principle is technically correct it is hardly justified by its inherent difficulties, as each note will require a judgment as to whether or not it wants a full-stop, and an ungainly incongruity will obtain when notes with initial capitals and full-stops and notes without are placed together. A simpler policy of starting every footnote with a capital letter, save for i.e., e.g., ibid., cf., p., etc.,will prove much less inconveniencing or complicated than allowing certain phrases to begin in lower-case because they are parenthetical or they're not complete sentences or may be, as in Rees's rule 346, 'a simple reference to the source of the quotation'.†

The sequence of symbols is: * † ‡ § ‖ ¶. The standard Macintosh, Windows and ISO Latin-1 character-sets do not contain the fifth symbol (the parallel) and so a paragraph mark (the sixth symbol)‡ is nowadays used in its stead and then the symbols are doubled. If it is anticipated that doubled symbols (or worse, trebled!) will often be required, figures should be used. *The Oxford Guide to Style* states that 'Other symbols are possible, such as the degree mark (°) or star (★)', but neither of these symbols is suitable; the star is not contained in the standard character-sets and Bembo, Plantin, Spectrum, Times Europa, Trump Mediaeval, all have such solid stars for asterisks. The symbols should be of the same point-size as the text and align (as they should naturally do) with the caps or ascenders.

Both old-style (non-lining) figures and 'modern' (lining) figures are used for footnote/endnote notifiers. In QuarkXPress there is a 'selection' in the measurement palette by which any character can be reduced and raised to

* 'For aesthetic reasons, text indicators are placed after punctuation (except dashes), unless the reference is to a single word at the end of a sentence or a parenthetical phrase.' (Judith Butcher, *Copy-Editing* (Cambridge, 1981), p. 155.)

† But Burbidge takes the opposite view. 'Many authors, and some authorities, consider that these Latin conventional phrases – and some others, such as cf. (*confer*), e.g. (*exempli gratia*), and i.e. (*id est*) – need no capital letter when they are used to begin a footnote. The Latin language itself is normally printed without a capital at the beginning of a sentence, but it is difficult to see why this practice should be brought into the printing of footnotes which use a few conventional Latin words for cross-reference. It is better to begin all footnotes with a capital letter, except perhaps when an initial word is lifted bodily from a quotation in which it begins with a lower-case letter.' (*Notes and References*, p. 11.)

‡ In Oxford style the paragraph mark precedes the parallel mark. In the *Lund Humphries Desk Book* (1971) the order is: * † ‡ ‖ §.

the cap-line. The obvious disadvantage of using normal characters reduced in size as superiors is that they're too light. A number of digital types feature proper superior figures in 'expert' sets (which also contain non-lining figures, f-ligatures, fractions, superior letters) and these are of an appropriate weight and design (being all of the same height and alignment). In earlier days superior figures weren't included among the sorts of most founts and so superiors (most of which were supplied for setting fractions also) from an extensive selection of sizes, weights and styles were used. Many designers, typographers and connoisseurs have deemed such figures, which were usually of a 'modern' design, incongruous.* I find the superiors of many expert sets to be quite suitable (e.g. those of the Monotype Ehrhardt expert set: [123]) but I have chosen to use more conspicuous, heavier figures for this book for both the notifiers and fractions as they're more reader-friendly. I should hope they're not too disharmonious.†

Superior figures, as used in the text (as notifiers), are often used to number the footnotes also, though full figures (lining or non-lining), as specified in Jan Tschichold's Penguin Composition Rules, will look better: 'For the numbering of footnotes use normal figures followed by a full point and an en quad.' Alternatively (if one isn't obliged to follow the Penguin Rules), the full point may be omitted (as is done in the endnotes of this book). The footnotes may be indented, in which case the indention should be the same as that of the paragraphs of the text, or set full-out or with hanging (or reverse) indents (as in Rayner Heppenstall's *Journals*, fig. 2). Symbols should always be followed by word-space; either a word-space or an en should follow full figures but an en is too much space after superior figures.

Footnotes are normally set two points smaller than text but may be smaller still, especially if the notes are copious.

In this book the short footnotes are left-ranged and first lines are indented 11 points as the text is.‡ In books which are centre-orientated short single-line footnotes are usually centred within the measure and if two or more are short (and all are single lines) they are often left-aligned with the longest line which is centred. Two or more footnotes may be set on one line (as on our page 43); it may be well to align the final note with the right edge of the measure or indent it on the right by an em (especially in a symmetrical, centre-orientated book). An em, or more or less, might be inserted between them.

---

* 'A small matter, but one that is worth stating, is that it would be more in harmony to use old-face (hanging) figures with old-face types and lining figures only with modern faces; but printers and typefounders appear to prefer lining figures, and old-face figures are seldom forthcoming even when asked for.' (Seán Jennett, *The Making of Books*, p. 292.)

'Do not use modern face fraction figures in any old style fount. Either hanging or ranging figures may be used provided they are in harmony with the face used for the text. For books composed in any old face letter, we recommend Monotype Superior Figures F627, to be cast two points below the size of the face used.' (Jan Tschichold, *Penguin Composition Rules* (1947), p. 3.)

† I expect I've developed a prejudice against the too-small and filamentary figures which feature in so much of digital typography. In any case, one *turns back* from the endnotes to the text page nearly as often as one goes from text to notes and it is in this instance especially that too-light notifiers are discommodious.

‡ Among the 'faults' which were found in the books examined at the Exhibition of British Book Production 1970 (by uncredited writers on p. 7 of the *Monotype Newsletter* 88 (February 1971)) was 'The indent of the first line of a footnote'. But such an indent can be judiciously used to differentiate note from text and will prove happier than a full-out setting if the final line of the superjacent text happens to be indented.

Oxford style specifies that footnotes should be positioned on short pages not at the foot but close to the last line of text. *The Oxford Guide to Style* is indeed very specific: 'Footnotes to a short last page should be set 12 points below the last line of the text, *not* at the bottom of the page' (p. 52). It is not stated whether this should be 12 points from the last line of a text set 12/14 (i.e. with line-spacing of 14 points) or 12 *additional* points.* At any rate, one can conceive of circumstances in which the method would prove quite awkward. An article or letter etc., for example, ending on a short page with a date set on a line by itself, right-ranged and in brackets (square or round), spaced by a line or a half-line of white – or a closing ('Yours', etc.) – may look better with the footnote at the foot.

The opposite is advised by Oliver Simon in his *Introduction to Typography*: 'Notes to a short page must be brought down to the foot of the page and not "skied".'† But this can be quite as problematic if applied to a long short page. If there isn't very much space (only two or three lines) between text and footnote when the footnote is placed at the foot, it may look quite more awkward than to set the footnote close to the text.

A curious footnoting method is sometimes seen in books of letters or diaries wherein the particular entry or letter is marked (with figure or symbol) and the note is not placed at the foot of the page but at the end of the letter or entry. To make the matter more confusing the annotated parts of the letter or entry may occur, all or some of them, on a recto page with the letter or entry ending on the following verso page and the notes placed therein. It is an old style but not a very good one (fig. 22).

Composition of footnotes isn't nearly as troublesome nowadays as it was in pre-desktop days and the advantage of keeping notes within the text to avoid costly compositional difficulties is open to question. Nor is any aesthetic advantage attained by eliminating the small type at the foot of the page if the notes are set within the text or as sidenotes as in Robin Kinross's *Modern Typography* (fig. 23). Seán Jennett suggests however that when this is 'well done, in the few kinds of books this method suits, the result may be pleasantly decorative.'[7]

Sidenotes, which are uncommon in modern books, are not usually used for ordinary references but for commentary, to give glosses on the text. Figures are sometimes set in outer margins either for the purpose of numbering the lines of a text, often of a play or poetry,‡ to provide the reader with a guide (useful when endnotes refer to particular lines of text of a particular page) or to refer to illustrations in another part of the book. This might be an agreeable alternative to constantly interrupting a text with (fig. —).

In Quark and InDesign separate text boxes should be used for footnotes, the last lines of which should always align with the bottom of the text area (where the last line of the main text would normally fall). When the footnote must be carried over to the next page the text boxes can be linked. The note should break within a sentence and a thin rule ($\frac{1}{2}$ or $\frac{1}{4}$-point) may be placed over the continuation but this is more a matter of taste than rule. No rule but rather space is favoured by Oxford and, if the rule can be done without, the

---

* The line-spacing of the text of *The Oxford Style Guide* is 13 points.

† (Faber, 1945), p. 9 and later editions. This is also the Lund Humphries style.

‡ Usually by every five lines.

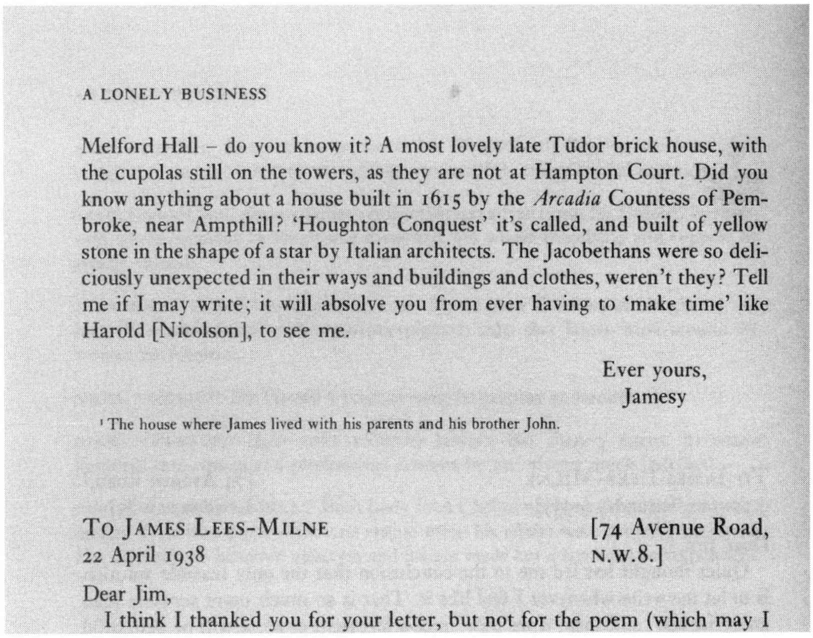

Fig. 22 Detail of p. 6 of *A Lonely Business: A Self-Portrait of James Pope-Hennessy*, edited by Peter Quennell (Weidenfeld & Nicolson, 1981), showing a note pertaining to the first line of text on the preceding page. Designed by Joyce Chester; set in Monotype Ehrhardt; printed by Butler & Tanner Ltd. Shown at 80 per cent.

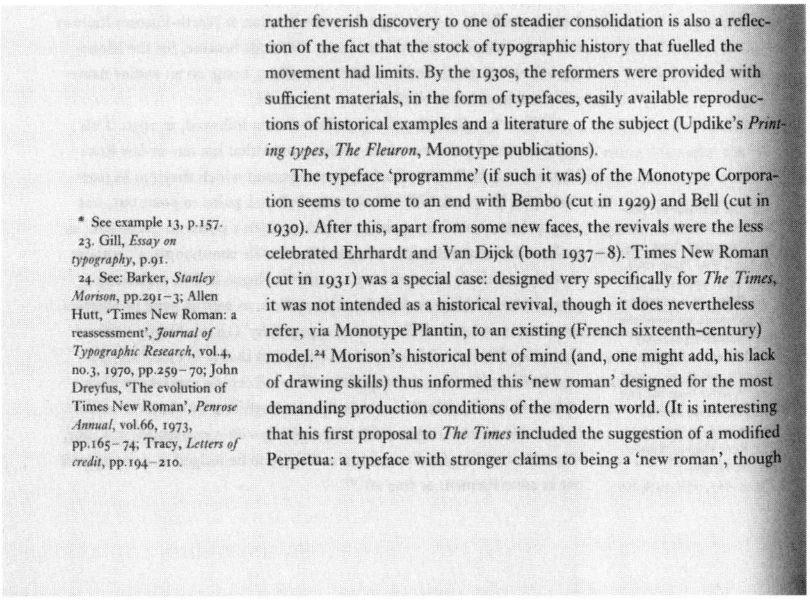

A LONELY BUSINESS

Melford Hall – do you know it? A most lovely late Tudor brick house, with the cupolas still on the towers, as they are not at Hampton Court. Did you know anything about a house built in 1615 by the *Arcadia* Countess of Pembroke, near Ampthill? 'Houghton Conquest' it's called, and built of yellow stone in the shape of a star by Italian architects. The Jacobethans were so deliciously unexpected in their ways and buildings and clothes, weren't they? Tell me if I may write; it will absolve you from ever having to 'make time' like Harold [Nicolson], to see me.

Ever yours,
Jamesy

¹ The house where James lived with his parents and his brother John.

To James Lees-Milne
22 April 1938

[74 Avenue Road,
N.W.8.]

Dear Jim,
I think I thanked you for your letter, but not for the poem (which may I

Fig. 23 Detail of p. 64 of *Modern Typography* by Robin Kinross (Hyphen, 1992; reprinted with minor corrections, 1994), set in Monotype Ehrhardt ('designed & typeset by the author in QuarkXPress 3·0'). The sidenotes are set 8/10 in an eight-pica measure (in other pages words are divided but not in this example). References are numbered by chapter; the numbers are not used in the bibliography. Symbols refer to illustrations in the final pages of the book. The notes are positioned at the foot of the page in short pages also. The notifiers in the text are set in old-style (non-lining) figures. Note the absence of spaces between pp., no., vol., and figures, but space added between en-rules and figures. Shown at 69 per cent.

* See example 13, p.157.
23. Gill, *Essay on typography*, p.91.
24. See: Barker, *Stanley Morison*, pp.291–3; Allen Hutt, 'Times New Roman: a reassessment', *Journal of Typographic Research*, vol.4, no.3, 1970, pp.259–70; John Dreyfus, 'The evolution of Times New Roman', *Penrose Annual*, vol.66, 1973, pp.165–74; Tracy, *Letters of credit*, pp.194–210.

rather feverish discovery to one of steadier consolidation is also a reflection of the fact that the stock of typographic history that fuelled the movement had limits. By the 1930s, the reformers were provided with sufficient materials, in the form of typefaces, easily available reproductions of historical examples and a literature of the subject (Updike's *Printing types*, *The Fleuron*, Monotype publications).

The typeface 'programme' (if such it was) of the Monotype Corporation seems to come to an end with Bembo (cut in 1929) and Bell (cut in 1930). After this, apart from some new faces, the revivals were the less celebrated Ehrhardt and Van Dijck (both 1937–8). Times New Roman (cut in 1931) was a special case: designed very specifically for *The Times*, it was not intended as a historical revival, though it does nevertheless refer, via Monotype Plantin, to an existing (French sixteenth-century) model.²⁴ Morison's historical bent of mind (and, one might add, his lack of drawing skills) thus informed this 'new roman' designed for the most demanding production conditions of the modern world. (It is interesting that his first proposal to *The Times* included the suggestion of a modified Perpetua: a typeface with stronger claims to being a 'new roman', though

page will not suffer. The rule, if it is used, is positioned full-left and normally extended to six ems or a quarter or half of the measure but it should not extend the full width.

Rather than causing difficulty, the footnote can be prove beneficial to pages which will otherwise end or start awkwardly: space can be added without adverse effect between text and footnote in circumstances wherein the next page would otherwise start with a widow.

There are a few different ways of numbering footnotes or endnotes – by the page (for footnotes but not endnotes), by the chapter or section, being the most common. In Virginia Woolf's *Diary* the footnotes are numbered by the month, in Harold Nicolson's *Diaries and Letters* by the year, in the Everyman Pepys footnote numbering begins fresh on each page and this is the most common practice (the least costly when notes are moved, added or deleted).

If there are just a few pages of endnotes* it shouldn't be necessary to use headlines referring to text pages. If the notes are not too numerous, numbering may not be necessary; an asterisk can be used in the text pages, even more than once in the same page, when the endnotes identify the referent word or phrase. The endnotes to the English translation of *L'Âge d'homme* by Michel Leiris (*Manhood*, Cape, 1968) follow the form of the Gallimard edition in which no indication whatever is given in the text pages but the noted word, phrases or passages are identified as follows in the Notes:

Page 47, line 8:... *in whose third act...*
     Actually, the fourth act, not the third.

These are the author's notes, not the translator's or editor's. As they're unmarked in the text, the reader may not be aware of their existence until the end of the book is reached. That may be desirable for both author and reader. An advantage of endnotes exists in their very unobtrusiveness and perhaps it is desirable if the reader, after reading all of the book, now re-examines and reflects on passages which were at first read without interruption.

The more common style is that which is used in this book: endnotes indicated in the text by number, numbered by chapter. The notes are set one size smaller than the text, distinguished by right-aligned figures and hanging indents.

I have omitted to describe some other peculiar treatments. But whatever the particular form, for every book it is a question of what is most suitable and reader-friendly; is a matter of *nicety*, which my old *Chambers* defines as 'delicate management: exactness of treatment: degree of precision: fineness of perception or feeling: critical subtlety: a matter of delicate discrimination or adjustment'.[8]

* 'If each chapter is by a different author it is advisable to print the notes after the chapter; otherwise they are better at the end of the book, where they can be turned to more easily.' (*Notes and References*, p. 12.)

Fig. 24 *The Diary of Samuel Pepys*, edited with an introduction by John Warrington, the Everyman's Library (Dent, 1953; reprinted 1973), vol. 3, p. 223. Beautifully set by the Aldine Press in Monotype Fournier 185 (though regrettably em-quadded between sentences). A shortened-capitals Fournier (series 285) was cut for the Nonesuch Press Shakespeare (1929) and this is now the ordinary version of the digital Fournier – the series 185 is available as an alternative called Tall Capitals. Note the centred note no. 4, and the rule, which is used to demarcate the carried-over note, going the full width of the measure.

May 1668   DIARY OF SAMUEL PEPYS

is not, modest. Here took up Knipp into our coach, and all of us with her to her lodgings, and thither comes Banister with a song of hers, that he hath set in Sir Charles Sedley's play for her,[1] which is, I think, but very meanly set; but this he did, before us, teach her, and it being but a slight, silly, short air, she learnt it presently. But I did get him to prick me down the notes of the Echo in 'The Tempest,' which pleases me mightily. Here was also Haynes, the incomparable dancer of the King's House. Then we abroad to Marylebone, and there walked in the garden,[2] the first time I ever was there; and a pretty place it is.

8th. The Lords' House did sit till eleven o'clock last night about the business of difference between them and the Commons in the matter of the East India Company. To my Lord Crewe's, and there dined; where Mr. Case, the minister, a dull fellow in his talk, and all in the Presbyterian manner—a great deal of noise and a kind of religious tone, but very dull. After dinner my Lord and I together. He tells me he hears that there are great disputes like to be at Court between the factions of the two women, my Lady Castlemaine and Mrs. Stuart, who is now well again, the King having made several public visits to her, and like to come to Court: the other is to go to Berkshire House,[3] which is taken for her, and they say a Privy Seal is passed for £5000 for it. He believes all will come to ruin. Thence I to White Hall, where the Duke of York gone to the Lords' House, where there is to be a conference on the Lords' side with the Commons this afternoon, giving in their reasons, which I would have been at, but could not; for, going by direction to the Prince's chamber, there Brouncker, W. Pen, and Mr. Wren and I met, and did our business with the Duke of York. But, Lord! to see how this play [4] of Sir Positive At-all, in abuse of Sir Robert Howard, do take, all the Duke's and every-body's talk being of that, and telling more stories of him, of the like nature, that it is now the town and country talk, and, they say,

---

Othello, Theodosia in *The Mock Astrologer*, etc. This actress seems to have quitted the stage before 1670, but it is not known when or where she died. Her residence for many years was at Hammersmith, in a fine mansion, built by Sir Nicholas Crispe, which had been purchased for her by Prince Rupert.

[1] The song in Sir C. Sedley's play, *The Mulberry Garden* is 'Ah, Cloris, that I now could sit.'

[2] On the site of Manchester Square.

[3] Afterwards called from the title of Cleveland conferred on Lady Castle-maine, and preserved in the names of Cleveland Row and Cleveland Square.   [4] *The Impertinents.*

223

Fig. 25 *The Sorcerer's Apprentice* by John Richardson (Alfred A. Knopf, 1999). You can easily find worse examples at the booksellers, but this is one of the ugliest books I own. It was designed by Iris Weinstein; typeset in New Caledonia (letter-spaced italic folios, headlines and captions in Diotima) by North Market Street Graphics at Lancaster, Pennsylvania; printed by Quebecor at Martinsburg, West Virginia. Greyish half-tones throughout intruding into the text which then suffers from measures too narrow and consequent monstrosities of word-space. I'm told it's a good read but unless a readable edition is printed, I'll never know. Reduced from 233 mm deep.

THE SORCERER'S APPRENTICE

DC with Fernand Léger in his Paris studio, 1949

greatest of all studio pictures, Velázquez's *Las Meninas.* Picasso did not draw on Douglas's colorful *Atelier,* but on one of the earlier monochrome versions. He envisioned Velázquez's studio in the gray light and tactile space of Braque's *Ateliers.*

Of the four cubists Douglas had chosen to collect, only one, Juan Gris, had died—too soon to meet the man who would devote much of his life to studying his work. Douglas's scholarly *catalogue raisonné* of Gris's oeuvre is the publication that does him the most credit. Rightly or wrongly, he felt he would have disliked Gris—"a wonderful artist, but a humorless whiner with terrible chips on his shoulder"—however, Douglas was fond of his widow, the beautiful Josette, who worked as a *vendeuse* in a French fashion house. She had also been the model for the magnificent 1916 portrait (bought for less than £100 at Christie's in the late 1930s), which was the *clou* of Douglas's Gris collection. Picasso, who had done much to encourage Gris when he was a poor illustrator, and quite a bit to discourage him when he became a successful cubist painter, regretted that he had never acquired any of his work. Hence his repeated efforts to persuade Douglas to sell him the *Portrait of Josette*—to no avail. Douglas left this masterpiece to the Prado.

To my surprise, Douglas's eyes turned out to have been opened to modernism not by Picasso but by Fernand Léger: specifically Léger's one-man show at Paul Rosenberg's Paris gallery in 1930, when Douglas had been nineteen. He did not actually meet the artist until May 1933, when Carl Einstein—the pioneer historian of modernism and primitivism, who committed suicide when the Nazis invaded France—took him to Léger's studio. Painter and patron became instant friends. For Douglas, this stalwart, outgoing, left-wing modernist from Normandy, with his tough-minded, architectonic theories and total lack of preten-

Illustrations, captions

The wonderments of digital technology notwithstanding, photos still look better on coated or art paper than on text paper. If the practice of printing photos and other artwork together on special paper which is inserted in the middle of a book (or at three intervals) is seen as antiquated (i.e. unenlightened), the practice of putting them into text pages and running text round them is hardly a step forward.* A case in point is *The Sorcerer's Apprentice* which should be regarded as a cautionary tale.

Of course, I'm not speaking of illustrated books whose typography is as well treated as the images, where the integrity of the text is never violated (as in such books as *About Face* or *The Ascent of Man*). No. It is the practice of running text round art which is to deplored. I recognise it's nothing new.

But other deplorable things are often done in the illustrations pages. It is seldom very easy to fit the photos into the pages and rather than reduce them drastically photos are given odd croppings (making them very narrow or short) or one photo is positioned over the corner of another in an area not occupied by the subject or essential contents. But if the designer resolutely abstains from these practices he/she can produce a more sensible and attractive page. It may mean editing (omission of a photo!), and that may prove a difficult business if not an impossibility, or re-writing or repositioning of captions, or reduction and (or) cropping of a reasoned, moderate, judicious nature.

The following are my own rules. The words 'photo' and 'illustration' are used here to indicate the same thing.

1 Type should not be placed over photos. (Reduce the photo or place the caption on a facing page.)
2 Type (whether text or caption) should not run round illustrations.
3 People should not be reversed (nor should anything else be).
4 Photos should not be overlapped.
5 Photos should not be tilted nor turned on their side.
6 The background should not be 'dropped out' or removed from a figure or figures.
7 Photos should be 'squared-up' within rectangles or squares, nor framed in ovals or circles. (This rule does not pertain to original images whose outer edges are ellipsoid or circular – but even then, if it can be done judiciously, it might be preferable to crop the image rectilinearly.)
8 Odd dimensions should be avoided. 'Portrait' (vertical) is preferable to 'landscape' (horizontal).

* 'Letterpress half-tones are best printed separately from all text other than captions. The glossy white paper which provides the most favourable colour and surface for these illustrations does justice to a limited number of type-faces only, and returns a dazzling reflection from bright light into the reader's eyes; text is better printed on toned paper with a matt surface. For these reasons, text and half-tone illustrations, which can be printed together by any process, have long been printed separately from each other in letterpress work of good quality. This has given rise to a convention that half-tone illustration need not appear at a relevant point in the text, but may be placed in a textually random position which suits the economics of binding but not the convenience of the reader.' (Hugh Williamson, *Methods of Book Design*, 3rd edn, p. 218.) This is a good explanation for why we find such a convention, but I rather think that separating illustrations from text, in most cases, causes the reader no inconvenience at all.

9 Captions should not be placed any nearer to illustrations than an em of their point-size. Better to give even more space (at least two ems) when this is possible.

10 The measure of a caption positioned under a photo should not exceed the photo's width. Captions should be set, in most cases, in a smaller size than the text.

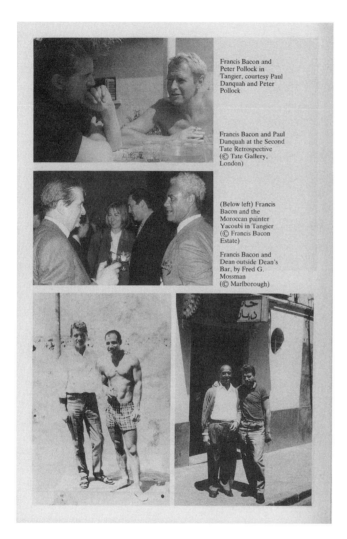

Fig. 26 Photos from *The Gilded Gutter Life of Francis Bacon* by Dan Farson (Century, 1993). Captions set rather large; credits might have been smaller. Reduced from 233 mm deep.

Fig. 27 The Vintage paperback (1994). See rule 4. Reduced from 197 mm deep.

3 On book design and typographic style: books by Richard Hendel and Robert Bringhurst

Richard Hendel, a designer of books and the associate director of design and production manager at the University of North Carolina Press, Chapel Hill, has written a unique and appealing book called *On Book Design*.*

The idea for this book came from my own curiosity about how designers conceptualize what a book should look like as well as how they actually *do* their work. I consulted British and American designers whose work I admire and asked if they would contribute design samples and describe their working methods.[1]

On Book Design is itself a study in book design and it is quite as interesting as the design samples of his fellow designers. It is 210 pages but it is large and rather heavy ($11 \times 7\frac{1}{2}$ in.); it is printed on antique paper and designed by the author. The 'typesetting specifications' of it are given on pages 84–6:

The 'main text' is $11 \cdot 2/15$ Monotype Garamond in a measure of 27 picas, 44 lines of text to a page ('1 line short facing pages' are 'OK'); the paragraphs are indented 12 points (rather than $11 \cdot 2$ points, the size of the type); '$\frac{3}{4}$-em dashes, thin-spaced left and right'; 'Fractions set as on-line fractions (1/2)'. It is not noted but Garamond italic series 174 is used, rather than 156 (the former is currently sold by Monotype as Garamond Italic and the latter is now called Garamond Italic Alternative, which may be a reason).† Narrow columns, such as I spoke of in the previous chapter, containing subsidiary text (short commentaries, quotes), are run alongside the text ('Sidebars: 7/10 Meta, ragged right, 6 picas + 7 points maximum'; 'paragraph indent: 6 points').

Mr Hendel prefers 'running feet to running heads' and they are set in $9\frac{1}{2}$-point Monotype Garamond small caps – left-ranged on verso pages with part titles following folios and right-ranged on rectos with chapter or section titles preceding folios. A number of pages are short by one line and where this occurs with facing pages the text areas of both the pages are shortened to align with one another (this is the matter of '1 line short facing pages' in the author's typesetting specifications which are stated by him as being 'OK'). There are a few instances of words breaking on recto pages and travelling across illustrated single or double pages before concluding (*contain-ing* starts on page 52 and concludes on page 56; *in-tegrating* is divided on page 67 and carried over to page 69). I think the short pages betray slovenly work but as they're allowed can't these awkward breaks have been avoided? Indeed if they can't have been corrected by other means the author might have

* New Haven, Yale University Press, 1998.

† 'The italic is unusual in its independent variation of angle and the free sweep of the kerned letters. The capitals show two or three distinct slopes and will not combine satisfactorily; but the conjunction of the erratic capitals with the erratic lower-case is charming. However, a regularised italic has also been cut.' (Seán Jennett, *The Making of Books*, p. 259.) The 174 series of a more even slant was designed specially to mitigate the variation of angle of the capital letters which was charming usually but ungainly at those uncommon instances when capital letters are set together.

dared 'take liberties' ('Being designer for myself as author, I could take liberties with the manuscript I would otherwise never have dared.')[2]

The matter of this is interesting, for the author who on page 33 observes inspiredly that 'Designers are to books what architects are to buildings' is elsewhere and at great length musing, muddling, worrying, wondering what a book designer does, should do, might do. He says: 'Book design is, indeed, an arcane subject' (page 1); 'Designers often work intuitively' (page 2). That is not architecture. There is a specially worrying muddling on pages 5 and 6.

By the mid-1990s many designers – even those who swore they would never use a computer – succumbed willingly. Never in the history of the printed book have most designers had a tool for working so easily with type. In the first century of the printed book, the designer not only set the type but also may have designed the typeface and done the printing. In time, the separation between typesetter and designer became a chasm. . . .

Computers may increase this separation between typesetter and designer. Many designers, knowing exactly how they want something to look, and not knowing how or wanting to bother to specify it, set their own type for some or all of the book. . . . Computers and computer fonts could not have come any too soon for me. I used to spend hours, even days, drawing out a title page. . . . No longer dependent on my ability to draw letters, I can see precisely what the letters look like and can control every detail of their final placement. . . .

Assuming that the designer prefers not to set all the type in a book, it is important to find a sympathetic typesetter. . . . Because the design and fit of letters can now be altered so easily, knowing who will typeset a book is as critical as planning the design itself. The same specifications followed by different typesetters often result in typography that is considerably dissimilar. Skilled and sensitive typesetters will always modify the faces they set – refining letterfit, kerning, awkward letter combinations, and even extensively re-drawing the typeface itself.

A curious use of the word 'typesetter'. 'Typographer' would be better. The definition of the one is considerably more specific than the other: in the United States, the UK and elsewhere in the English-speaking world, a typesetter is a compositor: someone who would be glad of such instructions or 'typesetting specifications' as Mr Hendel displays on his pages 84–6. It is misleading if not ridiculous to say the job of the typesetter ('who will typeset a book') entails altering 'the design and fit of letters', no matter how easily altered.

Typographer is a very indefinite term* but in England it has often been used interchangeably with book designer. This is instructive.

Mr Hendel gives the reader the impression that the book designer is inevitably remote or removed from the typography or typesetting of books. He ascribes to the 'typesetter' typographical functions which are not to do with typesetting (i.e. operative composition) but which are well within his own (the designer's) realm of responsibility. If he does not actually alter 'the design and fit of letters' himself, he is the only one to direct such an operation and this would have no necessary connection to the performance of typesetting in any event. Indeed all typographical decisions are his to make. Or to *specify*.

Only someone who is remote or removed from the typography and type-

* See Linda René-Martin, 'Variations on the typographer', *Penrose Annual*, vol. 56 (1962), pp. 24–30.

setting of books can make such a statement as 'The same specifications followed by different typesetters often result in typography that is considerably dissimilar.' What are specifications for if not to specify? It is either the fault of the designer's specifications or the incompetence of the typesetter: there is nothing inherent in the nature of typesetting which would cause considerably different typographical results from the 'same specifications'. That doesn't make any sense at all.

Nor does the statement that 'Skilled and sensitive typesetters will always modify the faces they set'. Again, modification of type is nothing to do with typesetting, but 're-drawing the typeface itself', whether extensively or just a jot – if not done by manufacturers (typefounders) and the type or character duly identified as an alternative or new type – is something to be opposed in strongest terms.

Nearly as soon as I had opened Mr Hendel's book and began to read it I noticed a modification, a *re-drawing* practised upon the Monotype Garamond type of his main text. I shall insert a parenthesis here concerning the choice of typeface before I describe the particular modification.

Though the digital Monotype Garamond faithfully follows the forms of the original design (of 1922), as did the 'Monophoto' version, both the Monophoto and digital versions are scandalously too light at normal text sizes, and it is a pity that Mr Hendel didn't share the view of his British colleagues.*

Some of my British colleagues who worked with the original metal version of Garamond consider the digitized version much too light. It doesn't feel so to me. A typographer friend fine-tuned the face for me.[3]

Unfortunately, current printing methods can't compensate sufficiently for the unsuitable lightness of this type (Mr Hendel's 'desert island choice'[4]) which the typographer friend's fine-tunings do not succeed in mitigating. (Note that Mr Hendel refers to a *typographer*.)

'Fine-tuned' is an interesting choice of words. Being typographically-orientated I saw straight away that the commas – all of them – were not those

* Even the metal version was quite light and a sufficiently heavy impression on suitable (soft) paper was essential. 'The general tone is light, and appropriate to books where daintiness is required. Good press-work is important to retain the beauty of this face . . . and the type as a whole is apt to look pale and anaemic if under-inked.' (John R. Biggs, *An Approach to Type*, 2nd edn (Blandford, 1961), p. 84.)

Mr Hendel's book features many quotations or 'marginal comments' (set as 'sidebars' in the outer margins) from book-designing and typographical folk and this marginal comment of Alan Bartram's is found on page 89: 'I suppose I do have current favorite types. . . . But practical considerations may have to override preferences. . . . if the typesetter holds mainly Monotype, I have to find one that hasn't been PostScripted out of sight (Monotype Garamond . . . is now so light as to be unusable).' Rather irksomely Mr Hendel does not give any reference beyond the marginal commenter's name, either with the quotation or in an endnotes or bibliography. It seems this was a design matter but an interesting one for a designer employed by a university press. The design matter did not escape the notice of his publishers: 'The Yale University Press editorial staff were unhappy about my desire to identify the source of these marginal comments in such a minimal way (using only the name of the person being quoted and not the location from which the quotation was taken), but any longer source would have made the sidebars unwieldy' (pp. 80–1). One expects in any case the quotation from Bartram is from a private correspondence.

Richard Hendel might also have read Alan Bartram's (and his co-author James Sutton's) view of Monotype Garamond in *Typefaces for Books*: 'Display sizes are about the same weight as the original hot metal version (although the letters are wider and the serifs lighter) but when reduced to text sizes the design is too light.' (p. 148.)

of Monotype Garamond but looked rather like those of Galliard.* There's
not the slightest mention of this in the book but I thought the matter curious
and remarkable enough to warrant writing to Richard Hendel, and he was
kind enough to reply:

I did not modify the Monotype Garamond comma, though some of the other
characters were slightly modified and kerning pairs adjusted. I don't see any difference in Monotype Garamond between what I have and what is offered by Monotype. I'd be *very* interested to see what examples you have.[5]

This confused me. I took it he didn't wish to tell me, for obviously the
commas were much different to those of the type as produced by Monotype
and I couldn't conceive that they were altered without his knowing. I then
sent him a list of books which are set in Monotype Garamond, the commas
in each example (whether from metal, Monophoto or digitised versions) all
essentially the same (i.e. proper Monotype Garamond commas). I also remarked that in the examples he shows in his book of his own design for another book, which is also set in Monotype Garamond, the commas appear
to be the type's proper commas.† I suggested to him that it might have been
a 'rogue version' (made by another manufacturer), though I quite doubted
that it was. In any case, all that was needed was to print his comma at a large
size and compare it to any comma set at the same size in a PostScript Monotype Garamond which hadn't been 'modified'.

Here is his e-mail to me:

I don't see the difference between your Garamond and mine . . . Not to say there
isn't a difference, only *I* don't see it. The Garamond on pages 74–75 looks different
I think because the illustration is made from a 600 dpi print out [*sic*] while the rest
of the job was disc to film.

This week I'm having lunch with Charles Ellerston, the gent who worked on the
font for me, and if he sees it differently than I do, I'll get back to you.[6]

He did that and this is the e-mail I then received from him – the second,
third, and fourth paragraphs are his colleague's:

My hat's off to you . . . here's what my friend tells me he did with the font.

Turns out the guy was right. I looked at the comma in the foundry Monotype
Garamond & the one in our modified font, and they are different. Apparently I used
a slightly modified Galliard comma for the Garamond. Galliard was based on a
typeface by Granjon, whereas Monotype "Garamond" is based on Jannon's font(s).
But, still, not that far apart. And I continue to think ol' Bringhurst‡ wrong, in that
he maintains the italic of Mono Garamond is based on Jannon's ital, whereas I think
it is based on a Granjon font. But we're talking about the roman, and the MG roman is surely based on Jannon's work.

BTW,§ in terms of what the old compositor's [*sic*] did with Monotype metal
fonts – what you put in the matrix case is your business. It wasn't that uncommon
for someone to use a different comma or period in the case. The more you used a
font, the more you made little touches like that.

I'd think that overall, this is one of the smaller changes I made to the font. More
obvious are the ascenders & descenders; more helpful was the re-weighting . . .[7]

---

* A 'modern revival of the types of Robert Granjon', designed by Matthew Carter and issued in 1978 by Mergenthaler Linotype (New York). Its commas are distinctive.

† The contents page and p. 135 of *High Lonesome*, by Cecelia Tichi (University of North
Carolina Press, 1994), reproduced in *On Book Design*, pp. 74–5.

‡ Robert Bringhurst, whose book, *The Elements of Typographic Style*, is considered below.
§ 'By the way'.

I can't make out anything from this which is sensible. 'Apparently' it's such a trivial thing, this slightly modified comma, that the fine-tuning friend can scarcely remember. From this 'Apparently' one might gather it was absent-mindedly if not unintentionally done. But the explanation which he troubles to deliver (in effect to say: well, at any rate, it's perfectly justified) is then doubly curious.* Worded and e-mailed as it was, I expect it was for my benefit as well as Mr Hendel's.

But isn't it interesting how the job was done without our Mr Hendel knowing? In the Glossary to *An Approach to Type* by John R. Biggs, Typographer is defined:

> Roughly what an architect is to building. That is, a person responsible for the appearance and character of printed matter and who therefore must be knowledgeable in all the processes of printing, paper, binding, etc., while possessing the good taste to use the materials effectively.[8]

Fig. 28 (*a*) Monotype Garamond set at 22½ points; (*b*) from p. 85 of *On Book Design*, by Richard Hendel, enlarged to 200 per cent, with modified Galliard commas which are quite unlike Monotype Garamond.

(*a*) Garamond, caps & lowercase,

(*b*) Garamond, caps & lowercase,

A little more than half of *On Book Design* (pp. 87–198) consists of résumés contributed by Richard Hendel's colleagues of their creative processes and working methods, views, tastes, etc., with examples of their work. Or as the inner flap says: 'In this unique and appealing volume, the award-winning book designer . . . and the eight other designers, who represent extensive experience in trade and scholarly publishing in the United States and Great Britain, show how they aim to find the most effective visual presentation of words, offering many examples to illustrate their choices.' They are: David Bullen, Ron Costley, Richard Eckersley, Sandra Strother Hudson, Mary Mendell, Anita Walker Scott, Humphrey Stone, Virginia Tan. Five are American, two are Brits and Richard Eckersley is of Irish origin ('has taught or been a visiting critic at many art schools in Britain, Ireland, and the United States' and in 1981 became senior designer at the University of Nebraska Press). The résumés are each six or seven pages and one is glad of that for they tend to get just a bit boring. It shouldn't, of course, be surprising that similar views and approaches are taken. A predictable mix of 'intuitive reactions'[9] and the essential mundane labours, but it is remarkable that the designers do not complain of being denied 'creative control' by editors or publishers and they give an impression of being architects of books.

Their ages aren't given but the contributors seem to have in common with their colleague, Richard Hendel, the experience of pre-digital book design and in 1998 we find them at different stages of involvement with desktop publishing. The American designers, like their colleague, do not seem terribly typographically orientated and here is a striking contrast between them and the British designers Ron Costley and Humphrey Stone. One takes into

---

* Matrix-cases such as would be used for large hand-set type or for machine-composed 11·2-pt type? I'd be very interested to see an example of machine-composed Monotype Garamond with such little touches as *wrong founts* which Mr Ellerston mentions.
  The changes to the ascenders and descenders are *not* more obvious.

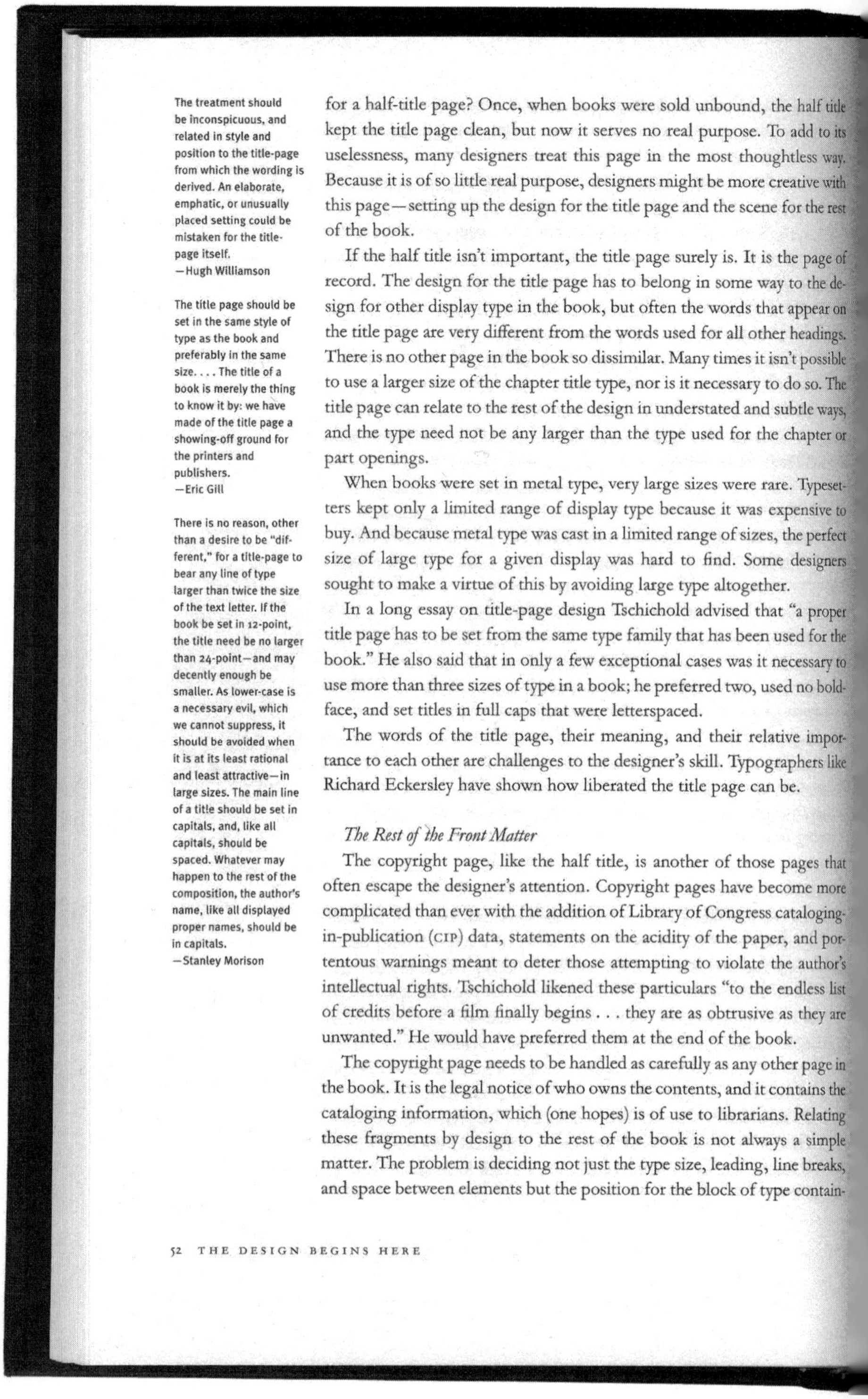

Fig. 29 The feet are running. *On Book Design*, by Richard Hendel (New Haven, Yale University Press, 1998), designed by himself and typeset in modified Monotype Garamond and Meta (designed by Erik Spiekermann, issued by FontShop International in 1993) by Julie Allred, B. Williams and Associates of Durham, North Carolina; printed at Dexter, Michigan by Thomson-Shore. Reduced from 278·5 mm deep.

The treatment should be inconspicuous, and related in style and position to the title-page from which the wording is derived. An elaborate, emphatic, or unusually placed setting could be mistaken for the title-page itself.
—Hugh Williamson

The title page should be set in the same style of type as the book and preferably in the same size. . . . The title of a book is merely the thing to know it by: we have made of the title page a showing-off ground for the printers and publishers.
—Eric Gill

There is no reason, other than a desire to be "different," for a title-page to bear any line of type larger than twice the size of the text letter. If the book be set in 12-point, the title need be no larger than 24-point—and may decently enough be smaller. As lower-case is a necessary evil, which we cannot suppress, it should be avoided when it is at its least rational and least attractive—in large sizes. The main line of a title should be set in capitals, and, like all capitals, should be spaced. Whatever may happen to the rest of the composition, the author's name, like all displayed proper names, should be in capitals.
—Stanley Morison

for a half-title page? Once, when books were sold unbound, the half title kept the title page clean, but now it serves no real purpose. To add to its uselessness, many designers treat this page in the most thoughtless way. Because it is of so little real purpose, designers might be more creative with this page—setting up the design for the title page and the scene for the rest of the book.

If the half title isn't important, the title page surely is. It is the page of record. The design for the title page has to belong in some way to the design for other display type in the book, but often the words that appear on the title page are very different from the words used for all other headings. There is no other page in the book so dissimilar. Many times it isn't possible to use a larger size of the chapter title type, nor is it necessary to do so. The title page can relate to the rest of the design in understated and subtle ways, and the type need not be any larger than the type used for the chapter or part openings.

When books were set in metal type, very large sizes were rare. Typesetters kept only a limited range of display type because it was expensive to buy. And because metal type was cast in a limited range of sizes, the perfect size of large type for a given display was hard to find. Some designers sought to make a virtue of this by avoiding large type altogether.

In a long essay on title-page design Tschichold advised that "a proper title page has to be set from the same type family that has been used for the book." He also said that in only a few exceptional cases was it necessary to use more than three sizes of type in a book; he preferred two, used no boldface, and set titles in full caps that were letterspaced.

The words of the title page, their meaning, and their relative importance to each other are challenges to the designer's skill. Typographers like Richard Eckersley have shown how liberated the title page can be.

The Rest of the Front Matter

The copyright page, like the half title, is another of those pages that often escape the designer's attention. Copyright pages have become more complicated than ever with the addition of Library of Congress cataloging-in-publication (CIP) data, statements on the acidity of the paper, and portentous warnings meant to deter those attempting to violate the author's intellectual rights. Tschichold likened these particulars "to the endless list of credits before a film finally begins . . . they are as obtrusive as they are unwanted." He would have preferred them at the end of the book.

The copyright page needs to be handled as carefully as any other page in the book. It is the legal notice of who owns the contents, and it contains the cataloging information, which (one hopes) is of use to librarians. Relating these fragments by design to the rest of the book is not always a simple matter. The problem is deciding not just the type size, leading, line breaks, and space between elements but the position for the block of type contain-account that the contributors would be keen to show more interesting examples of their work than pages just of words and there are many examples of ornamented, decorated, illustrated books, but here also one finds the American designers and Ron Costley and Humphrey Stone with quite different tastes, approaches, ideas or ethos. The Americans in Richard Hendel's book (prize-winners all), seem to be practising a form of magazine design. And not very competently. Their words, in any event, are more to be recommended than their examples.

There is an interview with Ron Costley (pages 105–25) rather than a résumé and it is, with Humphrey Stone's contribution (pages 177–88), the most recommendable part of the book. Mr Costley was interviewed while at Fabers and one gets a much better picture of the inside of publishers than from the other contributors. Humphrey Stone's section is notable for the samples of his first-rate work (his catalogue of the Sainsbury Collection, published by Yale University Press, particularly).

The Elements of Typographic Style

The principles of typography as I understand them are not a set of dead conventions but the tribal customs of the magic forest, where ancient voices speak from all directions and new ones move to unremembered forms.[10]

These words are from the Foreword to *The Elements of Typographic Style* by Robert Bringhurst. It is a book of narrowish dimensions: $9\frac{1}{8} \times 5\frac{1}{4}$ inches ($231 \cdot 8 \times 133 \cdot 3$ mm); it was designed by Robert Bringhurst and 'set into type' in 10/12 Adobe Minion (but ampersand whenever it appears in Minion italic) in 21 picas by himself and Susanne Gilbert at The Typeworks at Vancouver, Canada; printed and bound by Quebecor at Kingsport, Tennessee. 'The paper – which is Glatfelter laid – was made at the Spring Grove Mill in Spring Grove, Pennsylvania. It is of archival quality and acid-free.' There are sideheads and sidenotes (described by Alan Bartram who admires them in *Making Books*: 'a battery of chapter heads, side-heads, sub-heads and cross-heads, clearly differentiated and ordered both typographically and by the numbering system'[11]). Captions are set in a sans-serif face called Scala Sans. It is a singular book. It is a manual and a meditation. It considers every detail, every curious leaf, twig, dew-worm of the magic forest. It answers every typographical question. It never puts a foot wrong.

Richard Hendel is one of the friends of Robert Bringhurst whom he thanks in the Afterword to the Second Edition, but the two writers and the two books are very different. Robert Bringhurst (who is, according to the back cover, 'one of Canada's most highly regarded typographers and book designers, as well as one of its most respected and best-known poets', who has 'taught literature, art history and typographic history at several universities and held fellowships from the Canada Council and Guggenheim Foundation') has done his home-work; he is knowleageable. The venerable Hermann Zapf says on the back cover that Robert Bringhurst is an 'expert'. *The Elements of Typographic Style* will mark our cards for us, guide us, enlighten us. For just a moment, though, on the first page of the Foreword, he wonders (lest we think him insensitive?) whether it's right to write a 'rule-book'.

One question, nevertheless, has been often in my mind. When all right-thinking human beings are struggling to remember that other men and women are free to be different, and free to become more different still, how can one honestly write a rule-book? What reason and authority exist for these commandments, suggestions and instructions?[12]

But he manages to overcome that moment of doubt and goes on to write honestly a book which is a book of rules – commandments, suggestions and instructions – and moral precepts *par excellence*. It is a sort of typographical Scout Manual.* (It should be noted, however, that the question of 'what reason and authority' is not left unanswered and he says sagely, 'If you use this book as a guide, by all means leave the road when you wish. That is precisely the use of the road: to reach individually chosen points of departure.') The rules (there are 129 of them), or let's call them articles so as not to call them rules, are numbered and organised in the style of *The Chicago Manual of Style* or *The Oxford Guide to Style*. Most of the rules are injunctive; I counted just eighteen proscriptive rules but that is a matter of wording. A few examples:

2.1.6 Letterspace all strings of capitals and small caps, and all strings of digits.

3.2.2 For abbreviations and acronyms in the midst of normal text, use spaced small caps.

3.4.1 To the marriage of type and text, both parties bring their cultural presumptions, dreams and family obligations. Accept them.

5.5.1 Use the accents and alternative sorts that proper names and imported words and phrases require.

The rules or articles are individually taken and considered, expounded upon, explained, elaborated methodically, and then they are listed in the final pages in Appendix E: Recapitulation.

Robert Bringhurst is a fancier of accents, diacritics, foreign characters, tribal runes. On the paper cover of the second edition, between the title and the author, there's a line of bright red a's accented acutely, gravely, brevely, circumflexedly, and with háček, trema or umlaut, ring, tilde, ogonek attached aduncously, ogonek with acute overhead, and bang in the middle a bright red æsc. There's also a lower-case eth, a thorn, a kreska ukośna and a cedilla. Even funnier things on the title page.

And in the inner matter the reader will learn that the 'a' to which ogonek and acute are affixed isn't a special Polish character but a common-or-garden Navaho letter. 'Navaho, for example, involves twelve forms of a – a, aa, ą, ąą, á, áá, áa, aá, ą́, ą́ą́, ą́ą, ąą́ – all easily distinguished.'[13] The reader will learn also that 'In North America, for example, Navajo, Hopi, Tlingit, Cree, Ojibwa, Inuktitut and Cherokee, among others, have evolved quite stable writing systems, in which a substantial printed literature has accrued.'[14]

The accent separates the unaccented and unexotic American/English culture from the Vietnamese, Navajo, Cherokee, Basque, Lapp, Lettish, Lithuanian, Albanian, Fijian, Romany, Malay, Polari, and here is the sub-text or the sub-message of *The Elements of Typographic Style* (but *secondary* or *other-teaching* might be better than 'subtext', for it is not conveyed abstrusely nor subliminally nor subtly); the smell of dogmatism (to borrow

---

* On the back cover of the second edition, Hermann Zapf says 'I wish to see this book become the Typographers' Bible'.

Fig. 30 A page for order. *The Elements of Typographic Style*, by Robert Bringhurst (2nd edn, Point Roberts, Washington, Hartley & Marks, 1996), designed and set into type by himself and Susanne Gilbert at The Typeworks at Vancouver, in Adobe Minion and FontShop Scala Sans. It is a book of rules and moral teachings but none of the rules forbids putting right-ranged hyphenated matter in the outer margin. Reduced from 231 mm deep.

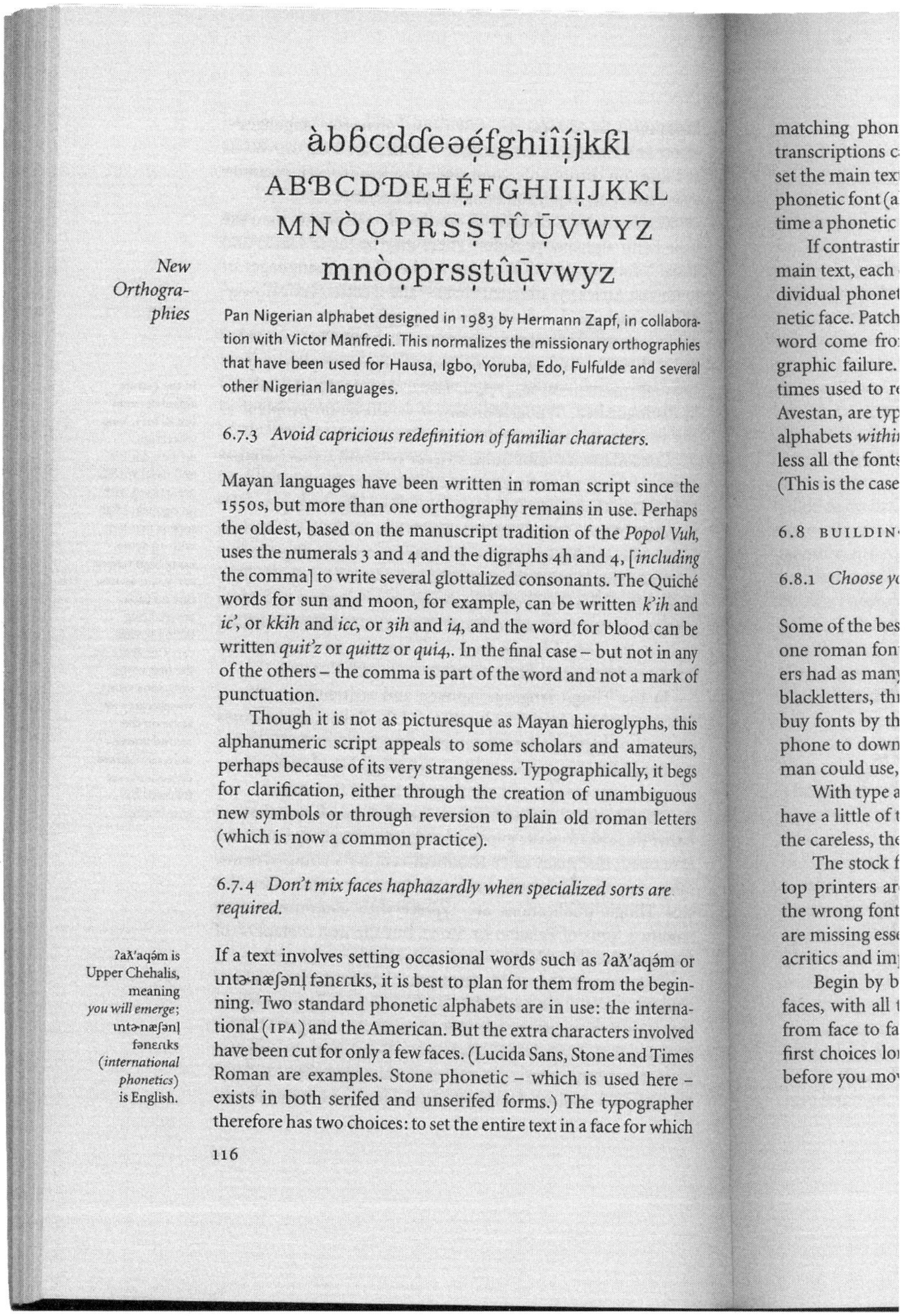

New Orthographies

àbɓcddɗeəḗfghiíịjkƙl
ABƁCDƊEƎÉFGHIỊJKƘL
MNÒỌPRSṢTÛỤṾVWYZ
mnòọprsṣtûụṿvwyz

Pan Nigerian alphabet designed in 1983 by Hermann Zapf, in collaboration with Victor Manfredi. This normalizes the missionary orthographies that have been used for Hausa, Igbo, Yoruba, Edo, Fulfulde and several other Nigerian languages.

6.7.3 *Avoid capricious redefinition of familiar characters.*

Mayan languages have been written in roman script since the 1550s, but more than one orthography remains in use. Perhaps the oldest, based on the manuscript tradition of the *Popol Vuh,* uses the numerals 3 and 4 and the digraphs 4h and 4, [*including the comma*] to write several glottalized consonants. The Quiché words for sun and moon, for example, can be written *k'ih* and *ic'*, or *kkih* and *icc*, or *3ih* and *i4*, and the word for blood can be written *quit'z* or *quittz* or *qui4*,. In the final case – but not in any of the others – the comma is part of the word and not a mark of punctuation.

Though it is not as picturesque as Mayan hieroglyphs, this alphanumeric script appeals to some scholars and amateurs, perhaps because of its very strangeness. Typographically, it begs for clarification, either through the creation of unambiguous new symbols or through reversion to plain old roman letters (which is now a common practice).

6.7.4 *Don't mix faces haphazardly when specialized sorts are required.*

ʔaƛ'aqám is Upper Chehalis, meaning you will emerge; ɪntə-næʃən̩ fənɛɾks (international phonetics) is English.

If a text involves setting occasional words such as ʔaƛ'aqám or ɪntə-næʃən̩ fənɛɾks, it is best to plan for them from the beginning. Two standard phonetic alphabets are in use: the international (IPA) and the American. But the extra characters involved have been cut for only a few faces. (Lucida Sans, Stone and Times Roman are examples. Stone phonetic – which is used here – exists in both serifed and unserifed forms.) The typographer therefore has two choices: to set the entire text in a face for which

116

---

matching phon
transcriptions c
set the main text
phonetic font (a
time a phonetic

If contrastir
main text, each
dividual phonet
netic face. Patch
word come fro
graphic failure.
times used to re
Avestan, are typ
alphabets *within*
less all the fonts
(This is the case

6.8 BUILDIN

6.8.1 *Choose y*

Some of the bes
one roman font
ers had as many
blackletters, thr
buy fonts by th
phone to down
man could use,

With type a
have a little of t
the careless, the

The stock f
top printers ar
the wrong font
are missing ess
acritics and imp

Begin by b
faces, with all t
from face to fa
first choices lon
before you mov

from Geoffrey Grigson*): there is a concentration of it on pages 102–17 in sections called The Multicultural Page and New Orthographies.

> Every alphabet is a culture. Every culture has its own version of history and its own accumulation of tradition . . . The Arabic, Armenian, Burmese, Cherokee, Cree, Cyrillic, Devanagari, Georgian, Greek, Gujarati, Hebrew, Japanese, Korean, Malayalam, Tamil and Telugu alphabets and syllabaries – to name only a few – have other histories of their own, in some cases every bit as intricate and long as – or longer than – the history of Latin letterforms.[15]

One wonders why Mr Bringhurst uses the Western, eurocentric word 'alphabet' rather than 'character-set'. The reader is told that 'typography and typographers must honor the variety and complexity of human language, thought and identity, instead of homogenizing or hiding it.'

> But typographical ethnocentricity and racism also have thrived in the last hundred years, and much of that narrow-mindedness is institutionalized in the workings of machines. Unregenerate, uneducated fonts and keyboards, defiantly incapable of setting anything beyond the most rudimentary Anglo-American alphabet, are still not difficult to find.'[16]

Defiantly incapable, mind you. One finds oneself now wondering uneasily whether it might be insensitive if not unregenerate to write Rudolph Ruzicka (as his name was spelt) rather than Rudolf Růžička.[17] Tang dynasty rather than Táng (in my *Chambers* it is 'T'ang, Tang'). Perhaps it's better to set one's Minion in Pinyan (than the Wade-Giles of doubtful sensitivity).

It is a pity that so many of the world's type designers are (were) White European Males. But there it is. Their names (mitigated by a few women's names and a few háčeks and a mäkčeň), intermixed with the names of poets, painters and sages, are dropped everywhere and constantly, habitually, Robert Bringhurst writes: 'Adrian Frutiger's Méridien', 'José Mendoza's Photina', 'Rudolf Růžička's Fairfield', 'Morris Fuller Benton's Century Schoolbook', 'Hans Eduard Meier's Syntax', 'André Gürtler's Egyptian 505', etc. This, one expects, is a didactic method but it is awfully grating. It is an odd combination of familiarity and punctiliousness. It is remarkable how punctilious (of European type designer as much as of Bí Sheng): George W. Jones is uncommonly called George William Jones; in the Index, Liszt of the Hungarian Rhapsodies is called Ferencz.

Rather than use the terms of Vox or British Standards for typeface classification, the author uses Renaissance, Baroque, Neoclassical, Rationalist, Romantic, Rococo, Realist, Geometric Modernist, Expressionist, Elegiac Postmodernism, Geometric Postmodern. The types he calls Expressionist are 'in some respects the typographic counterparts of expressionist painters such as Vincent van Gogh and Oskar Kokoschka. More recent painters and type designers, such as Zuzana Ličko [*sic*], have proven that the genre is still richly productive.' It would seem he means this seriously. And it would seem he's not attempting to pull a leg when he says:

> Painters in the twentieth century rediscovered the physical and sensory pleasures of painting as an act, and the pleasures of making organic instead of mechanical forms. Designers of type during those years were equally busy rediscovering the pleasures of *writing* letterforms rather than drawing them.[18]

There are some other variant terminologies or definitions in the book,

* *The Contrary View* (Macmillan, 1974), p. 174.

though none of them terribly misleading. 'Solid' means not 'without additional lead' but without any leading; 'M/6' etc. for $\frac{1}{6}$-em or one sixth of an em etc. (M/4 for mid-space) is rather confusing.

Agreeable advice is given on the matter of those annoying initials and acronyms which are relatively recent aberrations of the English language.

Type is idealized writing, and its normal function is to record idealized speech. Acronyms such as CD and TV or USA and IBM are set in caps because that is the way we pronounce them. Acronyms like UNESCO, ASCII and FORTRAN, which are pronounced not as letters but as words, are in the process of becoming precisely that. When a writer accepts them fully into her speech and urges readers to do likewise, it is time for the typographer to accept them into the common speech of typography by setting them in lower case: Unesco, Ascii (or ascii) and Fortran. Other acronymic words, like *laser* and *radar*, have long since travelled the same road.[19]

Curiously, in another part of the book, he puts Nato in small caps,[20] though I'd have thought it a fellow-traveller of Ascii (how does one pronounce this word?) and Fortran.* At any rate he is right to use caps and lower-case rather than caps (or small caps), but use of small caps otherwise in *The Elements of Typographic Style* is inordinate. Element 3.2.2 states: 'For abbreviations and acronyms in the midst of normal text, use spaced small caps.'[21] AM and PM for a.m. and p.m.; USA, UK, Appendix A, Cambridge, MA (but Washington, DC, and Mexico, DF, it seems because the MA is a 'postal abbreviation' while DC and DF are not); 'World War II or WWII; but JFK and Fr. J. A. S. O'Brien'.† It is often argued that small caps are less obtrusive than full caps and to a certain extent this is true, but there's a kind of fussiness, I think, in Robert Bringhurst's Style, and when AM, PM, USA, etc., are used rather than a.m., p.m., USA, etc., the effect is distracting. It is well to recall Stanley Morison's dictum: 'No reader wishes to be made conscious at every other page of some typographical dexterity, however well intended.'[22]

It's not that one is put off by a 'rulebook'; one *enjoys* R. A. Hewitt, Oliver Simon, Hugh Williamson, Ruari McLean, G. V. Carey, Judith Butcher, Herbert Rees, Eric Partridge, even *The Oxford Guide to Style*. It cannot be denied that *The Elements of Typographic Style* is full of useful things. There is much in the book that is correctly said and worthy of consideration if it can be suffered.

* '*Sets of initials.* One can punctuate all, none, or those that consist of lower-case letters; or one can distinguish those which are pronounced as a word (e.g. NATO, UNESCO, which can also be in the form of Nato, Unesco). . . . Small capitals may be used in place of full capitals. . . . However, if there are a number of capitalized words in the text or lining figures are used, the abbreviations may look incongruous and too insignificant, for example US Library of Congress, AD 1692.' (Judith Butcher, *Copy-Editing*, p. 85.)

The matter of this is discussed in greater detail in the chapter which follows.

† AM and PM are interesting because they're the only normally lower-case abbreviations which Mr Bringhurst puts in small caps, but it is a matter of omitting points in this instance (as prescribed in Element 5.4.4 ('Eliminate other unnecessary punctuation') on page 88) and one can't write 'am' (thus 'dpi' is lower-case in Mr Bringhurst's book), but no advice is given on what to do with 'e.g.', 'i.e'.

Fig. 31 More tribal runes here than in *The Elements of Typographic Style* (2nd edn): a page from the fount list of the Clarendon Press (reproduced from Richard Russell, 'Five centuries of the OUP', *Penrose Annual*, vol. 71 (1978/9), p. 60), showing Monotype Imprint for which over 8,000 special sorts were cut.

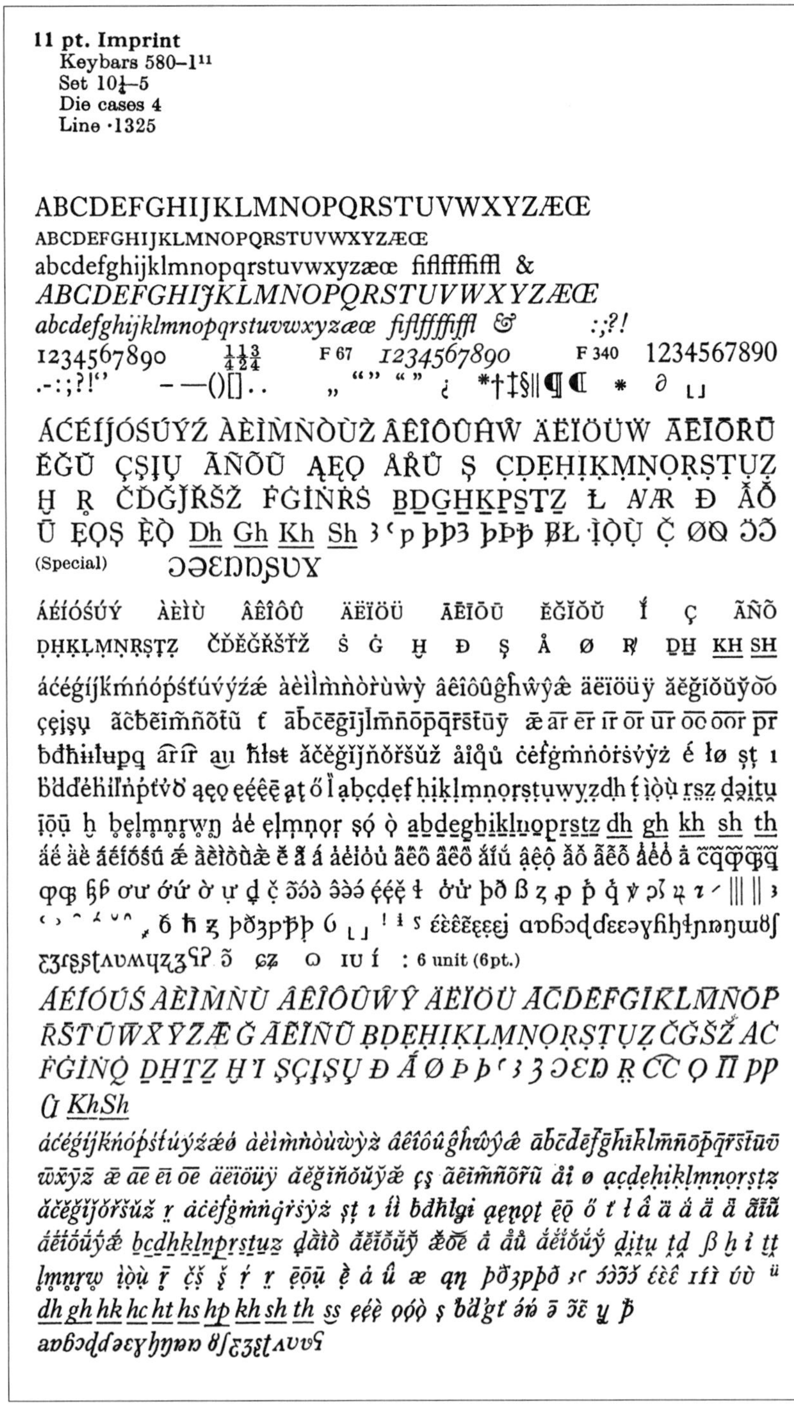

11 pt. Imprint
 Keybars 580–1[11]
 Set 10¼–5
 Die cases 4
 Line ·1325

ABCDEFGHIJKLMNOPQRSTUVWXYZÆŒ
ABCDEFGHIJKLMNOPQRSTUVWXYZÆŒ
abcdefghijklmnopqrstuvwxyzæœ fiflffffiffl &
ABCDEFGHIJKLMNOPQRSTUVWXYZÆŒ
abcdefghijklmnopqrstuvwxyzæœ fiflffffiffl &   :;?!
1234567890   11¾/42¼   F 67   *1234567890*   F 340   1234567890
.-:;?!'   – —()[]··   „ " " " ¿ *†‡§‖¶❲ * ∂ ⌐⌐

ÁĆÉÍJÓSÚÝŹ ÀÈÌMÑÒÙZ̀ ÂÊÎÔÛÂ̂Ŵ ÄËÏÖÜŴ ĀĒĪŌRŪ
ĔĞŬ ÇŞIŲ ÃÑÕŨ ĄĘǪ ÅRŮ Ş ÇDĘHĮKMNǪRŞTUZ
Ḩ Ŗ ČĎĜJŘŠŽ FGIŃRS BDGHKPSTZ Ł ᴎÆR Đ ÅÕ̊
Ū ĘǪS ĘǬ Dh Gh Kh Sh ꜫ ' p þþꜫ þÞþ ẞŁ IQÙ Ç ØQ ᴐᴐ
ᴄꜰ (Special)   ᴐꜱEⅅⅅꙅ∪X

ÁÉÍÓSÚÝ   ÀÈÌÙ   ÂÊÎÔÛ   ÄËÏÖÜ   ĀĒĪŌŪ   ĔĞĬŎŬ   Ì̊   ç   ÃÑÕ
Ḍ̣HᴋḶMNRŞTZ   ČĎĚĞŘŠ̌Ž   Ṡ Ġ   Ḩ   Đ   Ş   Å   Ø   ᴎ   DH KH SH

áćéǵíjḱḿńóṕśťúvýźǽ àèìl̀mǹòr̀ùẁỳ âêîôûĝ̂ĥŵŷǽ äëïöüÿ ăĕğĭŏŭẙŏ̊õ
çẹịşẉ ãčēĕïm̃ñõt̃ũ ꞇ ab̄cēḡijlm̄ñōp̄q̄r̄s̄tūy ǣ ar ēr ir ōr ur oo oor pr
b̄dĥiłłupq ar̄ir̄ au ĥłsꞇ ăčĕğïjňŏřšůž âiq̂ů cêfĝṁṅor̀śvýż é łø şꞇ ı
b̄ddĕĥil̃ńpꞇv̀b̆ ąęǫ ęếếệ ąꞇ ő Ĩ abçdęf hịḳlmnoṛṣtuẉyzdh ꞇ ìǫù rṣz dạịtu
ịǫū ḥ b̧ęlmṇrẉ̧n àė ẹlmṇoṛ ṩǫ̇ ȯ abdeghiklꙇ̇oprstz dh gh kh sh th
áé̊ àè̊ áéíóśú ǽ àèìôùæ̀ ĕ ᴈ̌ á àėíôù âêô âêŏ âīú âĕǫ âŏ̊ âᴈŏ̊ âᴈô̊ ã cq̃q̃p̃q̃q̃
φcᴘ ẞꝥ ɵⱳ óṹ ò ụ ḍ č ᴈ̃ŏᴈ̃ ᴈ̃ᴈ̃ó ẹ́ẹ́ẹ́ ꞇ ȯṹ þᴈ ẞ z ṗ p̆ ɋ ᴘᴈ̃ ц 2 ′ ‖‖ ‖ ꜫ
' ᷄ ᷃ ᷇ ᷅ ᵛ ᵛ , ᴘ g ' 6 ħ ꝫ þᴈꝫpÞþ 6 ⌐⌐ ¹ ¹ ꜱ ểẻ̃ễậẹẹj ɑ∪6ɔɖꝺꜫꜱꙅᴦᶃꜰĥꞁꞇꞃ̃ɱɐꞃⱳᴂꭍ
ꜩꙅᴦꙅꞇᴧ∪ꙏꝯᴈꝫꙅᴦꜱ ᴈ̃ ꜫᴈ ꝺ ꙇ∪ꞇ : 6 unit (6pt.)

ÁÉÍÓÚŚ ÀÈÌMÑŪ ÂÊÎÔÛẂŶ ÄËÏÖÜ ÁĆDÉFGIKLMÑŌP
RSTÚ̄ẂXÝZÆ Ğ ÂÊÎ̃ÑŪ BDEHIĶLMNǪRSTŲZ ČĞŠŽ ÁĆ
FGIŃǪ DHTZ Ḩ I ŞÇIŞŲ Đ Ă Ø Þ þ ' ꜫ ꜫ ᴐEⅅ Ŗ ĆĆ Q Π ꝑꝑ
Ĝı KhSh

áćéǵíjḱńóṕśťúýźǽ̊ àèìṁòùẁ̀ỳz̀ âêîôûĝĥẃŷǽ ab̄cēd̄ēf̄ghḡiklm̄ñōpqr̄s̄tūv
w̄xȳz̄ ǣ āē ēī ōē äëïöüÿ ăĕğĭňŏ̊ŭ̊ỹæ̆ çş āēìm̃ñõr̃ũ àì ø açḍeĥịḳlmnoṛṣtz
ăčĕğïjŏ̊řšůž ᴦ áćêfĝṁṅġr̀s̀ýż şꞇ ı fĩ b̄dĥłgi ąęŋǫt ēǭ ő ꞇ l å à ą̆ ä å äᴦ̃ũ̃
áêîôûýǽ̊ b̲c̲d̲h̲k̲l̲n̲p̲r̲s̲t̲u̲z̲ ḍàìɵ̄ äëïôüÿ̆ æ̆ŏ̊ē à åŭ áéíô̊úу̊ ḍịtu t̲ḍ ß ḥ ı̇ ꞇꞇ
lmnṛẉ ìǫù r̄ čš̆ š̆ ý ṛ ēǭū ę̀ á ů̆ æ ąꞇ þᴈ̃ᴈpÞð ꜫᴦ ᴈ̃ᴈ̃ᴈ̃ ểể̃ể̃ ıfĩ ùò ü
dh gh hk hc ht hs hp kh sh th ss ệệ̃ǫ́ǫ̀ǫ̀ ş b̄d̄ǵ̃ꞇ śṅ ā ᴈ̃ē y̆ ꝥ
ɑ∪6ɔḍꝺᴈᴦꭍ̃ÿ ꞁꞃꞃⱳ ᴈᴣᴈꝫ̃ᴦꙅ ꜱᴧ∪ꝯꜱ

I should like now to consider typographical treatments of punctuation and spacing, indentation, capitalisation, abbreviation, and the niceties of dashes, raised brackets, etc., which vex or fascinate designers or typographers, and the diverse opinions of the experts.

There are some rules which should serve as guiding principles rather than regulations which must never be transgressed. A common rule in bookwork is to spell out numbers under one hundred but another rule is to spell out one to ten.* The custom of spelling out numbers one to ninety-nine is probably better than spelling out only one to ten because of the likelihood of such numbers as twenty etc. occurring frequently in an ordinary text. In any event, 'nine- to 11-year-olds' won't do,† but perhaps a one-to-ninety-nine rule should be waived in such instances when either figures or words (e.g. 70 or seventy) could be alternatively used, as the ampersand is used by Dowding and Gill, to improve the spacing of a particular line.‡

G.V. Carey held the view that 'punctuation should serve the eye before the tongue and the ear, i.e. that it is concerned more with reading silently than with reading aloud.'[1] And so it would seem a matter of typographical interest. It seems also that it is often a matter of taste rather than rule (or as G.V. Carey says in *Mind the Stop*, 'I should define punctuation as being governed two-thirds by rule and one-third by personal taste'), or that there are acceptable variations just as there are for word-division. ('Rules of printed English? What impertinence! – until you reflect that rules are not dogmas, and that every rule is meant to be broken – some time or another.' – Herbert Rees, Preface to *Rules of Printed English*.) But of course word-division does not affect meaning and unless removal of a comma will (for instance) put to rights a typographical problem (without affecting meaning), or a house style prescribes omission of points from initials, etc., punctuation is not very much a typographical concern and questions of usage are matters to trouble proof-readers or editors but not designers or typographers. The books which treat of the subject are many (Fowler's, Carey, Herbert Rees, R. A. Hewitt, Partridge, Oxford, Cambridge, Chicago, etc.) and if the subject is your cup of cha they are mostly good reads.

* 'In text we set numbers as words when they are used simply, occurring only occasionally; and when starting a new sentence, or when the numbers are under ten. We print figures when the idea of measure or number is important, as in tables, dates, references or statistical use.' (The Eyre & Spottiswoode house style, quoted by Ruari McLean in *The Thames and Hudson Manual of Typography* (1980), p. 115.)

† Here is an example of hyphenating scorned by Sir Ernest Gowers. 'Avoid as far as possible the practice of separating a pair of hyphenated words, leaving a hyphen in mid-air. To do this is to misuse the hyphen (whose proper function is to link a word with its immediate neighbour) and it has a slovenly look.' (*The Complete Plain Words* (Penguin, 1962), p. 253.) And so one should write: 'nine-year-olds to eleven-year-olds'; '9–11-year-olds'.

‡ Either 42-line Bible or forty-two-line Bible will appear correct, but one would not normally write: twenty-four-hour clock.

Abbreviations and contractions. 'The Style of the House' of Mackays of Chatham states that:

> Where a full-point is not necessary to clarify the meaning, particularly in well-known abbreviations or contractions, it will be omitted.
> It will be omitted after Mr, Mrs, Dr, St (street or saint), Rd, Mme, Mlle – but M. (Monsieur) and S. (Signor, San, Santa) – and in general after all contractions in which the final letter of the word is the final letter of the contraction. Initials before names carry full-points, but may be omitted in display.[2]

This is common practice today in the UK and elsewhere but rarely seen in the United States. But there are some interesting variations. In the Lund Humphries style we find M (for Monsieur) without a point (though with a point is proper French style) and also Co and Inc, neither of which follow the final-letter rule; no point with St for Saint but a point with St. for Street.[3] We find in Herbert Rees's *Rules of Printed English* Rev. and Revd, Esq. and Esqre, Co. and Coy (as in Coy Commander).[4] *The Oxford Guide to Style* notes that the rules are broken in common usage:

> Traditionally, abbreviations were supposed to end in full points while contractions did not, giving both *Jun.* and *Jr* for Junior, and *Rev.* and *Revd* for Reverend. Handy though this rule is, common usage increasingly fails to bear it out: both *ed.* (for editor or edited by) and *edn.* (for edition) end in a point; Street is *St.* with a point to avoid confusion with *St* for Saint.[5]

I shouldn't expect such a confusion to occur very often, though this is why points are used in a.m. (and so p.m.), in., no. (No.).* These abbreviations however have had their points removed and restored in the past fifty years.

Letterpress: Composition and Machine-work in 1963 prescribes omission of the full-point 'from all abbreviations of counties, e.g. Hants, Bucks, Oxon'.[6] The new Oxford Style continues the Oxford custom: 'All British counties with abbreviated forms take a full point (*Oxon.*, *Yorks.*). Traditional exceptions were *Hants.* and *Northants.*, whose abbreviations were derived originally from older spellings, but this distinction no longer holds.'[7] (It doesn't say why the distinction no longer holds – it held in the *Oxford Guide to Style*'s predecessor, the 39th edition of *Hart's Rules*.)

UK, UN, USA are favoured nowadays in both British and American style; MP, QC, RSM are usually unpointed, as are such affixes as OBE, OM, CH, but M.D. more often than not retains the points.† In general, points are considered old-fashioned and many designers find them uncomely (no matter how useful they might be).‡

I wonder if the omission of points from etc., p., pp., vol., no., e.g., i.e., or from the initials of a name (e.g. A J Ayer), as James Sutton and Alan Bartram advise in *Typefaces for Books*, isn't something which pleases the tastes of designers rather than general readers. But they say that 'unnecessary use is dis-

---

* 'Dr (for Doctor but not after Dr. for Debtor as on a billhead)' (John Lewis, *Typography: Basic Principles* (Studio, 1963), p. 93).

† Though no points are used with honourable initials or professional degrees in James Jarrett's *Printing Style* (George Allen & Unwin, 1960).

‡ 'In assessing the need for certain uses of the full-point in a modern context, the book designer may bear in mind the probability that the author would have omitted them if he had realized in his printed text they might convey a slightly old-fashioned appearance.' (Hugh Williamson, *Methods of Book Design*, 3rd edn, p. 145.)

'e.g.', 'i.e.' need not be followed by commas or colons as used to be the common style.

turbing and confusing'. Alternatively (for p., pp., etc., but not for initials of a proper name) they advocate omission of space, which I think is even worse.

Use *either*: p 63, pp 80-95, vol 89, fig 204, pl 43, no 6 (no full point but half word space after). *No* without a full point can sometimes be ambiguous.

Or: p.63, pp.80-95, vol.89, fig.204, pl.43, no.6 (with full point but no space after).

Use *either*: *c*1900, *fl*1800, *d*1643 (in italic with no full point and no space after).

Or: *c*.1900, *fl*.1800, *d*.1643 (in italic with full point and no space after).

Print 6 am, 11.30 pm with half word space after figures, no full points within or following am, pm.[8]

I can't see how either treatment really improves the look of the text but it does seem that legibility is impaired.[*]

The p. and pp. are missing their points also in Robert Bringhurst's book but at least that is better than omitting word-space. I prefer, however, points and spaces for abbreviations and I follow to the letter the guide for capitalisation, punctuation and spacing (Table 6.1 – *The spacing of abbreviations*) on page 87 of Judith Butcher's *Copy-Editing*.

Capitalisations, large and small. Oliver Simon says that 'Figure, Number, Plate (Fig., No., Pl.) should each begin with a capital letter' (*Introduction to Typography*, p. 5) and this is also the form specified in *Hart's Rules* and *Collins*, though there is no mention of the matter in the current Oxford Style. It is not the Cambridge style. I cannot divine how these three abbreviations are different from p., vol., art., ch., etc., and so they are put in lower-case in this book (no. should be obvious if followed by figures).[†]

Overuse of small caps, which seems to be fashionable lately, is much in evidence in Robert Bringhurst's *Elements of Typographic Style*. Messrs Sutton and Bartram offer this advice:

Groups of initials consisting of more than three letters should be set in small caps if possible (possibly slightly letterspaced), although names of countries should perhaps always be in full capitals: UK, USA, USSR.

If a group of initials is followed by a word commencing with a capital, this group is best set in capitals: ICI Chemicals, not ICI Chemicals.

Roman figures can be a problem. Charles I looks diminutive, Henry VIII is rather strong. In this situation it is perhaps better to use full caps throughout; but otherwise, roman numerals are usually best in small caps.[9]

Two-letter initials and country names are put in small caps in *The Noël Coward Diaries* to irritating effect. A mixing of full caps and small caps on a

---

[*] It may also be considered that fewer errors are likely to result from a uniformity of style and that the half-word-spaces as well as closings-up or special deletion of points (usually contained in the keystrokes of an MS.) will bring 'double work' for compositor and reader.

'No. (number), fig., illus., p. (page), should be followed by a full point, but space should *not* be inserted between the full point and the figures which follow: No.234.' (*Lund Humphries Desk Book.*)

[†] 'Text illustrations are usually entitled *figures*, and textual references to them are all too often contracted to *fig*. Like contractions or abbreviations for *part*, *chapter*, *plate*, *volume*, and *page*, this has nothing to commend it, unless references occur in such numbers that to set words in full would appear uneconomical or unsightly or both. Nor is there any apparent need for an initial capital, as in *Figure*, within a sentence of text. Capitals are better reserved for specific purposes, and contractions and abbreviations, with their marks of punctuation, tend to interrupt the act of reading.' (*Methods of Book Design*, p. 276.)

page will prove quite more awkward than if full caps are normally used. (Sutton and Bartram suggest: 'A possible compromise is to use small caps up to V, small caps thereafter: vol IV, vols XVII–XXII. Thereby the confusion of vol II (two or eleven?) is avoided – at least if non-lining figures are used elsewhere.')

The reason for the former non-use of small caps in hot-metal typography was nothing to do with the trouble of changing founts, as small caps were included in most die-cases. Perhaps their present overuse is to do with their long exclusion from filmsetting types or their present inclusion in 'expert' sets. There is also an unfortunate tendency to render lower-case abbreviations (e.g. n.b.g., n/e, o.n.o.) in small caps. Should MoD (or M.o.D.) be rendered as MOD?

Sutton and Bartram prefer small to full caps.

BSC, PhD, FIInfsc, FIBiol are problems. Nevertheless, if many names with honours and awards are shown, the lesser evil is probably to use small caps, with lower case where necessary, rather than spattering the page with capitals and overwhelming the name.

I've seen such pages of names, honours and awards and I agree it is well to consider using small caps. But again: what pleases the designer may not please the reader.

This is not to protest against the judicious use of small caps. On page 262 of my own Journals there occurs:

Bethel Solomons, M.A., M.D., F.R.C.P.I.

With points and commas. Very old-fashioned indeed. While small caps without points should normally be letter-spaced as they are in this book (with 20 Quark units which is equivalent to two Monotype units), full caps in closely word-spaced text require less letter-spacing if any.*

A pleasing effect is obtained when the first word of a chapter opening is set with a single full capital and followed by small capitals but full and small capitals combined in other circumstances can look rather awkward (e.g. BOOK TYPOGRAPHY) when all full capitals or all small capitals (formerly called 'even smalls') or capitals and lower-case can be alternatively used. My own taste favours the most conservative use of small capitals and I would

---

* 'Small capitals used outside the actual context of a book, i.e. for headlines, chapter headings, sub-headings and in the preliminaries, should be letter-spaced two units. Where used in the text, except as the introductory words of a chapter, small capitals should be set solid. Set titles, credits, degrees of universities, etc, in small capitals in normal run-on text-matter.' (*Cowells House Rules* (Ipswich, W. S. Cowell, 1952), p. 20.) Note that Cowells have omitted the point from 'etc'.

'Words set in even small capitals in text matter should normally be hair (two-unit) letter-spaced. Displayed lines of capitals *above* twelve point should normally be letter-spaced only sufficiently to equalize the optical space between letters.' (*Lund Humphries Desk Book.*)

'Words in capitals must always be letter-spaced (except in Edward VIII, etc.). The spacing of capitals in lines from 10 pt upwards should be carefully equalized optically. The word spaces in lines either of capitals or small capitals should not exceed an en quad. Excessive word spacing in capitals is a frequent fault which should be avoided.' (*Editor's Manual of Penguin House Style* (1973), p. 103.)

'All words in capitals or small capitals will ALWAYS be letter-spaced with optically even spacing. About one-ninth of the body will normally be used. Thin or middle word-spaces will normally be used. Punctuation will be omitted unless essential to the sense. . . . Capitals and small capitals should not be mixed within a line.' (Mackays, *Type for Books* (The Bodley Head, 1976), p. xix.)

chose to follow initials in chapter openings with lower-case to avoid awkward caps and small caps combinations when chapters commence with proper names. A small capital should *not* in most cases be used for single letters (e.g. 30 °C; K. 201; pH; μA; A30).

Although *dropped initials* can be 'created' easily with current page-layout applications, examples of poor jobs are appallingly common. The initial used in modern books is a subdued and understated descendent of the incunabular illuminated letter but overstatement is very often the main defect or effect of inferior treatment. There is no better advice than Geoffrey Dowding's: 'Initials must, at all costs, be made to look as though they belonged to their texts.'* The conscientious designer will find the technical business – niceness of placement and spacing, the minute adjustments – relatively simple. The initial in the following paragraph was produced using the 'drop caps' function of QuarkXPress 4.

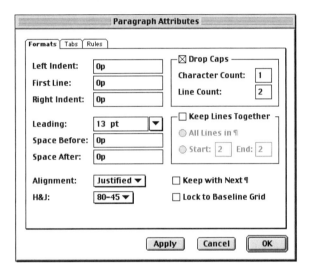

T HE 'drop caps' box is ticked and only the first letter of the paragraph is affected when the 'character count' is set to 1; when the 'line count' is specified (set to 2 for a two-line initial), the letter (which in this example is set in Monotype Octavian) is 'sized' or 'scaled' automatically. The program functions very nicely in the matters of sizing and fitting the initial snuggly against the text, but in this example the size was increased slightly from that of the default enlargement and the space between initial and text was increased slightly to be consonant with the spaced small capitals. The facility will cause the initial to align laterally with the text and so some manipulation is necessary, in this instance, to position the T so that the bar of the T overhangs into the margin and the vertical main-stroke is visually agreeable to the left edge of the text. This treatment accords with the style prescribed by Mackays (p. xiv):

Initials will range at the foot, and *must* either range at the top with the caps or small caps of the first line or rise higher than the caps. The initial will overhang into the margin far enough to give optical alignment.

* *Finer Points in the Spacing and Arrangement of Type*, p. 32.

A N INITIAL of three lines or more will usually demand more attention than a two-line initial. The letters A and L will want their shoulders mortised to bring the text close in. This can be achieved by various methods depending on which page-layout application is used. The 'drop caps' facility of QuarkXPress 4 will be unserviceable for the job and 'bézier' picture-boxes with 'runarounds' were employed to produce the example on this page. Only the first line of the paragraph in this example is positioned close to the initial. This is because the initial is part of the first line and if the paragraph commenced with a single A or I the treatment would be similar. This is the most common style and it is advocated by Geoffrey Dowding,* but a treatment whereby the succeeding lines are also positioned close to the initial so that no gap occurs is advocated by Seán Jennett.† While the initial is often set in the typeface of the text, a different type, especially a titling face, may produce a happier effect, particularly as digital versions of text types may be too heavy at larger sizes. There are a number of digitised versions of handsome types which are suitable for bookwork: Castellar (which is used for the initial of this paragraph), Monotype Bold Face Outline (which is now misleadingly called Old Style Bold Outline), Albertus, Columna, Chisel, Bembo‡ and Perpetua titling fonts, and others (a digitised version of Van Krimpen's Open Roman Capitals has yet to be produced). This is to name but a few and of course less conventional types might be used.

If the type which is used for initials is to be used for other display elements it must of course have a suitable range of letters and figures (if figures are to be used). Whether or not capitals, small capitals or lower-case should follow an initial and how many words (the first or first two or the entire first line) should be set in capitals or small caps is a matter very much to do with the special qualities of the book (typeface, line-length, etc.).

Sections of chapters can be distinguished (in lieu of subheading) by line-space and full-out setting and small capitals may seem ostentatious here.

It is a common practice to reduce the word-space between initials of names (J. H. Mason, J. H. Mason, S. L. Hartz, S. L. Hartz) but this may affect the colour of a line adversely.

In musical matter *The Oxford Guide to Style* prescribes that initial caps be used with op. or opus, no.; lower-case is sanctioned by Cambridge and this style is used in *The New Penguin Dictionary of Music*. Keys should be put in caps whether major or minor. In titles of works, 'flat' and 'sharp' etc. should be used rather than symbols (e.g. E flat minor – no hyphen). If String Quartet is the name of the work it should have initial caps.§

Special symbols and figures. Words are preferable to symbols in text. Feet or inches (spelt out or abbreviated) are preferable to minute (′) and second marks (″).‖ 48 by 72 might be used instead of 48×72 but the symbol is so commonly seen in modern text composition that it is more agreeable and of

---

* *Finer Points*, pp. 30–2. † *The Making of Books*, pp. 324–5.

‡ It does not retain the original, very useful design of the non-descending J and Q.

§ 'Initial capitals should be used for Piano, String, etc, when part of a title of a work, e.g. Brahms's Piano Quintet, no. 25, Beethoven's String Quartet, op. 59; but Dvořák's Quintet for piano and strings. Also for First, Second, etc, if again, it forms part of the generally accepted title of a work, e.g. Brahms's First Piano Concerto; but Cherubini's seventieth quartet, since the two words do not form a title in everyday usage.' (*Cowells House Rules*, p. 18.)

‖ 'Do not use ′ and ″ to mean feet and inches.' (*Copy-Editing*, p. 84.)

a different class than minute and second marks. Per cent (without point) is usually to be preferred to %. The degree mark should be used with a figure for temperatures (e.g. 30 °C – the figure should be separated from degree mark, the degree mark should be closed up to the symbol – though Cox & Wyman and many others wrongly set: 30° C); degrees of angle etc. can be spelt out or abbreviated to deg.

David Jury says that 'A full point should not be used between numerals. A decimal point should be positioned to separate a whole number from a proportionate number as in 10·5pt.'[10] A decimal should be set in this way for metric numbers indicating quantity but not for times (10.15 p.m.) or section numbers. The raised-point decimal is alien to American style and an ordinary full point is used. Herbert Rees recommends a full point for coinage.* Noughts's should go before decimals when the number less than 1 (0·25).

Figures in thousands are sometimes rendered 10 000 (etc.) with thin spaces or hair spaces. This is often done in scientific or financial work and though it looks well in ordinary books the comma is preferable if only for being less typographical trouble (the space should be less than word-space and thin spaces will be too much while hair-space may be insufficient). In ordinary texts, however, the comma is often omitted from four-digit numbers (when five and more digits take commas) and no extra space is inserted.

When noughts amount to naught they ought to be omitted (not $100.00 but $100; not 4.0 a.m. (nor 4.00 a.m.) but 4 a.m.).

Other odd points. There was an ellipsis key (or a *points of suspension* or *points of omission* key) on the Monotype keyboard, and there is an ellipsis mark in the Macintosh and Windows character-sets, but more often than not the three points are tapped out with word-spaces or fixed space (e.g. quarter-ems) put between them. This may look well or it may not look well depending on the available space of a given line. And depending also on whether other ellipses appear in nearby lines, for (if word-space is inserted) even the slightest variation of space between the points can be conspicuous. Ideally one should have three or more versions of ellipsis marks to choose from as suits the circumstances and these could be fashioned as alternative characters and added to the font or character-set quite easily and without being disloyal to the design of the type... ... ...

For parenthetical matter in text settings I prefer en-dash (with word-space either side) to em-dash (set close up or with hair-space or equivalent of Monotype 2-unit space). We are concerned here with the typographical appearances but it is interesting that Herbert Rees shows two different uses of en-dashes and em-dashes, though normally the em-dash is not used in books where an en-dash is parenthetically used.

---

* 'In decimal numbers, use decimal (raised) points normally; but in decimal coinage – dollars, francs, deutschmarks, etc. – use full points on the line:

　　10·85　　*but* $10.85　NF 6.25　DM 8.30'

A medially positioned decimal is never used with a US dollars amount and, of course, a comma is used in continental decimal numbers; sterling sums which are missing from Herbert Rees's example are none the less often set with raised points. The medial decimal was not very widely used until the time of currency metrication when The British Standards Institution and the Decimal Currency Board recommended its use. It may be less often used nowadays but I would not agree with *Oxford Style* that it 'has long been out of favour ... and should not be used unless reproducing a facsimile' (p. 171).

The en rule is also used to prolong the sound of a word in speech, or to represent a stutter:

'We – ell', he drawled.

'Have you sp – potted my p – pipe anywhere?'

The em rule is used to mark an interruption or a change of thought:

Why on earth have you—but there! what's the use of arguing?

Vanished! Just as we were about to—Good heavens, there he is again!

The em rule is also used for dramatic or rhetorical effect:

Condemned unheard! and they call that—justice.

It may also be used before a final phrase or sentence, to sum up previous phrases:

. . . the pursuit of the arts, the rule of law, love of country, reverence for the gods—all this makes up civilization.[11]

We might also note that dashes, em or en, are sometimes used for dialogue, as in James Joyce's *Ulysses* and Flann O'Brien's *The Hard Life* (translated from the Irish by himself) and so that is another category:

–Well, merciful martyrs in heaven, Father Fahrt, Mr Collopy said gleefully, did you ever hear the like of it? Drinking whiskey in a first-class carriage and us on a pilgrimage to kneel at the feet of the Holy Father![12]

En-dashes could conceivably be used in each of the cases cited (above) by Herbert Rees; the distinction seems negligible. The parenthetical use of en-dashes is none the less a relatively recent thing: it is not mentioned by Carey in *Punctuation* (Cambridge, 1957)* nor by James Jarrett in *Printing Style* (Allen & Unwin, 1960), but it is specified as house style at Cowells in 1952.† Its frequent use in British typography is likely owed to Jan Tschichold's Penguin style (1947).

Robert Bringhurst favours the en-dash. ('Used as a phrase marker – thus – the en dash is set with a normal word space on either side.') And he has no time for the em-dash.

The em dash is the nineteenth-century standard, still prescribed in many editorial style books, but the em dash is too long for use with the best text faces. Like the oversized space between sentences, it belongs to the padded and corseted aesthetic of Victorian typography.[13]

But the customary use of word-space with en-dashes can create the same sort of unhappy effects as occur in word-spaced points of omission. Monotype advised using a 5-unit fixed space.

The typographical appearance of the parenthetical dash poses something of a problem to designers, particularly in the context of justified setting. The old custom of using an em rule with a word space on each side is fortunately almost obsolete today, but it is difficult to lay down one precise typographical rule for all to follow. . . .

But by far the most general practice today is to use an en rule with word space on

---

* *Punctuation* uses em-dashes (following former Cambridge style). The Penguin edition of *Mind the Stop*, originally published by Cambridge, uses en-dashes (following Penguin style) but there is no mention of either species of dash in the discussions on dashes in either of the two works (the former using en-dashes none the less with figures).

† Em-dashes were favoured by Mackays (1976), Oliver Simon and The Curwen Press, Clowes (1970), Western Printing Services, HMSO, and Oxford. They're seen in the 1966 edition Hugh Williamson's *Methods of Book Design* but en-dashes are used in the 1983 edition. Oxford style still prescribes em-dashes but they are no longer prescribed by Cambridge. But in Lund Humphries style (1971): 'The en dash should be used with normal word-space either side of it. The practice of using an em dash without spaces should be strictly avoided.'

each side. In fixed space setting this looks quite satisfactory, but in justified setting the appearance will vary according to the width of the justified word space.[14]

It appears the en-dash is still something foreign to American tastes and few designers are disposed to using it: 'But British style uses an en dash with space around it' (Richard Hendel).[15] I suspect that to many American designers it may look too much like a hyphen.

Em-dashes used parenthetically were still the prevailing custom when Geoffrey Dowding advocated their use in 1954.

Dashes must always be of sufficient length: the em dash is to be preferred to the en dash because very short dashes begin to look like misplaced hyphens, or minus signs. They should be separated from the word or words they relate to by a hair-space only. If too much space is inserted on either side of them they appear to be floating, and the line becomes too gappy.[16]

A dash not as long as an em but longer than an en might look happier than either. Monotype supplied rules of 12 units and 15 units centred on 18 units in special made-to-order matrices. Mr Hendel uses a custom-made three-quarter dash. ('It is also possible for the designer or typesetter to create a $\frac{3}{4}$-em dash with a small amount of space on either side – as has been done for this book.')

It is customary to use an en-dash unspaced to indicate 'and' or 'to' (e.g. Creutzfeld–Jakob; May–June; 10.30 a.m.–5.30 p.m.).* But hyphens are also used and it is disputable whether this is a practice to be deplored or an acceptable variation. *Typefaces for Books* must think a hyphen more comely than an en-dash, for they instruct to use one with a 'thin space (1 unit) either side'. In any event, I usually don't find it necessary to insert hair-space before and after en-dashes as some people do.

Judith Butcher suggests that 'spaced en rules may be used between groups of numbers and words to avoid implying a closer relationship between the words or numbers next to the en rule than between each of these' (September–January *but* 18 September – 19 January). It may be preferable to give the birth-date for of a living person as (b. 1920) rather than (1920–), so as not to 'connote undue anticipation'.†

An en-dash might be used for a minus sign, although a minus sign is properly a different sort: a bit longer, a bit thinner (−30 °C).

Geoffrey Dowding recommends that dashes when set with capitals should be raised 'to the centre on the depth of the face'. Hyphens, says Dowding, should also be thus treated; and brackets:

Both marks of parenthesis ( ) and brackets [ ] look perfectly satisfactory when enclosing matter set in upper- and lower-case but appear to have dropped if they are used with capitals. The printer should therefore be asked to lift and centre them on the depth of the face whenever they are used with capitals.[17]

Brackets (*round, square, angle*). Square brackets are normally used for editorial interpolations in quoted matter (though such bracketeering is usually best avoided) and stage directions, and 'may be used in bibliographies to

Rules shown in this article as available in Baskerville (169) 10 pt

— *standard en rule, 9 units*
—— *standard em rule, 18 units*
— *S10967, 9 units on 13 units*
—— *S3106, 12 units on 18 units*
—— *S3036, 15 units on 18 units*

Fig. 32 Detail of page 17 of the *Monotype Newsletter* no. 88 (February 1971), showing standard and special dashes.

---

* 'All good printers use it in figure ranges (30–50, 1952–54), probably because, being the same width as a figure, they have become familiar with its employment in tabular work, and take it without question.' (*Printing Style*, p. 38.)

† *The Oxford Guide to Style*, p. 180.

enclose an author's name, publication place or date that does not appear in the publication cited.'* In the United States they are also used when parentheses occur within parentheses (this is the style of the University of Chicago Press [*A Manual of Style*]).† Herbert Rees advocates this usage.‡ (But note: 'If square brackets are used for interpolations, they should not also be used to replace parentheses within parentheses: use double parentheses.')§

Another rather comely but even more specialised bracket is the angle bracket which is used to indicate a letter, word or phrase omitted or wrongly copied by a copyist. They look like this: ⟨ ⟩ but *The Oxford Guide to Style* calls both these and the less-than and greater-than signs (< >) 'angle brackets' ('narrow' and 'wide'). There are still other specialist or scholarly brackets which are described in *The Oxford Guide to Style* (p. 200) and *Copy-Editing* (p. 209) in predictably slightly different ways.

Italics. Parentheses when printed with italic matter should be set in roman (but this is a matter of taste more than an inviolable rule and one can find many examples of finest printing where italic round brackets are used). Square brackets should however never be slanted, nor should the asterisk and other reference symbols. When a word or title of a book, etc., is set in italics within otherwise roman text, the full-stop, comma, colon, semi-colon and quotation marks should be set in roman. The exclamation or interrogation mark may be italic or roman depending on whether the mark follows a word or phrase in a middle of a sentence, or is part of a title, or the whole sentence is italics. The *c.* (or *ca*) for *circa* should be italic. The italic tends to emphasise and so a special word or phrase might be indicated alternatively by quote marks (but see below!). Many typefaces feature italics which look too small or too light or otherwise incongruous with the roman.

Quotation marks, apostrophes. 'The use of quotation marks *never* improves text settings. Whenever the meaning is clear without them they should be omitted.' (Geoffrey Dowding.)[18] American style generally favours double quotation marks outside and single inside. The opposite style (usually but certainly not always seen in British printing) is preferable for saving space and maintaining colour. In printing of earlier days, even in many Penguins, opening quotation marks were excessively spaced. Geoffrey Dowding advises 'not more than a hairspace should be used after the opening one and this hairspace can be omitted before certain capitals, e.g. A, C, G, J, the 'd', and the non-ascending lower-case letters.'[19] But in most digital types there should be no need of any spacing. He also recommends hanging of them (or setting them outside the measure) and reducing indentions in paragraphs

---

* *Copy-Editing*, p. 109.

† 'Some American printers, objecting to marking a parenthetical element within a parenthetical element by parentheses, mechanically substitute square brackets for the internal parentheses, especially if the final internal one happens to precede immediately the final external one: they print, i.e., not "))," but "])," regardless of whether or not the internal parenthetical element is of the sort normally marked by square brackets (i.e., editorial matter and the like).' (Professor John W. Clark of the University of Minnesota, in his contribution to Eric Partridge's *You Have a Point There* (Hamish Hamilton, 1953), p. 218.)

‡ *Rules of Printed English*, rule 80. It is also sanctioned by Oliver Simon (*Introduction to Typography*, p. 4) and R. A. Hewitt (*Style for Print*, p. 55).

§ *Copy-Editing*, p. 109.

commencing with them. There is a particularly good passage in Walter Tracy's *Letters of Credit* on the matter of spacing of punctuation and he observes that quotation marks 'make their full effect when they stand slightly apart from the letters.'

The double opening quote, which is often followed by a capital, especially in conversational wording, should be given a unit or two of space on its right-hand side. If there is also a single opening quote in the font it should be treated in the same way; but if the single is the only one it should not have the extra space because a pair of them, set in response to a demand for double quotes, will look too close.[20]

The space between the two marks in the double-quotation character of many digital types is rather too tight and so I set two inverted commas (open quote) and apostrophes (close quote). When single and double appear together they should be separated by 20 or 30 Quark units, not by word-space: "'

Oliver Simon advises: 'A hair space should be inserted before the apostrophe in such phrases as that's (that is), colonel's (colonel is), in order to distinguish from the possessive case',[21] but this nicety is fortunately no longer practised.

Apostrophes should not be used to indicate plurals except in such cases when the word wouldn't be easily cognisable without them (e.g. i's, h&j's; O.A.P.s *but* OAP's).

Colons, semi-colons, interrogation and exclamation marks (spacing of them). If the side-bearings are not adjusted in the font,* these marks should be preceded usually by 20 Quark units; in very closely-spaced lines, however, this space might be reduced: it should not be greater than the word-space. In some settings, particularly Linotype settings, the semi-colon is not spaced (cf. the rules for *signes doubles* below).

Indention. There is something pleasing about an indention of an em: an en would be insufficient, two ems too much. Some writers, however, recommend two ems indention for paragraphs exceeding 27 ems.† If a double-em indention is used for the first lines of paragraphs how should footnotes or quoted matter be treated? Many writers counsel against indenting paragraphs which follow subheadings ranged left, but they are indented here because two unindented lines so close together do not look better.

Bold-face is rarely needed in an ordinary book of text but if the book is a medical or scientific text, set in a suitable type such as Plantin or Times New Roman, then it is certainly appropriate and helpful (to the underslept medical student swotting for exams) to use bold for subheadings etc.

Foreign languages. Should the style of our en-dash or em-dash be favoured over the *tiret cadratin* in a short quotation from the French, or a longer quotation, or when just one or two cases appear in a book? Should the *Eszett* (ß)

---

* In hot metal composition the hair spaces were inserted.

† 'Paragraphs will have the first line indented 1 em (pica) up to measures of 30 ems, beyond which 1½ ems will be used. Small type to the same measure as the text will have the same indention, not 1 em of its own.' (Mackays, pp. xvi–xvii.) 'It is rarely advisable to indent more than an em, but there are times when a larger indention is more successful – in conjunction with a very wide leading, for example.' (*The Making of Books*, p. 278.)

be used or *guillemets* or *virgolette basse*, or closely-spaced *points de suspension*? Should one ever use letter-spacing for e m p h a s i s (in lieu of italics) as is done in German? What if the book is an academic study of mainly French texts and mostly brief annotations in English, or a study of German texts of the same nature?*

Often non-English languages do not permit much choice (if indeed any choice at all) when it comes to word-division or punctuation, and so they're not the challenge that English is. Quark and InDesign feature reliable hyphenation routines for many languages.

It should be noted that there is disagreement in matters of style or typographical practice (apart from word-division or punctuation) in other countries just as there is in the anglophonic world. The *règles* for French marks of punctuation, for example, include the semi-colon among the *signes doubles* (semi-colon, colon, exclamation mark, interrogation mark) to be preceded by *espace double* (i.e. the spacing for each of these marks is the same fixed double space), but in a good deal of modern French printing the semi-colon is less often set apart from the word than the question mark or exclamation mark which are as often as not set with half as much space (or *espace fine insécable*) as the colon. The colon should always be spaced with *espace insécable* (if the rules are to be observed) and in closely-word-spaced settings the space before a colon is liable to be greater than the word-space.

It may be advisable, in any case, to consult the literature of the Imprimerie nationale (*Lexique des règles typographiques*), *Abrégé du Code typographique à l'usage de la presse* of the CFPJ (Centre de formation et de perfectionnement des journalistes), Yves Perrousseaux's *Manuel de typographie française élémentaire*, etc. (or the comparable German or Italian literature, etc., for German, Italian styles, etc.), rather than to rely just on Oxford, Chicago, etc., which will provide mainly general guidelines.

Certainly one wants to use a proper *háček, kroužek, čarka, ogonek, kreska ukośna, kropka, kra, dyet.*† Or such other oddments and oddities as found in fig. 32 and in Robert Bringhurst's book. In the old days you'd be lucky to find a *tilde* in a Compugraphic (an unregenerate, defiantly incapable Compugraphic, one should rather say) and it depended on which Monotype character-set you happened to possess but most of the accents, diacritics,

---

*The approach advised in *The Oxford Guide to Style* is the most commonly taken and the most sensible:

'Foreign-language quotations given in English writing follow the same rules as for English quotations: the information a quotation contains is most important. The style of quotation marks can be normalized (e.g. « » or „ " changed to ' '); so too can the relative order of punctuation surrounding it, though not that within it.' (p. 194).

† A *háček* being, in Czech and other languages, an inverted circumflex over a c (č) or an n (ň), an r (ř), s (š) or z (ž), or a small high comma to the right of a d (ď) or t (ť) or l (ľ) (in Slovak it is called a *mäkčeň*); a *kroužek* being a ring over a u (ů); a *čarka* being an acute accent (á); an *ogonek* being, in Polish, the hook attached to an ą or an ę; *kreska ukośna* being a short oblique stroke through an l (ł); *kropka* being a dot over a z (ż); a *kra* being a Greenlandic k (κ) without ascender (similar to a lower-case *kappa*); a *dyet* being the d with a bar (đ) of Croatian and the transliterated Serbian ђ.

We note that some writers say that the háček is not or should not be 'an inverted circumflex' (though it is called that by Robert Bringhurst) but that it is a unique mark with its own principles of shape, height, angle, etc., and the háček used in this text is therefore unsatisfactory. There are some interesting views on this matter on pp. 454–5 of Oldřich Hlavsa's excellent *A Book of Type and Design*.

special characters of many languages which use the Latin alphabet, are found in the standard Macintosh or Windows sets and missing special characters can be created by means of Fontographer or a comparable utility. One would do well, however, to do careful research and keep as close to established form as possible.

Adam Twardoch has published on the internet a great deal of literature on the peculiarities of Polish diacritics and advice on drawing them.* He observes that, differently to the angle of the acute (in many typefaces), the angle of the *kreska* (over ć, ń, ó, ś, ź) 'runs steeper and is shifted more to the right rather than centered above the base glyph';† he remarks quite rightly that the *ogonek* of many PostScript fonts is woefully incorrectly formed.

Typographical treatment of non-roman, mathematics, scientific material, phonetics and other 'specialist subjects' are beyond the scope of this book. A good deal of information regarding such matters can be found in *The Chicago Manual of Style* and *The Oxford Guide to Style*. There are particularly good discussions on the niceties of special symbols for transliteration of Arabic, Sanskrit and other languages, romanisation of non-alphabetic languages, in *The Oxford Guide to Style*.

For this book I considered carefully the question of whether to use 'Fig.' in the captions or do without it. They may have looked nicer without but as so many numerals appear in the captions and elsewhere I decided to use 'Fig.' to avoid unnecessary confusions. 'Page' is spelt out in the text but not in the captions where space must be saved. But the abbreviation is used following a work cited. Also 'point' is spelt out; inches is spelt out but not millimetres. I have omitted hyphens between sizes and points where it will look awkward (e.g. 6–12 point) but have inserted them in other instances in the interest of clarity. For parts of words (*-ly* etc.) I have used italics rather than quotes. An apostrophe is used with h&j's so that it might be more intelligible; I prefer it just slightly to using an italic 's' (h&j*s*). An ampersand is used where it saves space in names of publishers who officially use 'and' (Faber and Faber; Thames and Hudson; but Fabers themselves have many times used the ampersand and have also used the shortened 'Faber' officially).

* studweb.euv-frankfurt-o.de/twardoch/f/en/typo/ogonek/intro.html
† The accents (over c, n, o, s, z) on this page are accordingly incorrect.

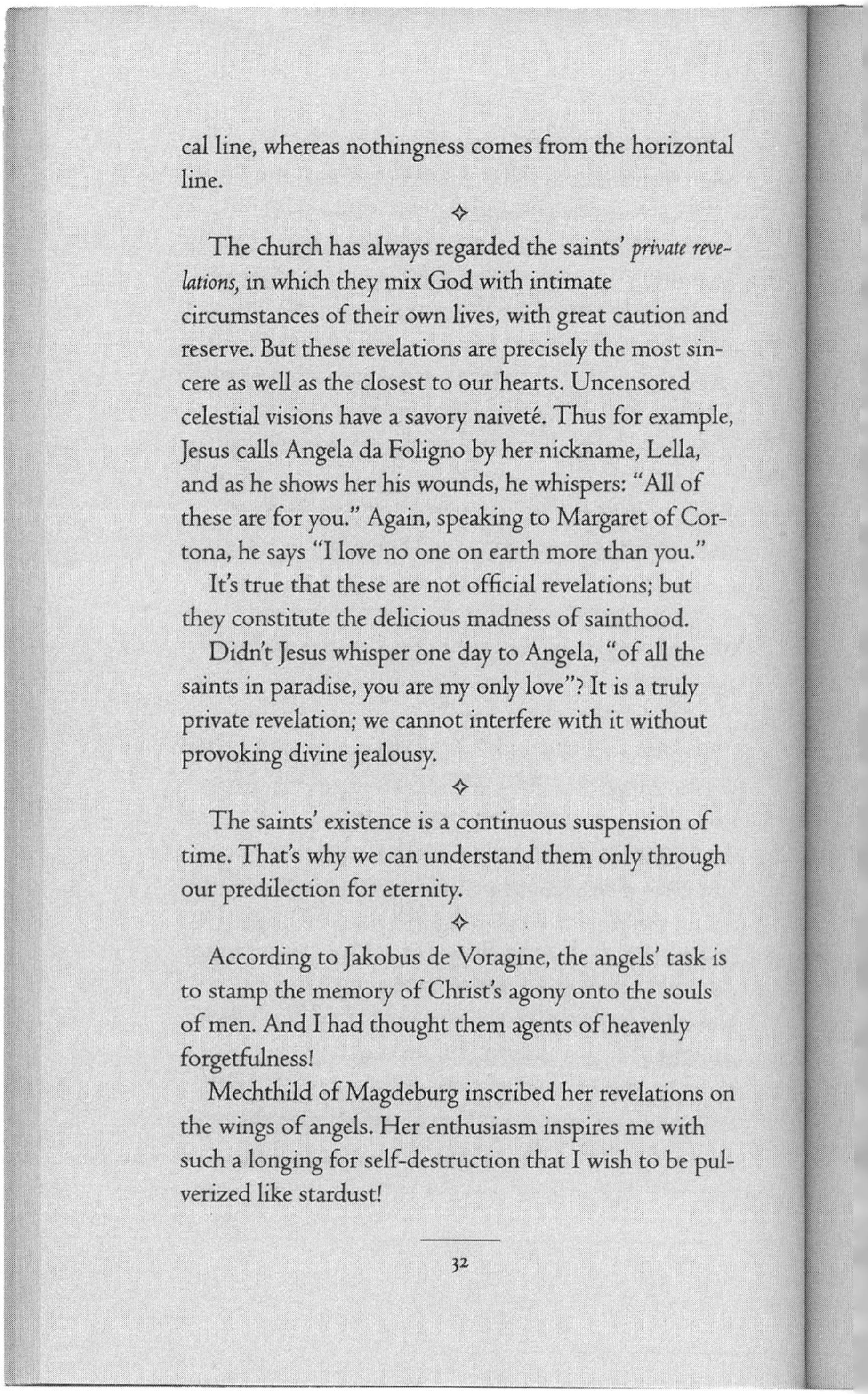

Fig. 33 E. M. Cioran's *Tears and Saints*,
trans. Ilinca Zarifopol-Johnston (University of Chicago Press, 1995), set in ragged-right and 'kerned' Centaur. It is a type
which will be used to good effect only in
special contexts and conditions and it
would look well in this book (size and
leading are agreeable in the narrow measure) if only more care had been taken
with the details. Note the end of a divided
word (verti–cal) starting the first line and
the undivided 'circumstances'. The i in
'naiveté' could do with a trema; double-f
ligatures were available when this job was
done but were not used. Reduced from
215 mm deep.

cal line, whereas nothingness comes from the horizontal
line.

❖

The church has always regarded the saints' *private revelations*, in which they mix God with intimate
circumstances of their own lives, with great caution and
reserve. But these revelations are precisely the most sincere as well as the closest to our hearts. Uncensored
celestial visions have a savory naiveté. Thus for example,
Jesus calls Angela da Foligno by her nickname, Lella,
and as he shows her his wounds, he whispers: "All of
these are for you." Again, speaking to Margaret of Cortona, he says "I love no one on earth more than you."

It's true that these are not official revelations; but
they constitute the delicious madness of sainthood.

Didn't Jesus whisper one day to Angela, "of all the
saints in paradise, you are my only love"? It is a truly
private revelation; we cannot interfere with it without
provoking divine jealousy.

❖

The saints' existence is a continuous suspension of
time. That's why we can understand them only through
our predilection for eternity.

❖

According to Jakobus de Voragine, the angels' task is
to stamp the memory of Christ's agony onto the souls
of men. And I had thought them agents of heavenly
forgetfulness!

Mechthild of Magdeburg inscribed her revelations on
the wings of angels. Her enthusiasm inspires me with
such a longing for self-destruction that I wish to be pulverized like stardust!

[1]

Centaur, which was designed by Bruce Rogers in 1912–14, is the only type from among the Jensonian revivals – others being William Morris's Golden Type, the Doves Type – which can nowadays be considered seriously for book typography; but for all its merits and estimation it is not a satisfactory type for ordinary books and it is seldom used.

Its design derives from drawings made from photographs, enlarged five times, of the letters which were cut by Nicolas Jenson and printed by him in the *De Praeparatione Evangelica* of Eusebius in 1470. Unlike Morris's heavy medievalist monstrosity (of 1890), Rogers's type is rather too light. The letters were redrawn deliberately rather freely with a brush and broad-nibbed pen in an attempt to capture the inscrutable qualities of the original but Rogers's type (unlike the Golden and Doves types) does not feature the unbracketed serifs (most noticeable in the T and M) which 'are characteristic of all Venetian romans until the coming of Aldus' (Stanley Morison).[1] This greatly lightens the type (apart from other lightenings) but also renders it more agreeable to modern tastes, frees it of much of the unmarketable eccentricity of the other neo-Jensonians which made them suitable only for handmade editions. The Centaur type was originally a 16-point titling fount (Jenson's roman of 1470 was about 16½-point) designed for the Metropolitan Museum of New York* and that may (or may not) account for its shortcomings in present-day ordinary text sizes (10 to 14 point) despite the expert work of Monotype in its manufacture for machine composition (commencing in February 1928 and completed exactly a year later).

Seán Jennett has said of it: 'it has, unfortunately, turned out weaker than the original, having lost most of the quality and sturdy common sense of Jenson. It is lighter and more feminine, and is inclined to be self-conscious where Jenson was self-sufficient.'† John R. Biggs calls it 'gentlemanly'.[2] Hugh Williamson said of it: 'Below 16-point, the style of type drawing begins to become imperceptible, and the text sizes are too thin and irregular to have achieved popularity.'[3] The designer himself said of it: 'It is a little too elegant and thin for our modern papers and methods of printing.'[4]

The 22-point machine setting of the Oxford Coronation Bible of 1935 is indeed a masterpiece of modern typography, and if we were considering types for settings in such sizes perhaps I would view this type more favourably. Another very beautiful example of it – set in 16-point – is to be found in the Officina Bodoni's *Candide* of 1944. The italic (or cancellaresca), called *Arrighi*, was designed by Frederic Warde at Rogers's request and Stanley Morison's instance. It derives from the chancery fount designed in 1524 by the calligrapher and printer Ludovico degli Arrighi. Italics did not exist in

---

* Cut in 1914 by Robert Wiebking of Barnhart Brothers and Spindler in Chicago.

† *The Making of Books*, p. 255. The readers surveyed by Sir Cyril Burt also found it '"self-conscious" and "arty"' (*A Psychological Study of Typography* (Cambridge, 1957), p. 36).

1470; Frederic Warde's design however 'consorts excellently with Centaur' (Seán Jennett). But it is even less well disposed to text-setting in normal sizes (12-point and smaller), admirable as it is.

Monotype have produced PostScript versions of Centaur and Arrighi (called Centaur Italic) which are at present sold by AGFA-Monotype and Adobe. To my knowledge the types were never adapted for filmsetting nor for the Lasercomp. A bold and a bold italic have been designed (perhaps because the manufacturers anticipated customers' dissatisfaction with the digital version's lightness).

The digital versions were used by the University of Chicago Press in 1995 for a book by E. M. Cioran called *Tears and Saints* (one expects the choice of type was influenced by the theme of the book). It is a book of aphorisms, set unjustfied and ranged leftwise but not a very good job (many endings of divided words carried over to verso pages). Diamonds from a set of ornaments called ITC Zapf Dingbats (◇) are placed between the aphorisms rather than the more saintly Centaur asterisk (✳).

In the chapter on text types of the second edition of Hugh Williamson's *Methods of Book Design* the types are individually described and commented upon in specimen settings: Monotype Centaur is shown on page 80; a paragraph set in Arrighi follows on the top of page 81, and below that are two paragraphs set in Monotype *Bembo*. The juxtaposition is instructive, for here is one of Monotype's most successful faces, used perhaps in more books than any other Monotype face. It was also manufactured and issued in the same year (1929) as Centaur. It is a revival of the type cut by Francesco Griffo and used by Aldus Manutius in the *De Aetna* by Pietro Bembo, printed at Venice in 1495; it is, as Centaur is, a modified revival.

Earlier, in 1923, Monotype had produced a revival of another of Aldus's type which was used by him in the *Hypnerotomachia Poliphili* of 1499. This (Aldus's) type was a recutting of the type used for *De Aetna*; the lower-case letters were essentially of the same design but the capitals are rather more eccentric. Monotype's *Poliphilus*, which is currently available in a digital version, is a facsimile – and quite a technical achievement in 1923 – which retains the roughness and irregularities as well as the ink-spread of the letters of 'rather less well-printed portions'[5] of the *Hypnerotomachia Poliphili* of 1499, and as such its appeal is limited: it is 'suitable for specialized and careful use only'.[6] In *A Tally of Types* Stanley Morison said: 'Everything taken into account, the recutting of the Poliphilo roman must be judged as a moderate success only, redeemed by the cutting of Bembo.'

And so Bembo, whose model was already more refined than the Poliphilo type, was regularised to suit twentieth-century tastes but only in such a careful and subtle way as to preserve the qualities of the original. This is a testament to Stanley Morison's acumen and fine judgment. The character width is mid-way between Centaur and Monotype Garamond. The capitals are shorter than the ascenders. They're more harmonious, one might say, than the capitals of Poliphilus (which are rather eccentric).* There are two Rs;

---

* Poliphilus is used to rather good effect in *Frank Auerbach* by Robert Hughes (Thames and Hudson, 1992), designed by Ruth Rosenberg. The type is heavier than Bembo and looks well on coated paper. Thames and Hudson used the type for many of their books in the 1950s

R

R

the alternative short-tailed R has been much preferred to the long-tailed R. Curiously Adobe supplies the type with only the long-tailed R. There are also a long-tailed and short-tailed italic R but the difference between them is much less pronounced. The metal version had a ligatured ct, non-descending J, a gj and italic gg, and alternative long-tailed Qs.

The type originally featured a small (x-height) question mark and other 'oddities' which are noted by James Moran:

> Not all the oddities were erased at first, including the eccentric capital M and a question mark the same size as the colon. The more normal M with two serifs was marketed from the beginning and has been allowed to take over, and a few years after Bembo was first issued the University Press, Cambridge asked for a more normal-sized question mark, which is now available, with the smaller one as an alternative sort.[7]

Morison was not very pleased with the design of the Bembo italic ('while not disagreeable, it is insipid'). The Blado italics* which were chosen to accompany Poliphilus are clearly superior to the Bembo† but save for the Bembo italic g (which I think is happier than the Blado) the two designs are quite similar and so the superiority of the Blado would seem to be owed to its heavier weight and more condensed form.

Another Bembo type was designed in 1929. This was Giovanni Mardersteig's *Griffo*, which followed the *De Aetna* type more closely than Morison's version, and which Dr Mardersteig used for the Latin text of his Officina Bodoni edition of *De Aetna* (1969), with an English translation set in Monotype Bembo.

> Despite the excellence of Monotype Bembo, Morison regretted that in the mechanical recutting something of the supple elegance of the original had been lost. When I talked to Morison about my plan to have a fine old type recut by that wonderful punch-cutter Charles Malin for use on my hand press, Morison strongly advised me to take the *De Aetna* type as a model too.[8]

The digitised Bembo is serviceable (if used over 12-point). A pity it wasn't supplied with three designs for ranges of size as the Monophoto was.

The Monotype *Garamond* of 1922 was Stanley Morison's first revival and it also proved a very successful type. The model, known as the *caractères de l'Université*, residing in Paris at the Imprimerie Nationale, was assumed to be a type of Claude Garamond's but it was discovered in 1926 to be a type cut by Jean Jannon of Sedan in 1621, more than fifty years after Garamond's

and 1960s. It was employed rather nicely in the Penguin edition of Hermann Hesse's *Steppenwolf*, printed by Cox & Wyman in 1965 with straight hyphens rather than the normally supplied slanted hyphens. Straight hyphens are also found in the *Tally of Types* setting. Both straight and slanted hyphens are found in the *Hypnerotomachia Poliphili* of 1499.

* Based on the chancery letters of the *Vita Sfortiae* of Paolo Giovio printed by Antonio Blado in 1539.

† 'An italic for Bembo having less personality was searched for, and found in the publication of the writing-master, Giovanni Tagliente, practising in Venice from 1524.' (*A Tally of Types* (Cambridge, 1953), p. 52.) There was a good deal of groaning and travail involved in the creation of the italics, a brief account of which is given in Nicolas Barker's *Stanley Morison* (Macmillan, 1972), pp. 242–4. The first version to be considered was designed by Alfred Fairbank; it was rejected for the Bembo type but issued independently of the series and called Narrow Bembo Italic (series 294). Morison liked the type, but it seems Fairbank was never paid for it (see James Moran, *Stanley Morison* (Lund Humphries, 1971), pp. 140–1).

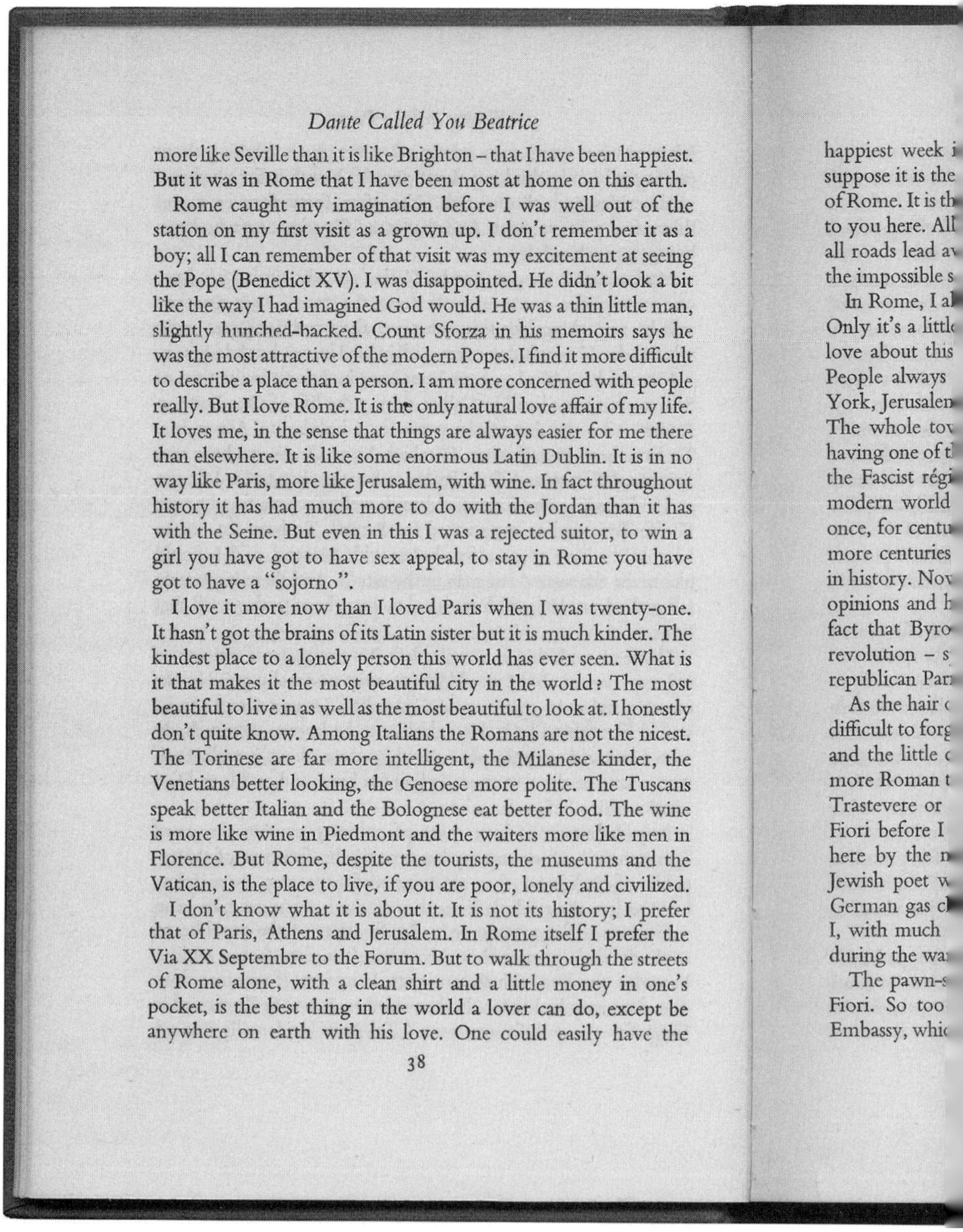

Dante Called You Beatrice

more like Seville than it is like Brighton – that I have been happiest. But it was in Rome that I have been most at home on this earth.

Rome caught my imagination before I was well out of the station on my first visit as a grown up. I don't remember it as a boy; all I can remember of that visit was my excitement at seeing the Pope (Benedict XV). I was disappointed. He didn't look a bit like the way I had imagined God would. He was a thin little man, slightly hunched-backed. Count Sforza in his memoirs says he was the most attractive of the modern Popes. I find it more difficult to describe a place than a person. I am more concerned with people really. But I love Rome. It is the only natural love affair of my life. It loves me, in the sense that things are always easier for me there than elsewhere. It is like some enormous Latin Dublin. It is in no way like Paris, more like Jerusalem, with wine. In fact throughout history it has had much more to do with the Jordan than it has with the Seine. But even in this I was a rejected suitor, to win a girl you have got to have sex appeal, to stay in Rome you have got to have a "sojorno".

I love it more now than I loved Paris when I was twenty-one. It hasn't got the brains of its Latin sister but it is much kinder. The kindest place to a lonely person this world has ever seen. What is it that makes it the most beautiful city in the world? The most beautiful to live in as well as the most beautiful to look at. I honestly don't quite know. Among Italians the Romans are not the nicest. The Torinese are far more intelligent, the Milanese kinder, the Venetians better looking, the Genoese more polite. The Tuscans speak better Italian and the Bolognese eat better food. The wine is more like wine in Piedmont and the waiters more like men in Florence. But Rome, despite the tourists, the museums and the Vatican, is the place to live, if you are poor, lonely and civilized.

I don't know what it is about it. It is not its history; I prefer that of Paris, Athens and Jerusalem. In Rome itself I prefer the Via XX Septembre to the Forum. But to walk through the streets of Rome alone, with a clean shirt and a little money in one's pocket, is the best thing in the world a lover can do, except be anywhere on earth with his love. One could easily have the

38

Fig. 34 Page 38 of *Dante Called You Beatrice* by Paul Potts (Eyre & Spottiswoode, 1960), set in Monotype Bembo by Billing & Sons Ltd, Guildford, on which can be seen the alternative R and also the small question mark (in the sentence: 'What is it that makes it the most beautiful city in the world?'). Reduced from 215 mm.

death.* A Garamond (also based on the *caractères de l'Université*) had been cut in 1917 by the American Type Founders Company and was received with such enthusiasm that Linotype in New York and both the London and Philadelphia Monotype offices decided to produce their own versions. Morison's work in the Monotype project at Fetter Lane† led to his appointment as 'typographical adviser' and thence to the undertaking of his 'programme of typographical design, rational, systematic, and corresponding effectively with the foreseeable needs of modern printing',[9] i.e. the production of revivals of historic typefaces and original types of the highest quality.

The italic fount of the Imprimerie Nationale was not used for the Monotype Garamond (Morison having decided that it was neither contemporary to the roman nor of a commensurate quality), but the model which was used appears to be one of Jannon's italics and not, as Morison believed, from Robert Granjon.‡

A long-tailed Q was designed for the roman and italics. The swash letters and most of the special italic lower-case letters (*as, ct, e, et, fr, gg, gj, gy, h, ij, is, k, ll, m, nt, q, f, fb, fh, fi, fk, fl, ft, fp, st, ta, tt, us, v, z, zy*) are available in the current digital version. The type was one of the most successful of the Monotype revivals (used to very good effect in many Penguins) and a digital recutting of a form appropriate for ordinary text settings is still much needed.§

Linotype & Machinery Ltd were also keen to produce a Garamond bookface and an admirable type was designed under the supervision of their adviser George W. Jones and issued in 1924. It was modelled upon a type which Jones had found in Thomas Bourchier's *Historia ecclesiastica de martyrio fratrum ordinus divi francisci*, printed by Jean Poupy in Paris in 1582 (Jones was a great book collector), and called *Granjon* 'by way of compliment to the sixteenth-century punch-cutter, and not because it was thought that he was in any way connected with the type'.[10]

When Beatrice Warde discovered in 1926 that Jannon was the author of the Imprimerie Nationale model for Monotype Garamond, the type used for the *Historia ecclesiastica* was also found, duly ascribed to Claude Garamond, on a specimen sheet printed in 1592 by the Egenolff–Berner foundry

Biolog y Biology

The extremely useful gy of the Monotype Garamond italic which is included in the current digital swash characters set.

* 'The Monotype reproduction of Jannon's roman is faithful and exact. That the name Garamond was given to the roman in 1922 is to be regretted, but the huge commercial success of the series is due to the merits of the design, which, it has been established, is Garamond's though at a distant remove.' (Morison, *A Tally of Types*, p. 66.) In Harry Carter's note to the 1973 edition of Morison's *Tally* (p. 129), he says 'There is no reason to think that Jannon tried to copy Garamond's types. His design is original and characteristic of the seventeenth century insofar as he increased the x-height.'

† The London offices of the Lanston Monotype Corporation were located at 43 Fetter Lane, EC4.

‡ 'Anyone who looks at the reproduction of the specimen of the Imprimerie Royale of 1643 . . . will find it hard to believe that the italic of Monotype Series 156 renders the design of Granjon's gros canon and not that of Jannon's *petit canon* or *gros paragon*. It has evident features of Jannon's style, the wide *A*, the serifs of his *R*, the multiplicity of extravagantly swash letters, besides the generally cramped look instead of the ease and fluency of Granjon.' (Harry Carter, note to *A Tally of Types* (1973), pp. 131–2.) After the Revolution the Imprimerie Royale became the Imprimerie Nationale.

§ 'Display sizes are about the same weight as the original hot metal version (although the letters are wider and the serifs lighter) but when reduced to text sizes the design is too light. This once-popular type deserves a strengthened version for text sizes to make up for the ink squash missing from today's printing techniques.' (James Sutton and Alan Bartram, *Typefaces for Books*, p. 148.)

at Frankfurt.* Mrs Warde (under the name of Paul Beaujon) then published her findings in Stanley Morison's and Oliver Simon's *The Fleuron* and identified the Linotype Granjon as a true Garamond.†

While the Granjon type is indeed faithful to the Garamond, something none the less seems to have got lost in translation: it has a certain refinement of the kind which also inhibits the design of Centaur. It is light, it is refined, it is oddly stiff. Seán Jennett says it's 'at its best in sizes over 12-point', but I've seen many settings at larger sizes which don't look as good as the 10-point settings found in Penguins.

It was supplied with twenty-six f-ligatures (though these were seldom used by printers).‡ In *Letters of Credit* Walter Tracy writes: 'The measure of a designer of type for line-casting was his ability to design a respectable non-kerning f. G. W. Jones and Harry Smith at Altrincham managed it very well in the Granjon and Georgian romans.'[11] The truncated f was redrawn for the filmsetting and current digital versions. The design of the italics suffered greatly because the letters had to be all the same set-width as the roman letters (the capital italics being 'duplexed' with the capital romans, the lower-case italics with the lower-case romans). If used only intermittently in roman text they are tolerable. The matter of this was somewhat mitigated by a redrawing done for the filmsetting and digital types but they aren't nearly as good as the Monotype Garamond italics. Linotype's digital types do not include the double-f ligature in their character-sets. I find the italic *k* rather irksome (as did some of the test subjects (or 'readers') interviewed for Sir Cyril Burt's Psychological Study).[12]

Monotype *Plantin* is a twentieth-century type designed and cut in 1913 under the supervision of the manager of the works at Salfords, F. H. Pierpont. It is an adaptation of a short extenders *Grosse Mediane Romaine* by Granjon *c*. 1567 (preserved in the collection of the Plantin-Moretus museum in Antwerp). It appears that Christophe Plantin never used the entire fount but used the ascending and descending characters to modify Garamond's *Augustine Romaine*. Monotype Plantin is considerably heavier than any of the later Monotype revivals and most of the original designs commissioned by Morison. It proved particularly good for use on art paper.

Indeed, when Pierpont had finished the design had perhaps as much in common with a nineteenth-century Clarendon as with a sixteenth-century Garamond. Although the classic old-face text design was preserved in the structure, the strength

* See Nicolas Barker, *Stanley Morison*, pp. 203–4, and also Beatrice Warde's own account in John Dreyfus, 'Beatrice Warde: the First Lady of Typography', *Penrose Annual*, vol. 63 (1970), pp. 71–4.

† 'But fortunately a true Garamont design has been given to the public: that admirable "later" Garamont of the Egenolff sheet which so distinguished French books from 1550 on, and had so good an influence over Dutch and hence English taste. The first and immeasurably the best of modern revivals of this letter was that of the English Linotype Company. . . . For some reason the face is called "Granjon". It would seem that Garamont's name, having so long been used on a design he never cut, is now by stern justice left off the face which is undoubtedly his.' (Paul Beaujon, 'The "Garamond" Types: sixteenth and seventeenth century sources considered', *The Fleuron*, no. 5 (1926), pp. 173–6.)

‡ 'To offset the unfortunate inability of the Linotype to cast a kerned f, no fewer than twenty-six f-ligatures are provided. After such a gallant sacrifice of practicality to beauty, it would be ungenerous for an author to mention Afghanistan and so call out the "button-hook" f that is the family spectre of Linotype designers.' (Paul Beaujon, p. 176.)

Book VI

CHAPTER TWENTY-THREE

AFTER FIVE months of exile in Sicily, Michael Corleone came finally to understand his father's character and his destiny. He came to understand men like Luca Brasi, the ruthless *caporegime* Clemenza, his mother's resignation and acceptance of her role. For in Sicily he saw what they would have been if they had chosen *not* to struggle against their fate. He understood why the Don always said, 'A man has only one destiny.' He came to understand the contempt for authority and legal government, the hatred for any man who broke *omerta*, the law of silence.

Dressed in old clothes and a billed cap, Michael had been transported from the ship docked at Palermo to the interior of the Sicilian island, to the very heart of a province controlled by the Mafia, where the local *capo-mafioso* was greatly indebted to his father for some past service. The province held the town of Corleone, whose name the Don had taken when he emigrated to America so long ago. But there were no longer any of the Don's relatives alive. The women had died of old age. All the men had been killed in vendettas or had also emigrated, either to America, Brazil or to some other province on the Italian mainland. He was to learn later that this small poverty-stricken town had the highest murder rate of any place in the world.

Michael was installed as a guest in the home of a bachelor uncle of the *capo-mafioso*. The uncle, in his seventies, was also the doctor for the district. The *capo-mafioso* was a man in his late fifties named Don Tommasino and he operated as the *gabbellotto* for a huge estate belonging to one of Sicily's most noble families. The *gabbellotto*, a sort of overseer to the estates of the rich, also guaranteed that the poor would not try to claim land not being cultivated, would not try to encroach in any way on the estate, by poaching or trying to farm it as

326

squatters. In short, the *gabbellotto* was a *mafioso* who for a certain sum of money protected the real estate of the rich from all claims made on it by the poor, legal or illegal. When any poor peasant tried to implement the law which permitted him to buy uncultivated land, the *gabbellotto* frightened him off with threats of bodily harm or death. It was that simple.

Don Tommasino also controlled the water rights in the area and vetoed the local building of any new dams by the Roman government. Such dams would ruin the lucrative business of selling water from the artesian wells he controlled, make water too cheap, ruin the whole important water economy so laboriously built up over hundreds of years. However, Don Tommasino was an old-fashioned Mafia chief and would have nothing to do with dope traffic or prostitution. In this Don Tommasino was at odds with the new breed of Mafia leaders springing up in big cities like Palermo, new men who, influenced by American gangsters deported to Italy, had no such scruples.

The Mafia chief was an extremely portly man, a 'man with a belly', literally as well as in the figurative sense that meant a man able to inspire fear in his fellow men. Under his protection, Michael had nothing to fear, yet it was considered necessary to keep the fugitive's identity a secret. And so Michael was restricted to the walled estate of Dr Taza, the Don's uncle.

Dr Taza was tall for a Sicilian, almost six feet, and had ruddy cheeks and snow-white hair. Though in his seventies, he went every week to Palermo to pay his respects to the younger prostitutes of that city, the younger the better. Dr Taza's other vice was reading. He read everything and talked about what he read to his fellow townsmen, patients who were illiterate peasants, the estate shepherds, and this gave him a local reputation for foolishness. What did books have to do with them?

In the evenings Dr Taza, Don Tommasino and Michael sat in the huge garden populated with those marble statues that on this island seemed to grow out of the garden as magically as the black heady grapes. Dr Taza loved to tell stories about the Mafia and its exploits over the centuries and in Michael Corleone he had a fascinated listener. There were times when even

327

Fig. 35 You don't see this kind of thing nowadays. An original setting by Richard Clay (The Chaucer Press) of Bungay for the Pan edition of *The Godfather* by Mario Puzo (1969). I enjoyed the movie but I found the book disappointing save for the typography which is a very fine example of Monotype Garamond: nicely leaded, closely-spaced, judiciously inked and impressed. This book looks identical to a Penguin and that's hardly remarkable: Clays were one of the main printers of Penguins in 1969 and in that year their total paperback production (for Penguins and other publishers) came to nearly 28 million. Reduced from 180 mm deep.

Fig. 36 A specimen of Linotype Granjon and twenty-eight of its logotypes which Linotype called 'typographical refinement characters' from page 258 of *The Making of Books* by Seán Jennett (4th edn, Faber, 1967).

ABCDEFGHIJKLMNOPQRSTUVWXYZÆŒ

ABCDEFGHIJKLMNOPQRSTUVWXYZÆŒ

12345)   abcdefghijklmnopqrstuvwxyzæœ   (67890

ctstff,f.f-ff ff,ff.ff-fafefofrfsftfufyffaffeffoffrffsffy

fiff flffiffl&£?!,.:;

ABCDEFGHIJKLMNOPQRSTUVWXYZÆŒ

ABCDEGJMNPRTY

12345)   abcdefghijklmnopqrstuvwxyzææ   (67890

ctstff,f.f-ff ff,ff.ff-fafefofrfsftfufyffaffeffoffrffsffy

fiff flffiffl&£?!,.:;

and colour required by a face for display and jobbing were imposed. The combination was both deliberate and successful.[13]

Seán Jennett says of the Monotype design: 'It certainly possesses a typically Dutch stolidness and plainness and business-like ability, none of which were characteristic either of Garamond or Granjon.'[14] I have often heard the Dutch described as stolid (which my *Chambers* defines as: 'impassive: blockish: unemotional'), but earlier in his book Seán Jennett notes that Plantin* was a Frenchman and 'What is distinctive of different countries is not so much the type faces they used, as the manner in which they used them.'[15] In any event one assumes his 'stolidness' applies to type design and Monotype Plantin is certainly that – as it is 'a type with no fal-lals about it'. None the less it is attractive and looks well in Pevsner's Buildings of England series (designed for Penguin by Hans Schmoller), the Faber edition of Ruari McLean's *Modern Book Design* (1957) and Herbert Spencer's design for *Portrait of Picasso*. The type was admired by Sir Francis Meynell who thought well enough of it to use it at his Nonesuch Press.

I think its italic (which is not taken from antique models) is particularly well designed: it is quite as strong and readable as the roman. There is an example of the digital version in fig. 21 (chapter 2). A Plantin Light which was

* He was not a punch-cutter but a printer and publisher – the *first* publisher – who in 1555 established a printing office in Antwerp and a foundry in 1563. The house, employing twenty-two presses in 1576, became the greatest printing house in Europe. 'Plantin's agents went as far as North Africa where they sold his Hebrew Bibles to the numerous Jewish congregations' (S.H. Steinberg, *Five Hundred Years of Printing*, 2nd edn (Penguin, 1961), p. 179). In 1568–73 he printed an eight-volume Polyglot Bible (with texts in Hebrew, Latin, Greek and Armenian). Granjon, whose designs were much prized, became an international trader in types and Plantin was one of his main customers. The firm survived religious intolerance and official obstruction. Plantin left Antwerp when the town was sacked by Spanish soldiers in 1576, and worked as printer to the University of Leyden (1583–5). The press was kept going by his sons-in-law and their descendants for eight generations; the equipment survived and remained in the family until it and the printing office on the original premises was sold to the city of Antwerp in 1875, where it remains the most important museum of printing history.

deemed more suitable for use on antique paper was issued in 1914. There is also a digital version of this type but owing to the unnatural lightness of digital types it is perhaps too light while the normal weight, formerly too-heavy (for some tastes or uses), is in its digital version barely heavy enough.

The x-height is higher than most old-face types; the descenders are rather too short. A seldom-seen long extenders version (having both ascenders and descenders lengthened) which has a very different look was cut for the Nonesuch Press.*

Monotype *Van Dijck* is another old-face revival which is available in digital form. It is a very refined design with a small x-height and high ascenders. The opposite of Plantin. A short account of its history and the Monotype re-cutting of 1937–8, written by Netty Hoeflake, is given in the appendix to the 1973 edition of Morison's *Tally*. The Monotype design derives from the '*Augustijn Romeyn* (English-bodied roman) shewn in the specimen which the widow of Daniel Elsevier issued as a sale-catalogue in 1681'[16] and thought to be one of the types of the great Christoffel van Dyck (?1606–69). The punches and matrices for the italic *Text Cursijf* survive in the Enschedé foundry at Haarlem. It is not known for certain whether the roman or italics were cut by Christoffel van Dyck or by his son Abraham. Enschedé's type-designer Jan van Krimpen advised in the Monotype project – although he took a poor view of revivals – and when the Monotype version of the roman was completed he called it 'a doctored adaptation of a seventeenth-century Dutch face'. There are admirable examples of the Monotype Van Dijck notwithstanding and Netty Hoeflake says that, despite Van Krimpen's judgment of it, it 'merits inclusion among the historical faces brought out by the Corporation.' The italic *Q* is remarkable. The italic *J* is terribly wide and the *C* and *G* are quite narrow. The roman features a lovely leopard-tailed Q (but rather subdued in the digital version). Its design is really too light for non-metal adaptations. Harry Carter believed that the metal version was impaired by its tight letter-fit: 'The greatest defect of the 13-point size is that it is on too narrow a set. If it were more loosely spaced it would be much more comfortable to read and the letters would look much handsomer.'[17]

Nicholas (Miklós) Kis (1650–1702) was a Transylvanian who went to Holland in 1680 to study Calvinist theology and while there the Bishop Tofeus instructed him to have a Hungarian bible printed by Daniel Elzevier. Kis was to be a corrector but as he was not provided with funds for Elzevier he was obliged to do the printing himself and so became a punch-cutter and printer. After working for nine years in Amsterdam Kis returned to Transylvania, calling at Leipzig, which was on the way, to sell his matrices to the typefounder Johann Carl Edling. It seems the matrices were defective and Edling didn't want to buy them; Kis left the matrices with Edling, hoping that Edling might find a colleague who would take them at a discount. But presently Kis ran into a spot of trouble with a Polish count who imprisoned him as a heretic. The count released him and returned his property (bibles

---

* Called the 'Nonesuch Plantin'. It was cut in 10-point and cast on a 12-point body. It was used in the Nonesuch Herodotus (printed at Cambridge in 1936) and in Sir Francis Meynell's autobiography, *My Lives* (The Bodley Head, 1971). Long extenders (or 'long extruders') versions were also designed for 11-point Baskerville and Times New Roman.

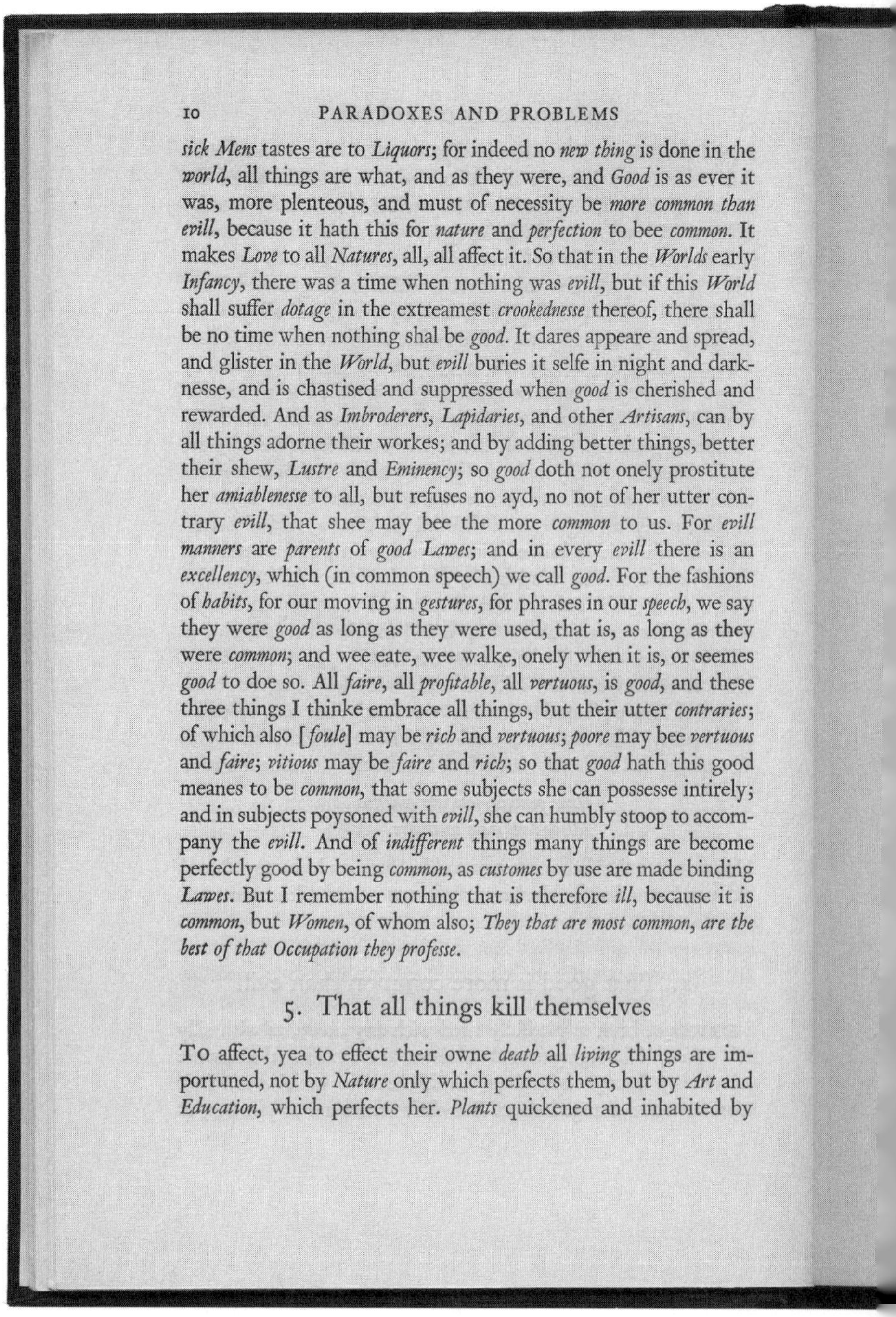

Fig. 37 A fine example of Monotype Van Dijck in *John Donne: Selected Prose* (chosen by Evelyn Simpson, edited by Helen Gardner and Timothy Healy), printed at the Clarendon Press by Vivian Ridler in 1967. The type has been supplied with Bembo figures since its introduction in 1937, but a set of figures designed by Matthew Carter in 1954 for Rowley Atterbury's Westerham Press (shown below) is digitally available as an 'alternate' figures set from Monotype. Cross-heads are set in Caslon Old Face. Reduced from 216 mm deep.

1234567890

---

10   PARADOXES AND PROBLEMS

sick Mens tastes are to *Liquors*; for indeed no *new thing* is done in the *world*, all things are what, and as they were, and *Good* is as ever it was, more plenteous, and must of necessity be *more common than evill*, because it hath this for *nature* and *perfection* to bee *common*. It makes *Love* to all *Natures*, all, all affect it. So that in the *Worlds* early *Infancy*, there was a time when nothing was *evill*, but if this *World* shall suffer *dotage* in the extreamest *crookednesse* thereof, there shall be no time when nothing shal be *good*. It dares appear and spread, and glister in the *World*, but *evill* buries it selfe in night and darknesse, and is chastised and suppressed when *good* is cherished and rewarded. And as *Imbroderers*, *Lapidaries*, and other *Artisans*, can by all things adorne their workes; and by adding better things, better their shew, *Lustre* and *Eminency*; so *good* doth not onely prostitute her *amiablenesse* to all, but refuses no ayd, no not of her utter contrary *evill*, that shee may bee the more *common* to us. For *evill manners* are *parents* of *good Lawes*; and in every *evill* there is an *excellency*, which (in common speech) we call *good*. For the fashions of *habits*, for our moving in *gestures*, for phrases in our *speech*, we say they were *good* as long as they were used, that is, as long as they were *common*; and wee eate, wee walke, onely when it is, or seemes *good* to doe so. All *faire*, all *profitable*, all *vertuous*, is *good*, and these three things I thinke embrace all things, but their utter *contraries*; of which also [*foule*] may be *rich* and *vertuous*; *poore* may bee *vertuous* and *faire*; *vitious* may be *faire* and *rich*; so that *good* hath this good meanes to be *common*, that some subjects she can possesse intirely; and in subjects poysoned with *evill*, she can humbly stoop to accompany the *evill*. And of *indifferent* things many things are become perfectly good by being *common*, as *customes* by use are made binding *Lawes*. But I remember nothing that is therefore *ill*, because it is *common*, but *Women*, of whom also; *They that are most common, are the best of that Occupation they professe.*

5. That all things kill themselves

To affect, yea to effect their owne *death* all *living* things are importuned, not by *Nature* only which perfects them, but by *Art* and *Education*, which perfects her. *Plants* quickened and inhabited by

---

and chattels-personal) to him in exchange for his promise 'not to send robbers again' (it appears the count believed that the robbers making raids in Poland at the time were sent in from Hungary), whereupon Nicholas Kis proceeded directly to Transylvania without going back for the matrices.

Edling was the successor to the Dutch typefounder Anton Janson (settled in Leipzig in 1659), having married his widow. There is no evidence that Kis and Janson ever met one another or had any dealings. Upon Edling's death the foundry was taken over by his foreman, Wolfgang Dietrich Ehrhardt. It was thereafter called the Ehrhardtische Giesserey and a specimen printed by them in 1720 shows a set of types called *holländische Schriften* which are now known to be the types of Kis but which until the 1950s were attributed to Janson. The types descended from Ehrhardt to the firm of Wilhelm Drugulin (*c.* 1868). The original copper matrices were bought from Drugulin by the Stempel foundry of Frankfurt in 1919 and called *Janson*.[*] A version of the Stempel type was designed for Mergenthaler Linotype by Nils Larson (under the supervision of C. H. Griffith) and issued in 1933. It was called Janson. A much remodelled version was designed by Monotype (under Fritz Steltzer) and issued as *Ehrhardt* in 1937–8. The Linotype Janson is rather wide; the Monotype Ehrhardt is much narrower than any seventeenth-century Dutch letters. The Monotype is also heavier than the original and Linotype Jansons. Harry Carter says that the design of Monotype Ehrhardt 'belongs to a late phase in Morison's thinking where he was less interested in the reproduction of an old type than in the production of one that gave good value in legibility.'[18] He relates that 'The works at Salfords were instructed to make the Ehrhardt as big for its body as Imprint and in weight intermediate between that and Plantin.' The type proved highly successful. Hugh Williamson notes that 'Ehrhardt, in company with Plantin, appeared more often in the British National Book League's exhibitions of book design and production between 1978 and 1980 than did the previous favourites of the 1945–1963 period, Bembo and Baskerville.'[19] And the Stempel Janson was quite successful also, as Horst Heiderhoff notes: 'A listing by *Stiftung Buchkunst* of the most frequently used typefaces in the years 1951 to 1975 shows Janson ranking fourth after Garamond, Walbaum, and Bembo.'[20]

Hugh Williamson notes that the Monophoto Ehrhardt is 'a little heavier still but less narrow and less closely fitted.' In our comparison in fig. 6 the digital version seems to be extremely close to the 11-point metal version.

The bar of the capital A curves downwards. This is very nice touch which doesn't seem to be connected to Kis's type. Also distinctive and quite different to the Janson types is the turn of the G and the high placement of the bar. The italics, in the digital version especially, are rather too light.

There were also a British Linotype Janson and an American Lanston-Monotype Janson. A Janson designed by Hermann Zapf from the original founts was issued by the German Linotype company in 1952. Linotype's filmsetting version was made from the Larson/Griffith design. A later Linotype (Frankfurt) design which was supervised by Adrian Frutiger and issued in 1985 as Janson Text, restored some of the oddities (the wide W), exaggerated others (the splay of the M) but erased more of its character than any of the earlier versions. It was a digital design but curiously it preserves the severely truncated tails of the original Linotype roman and italic capital Qs which were drawn in such a way to accommodate the limitations of the slug-casting equipment.

[*] The type's provenance was established by Harry Carter and George Buday in 'Nicholas Kis and the Janson Types', *Gutenberg Jahrbuch* (Mainz, 1957), pp. 207–12. A fascinating account of the type's origins and the 'Janson puzzle' was written by Horst Heiderhoff and a translation of it by Gertraude Benöhr was published as 'The Discovery of a Type Designer: Miklós Kis' in *Fine Print*, vol. 10, no. 1 (January 1984), pp. 25–30, and reprinted in *Fine Print on Type* (San Francisco, 1989), pp. 74–80.

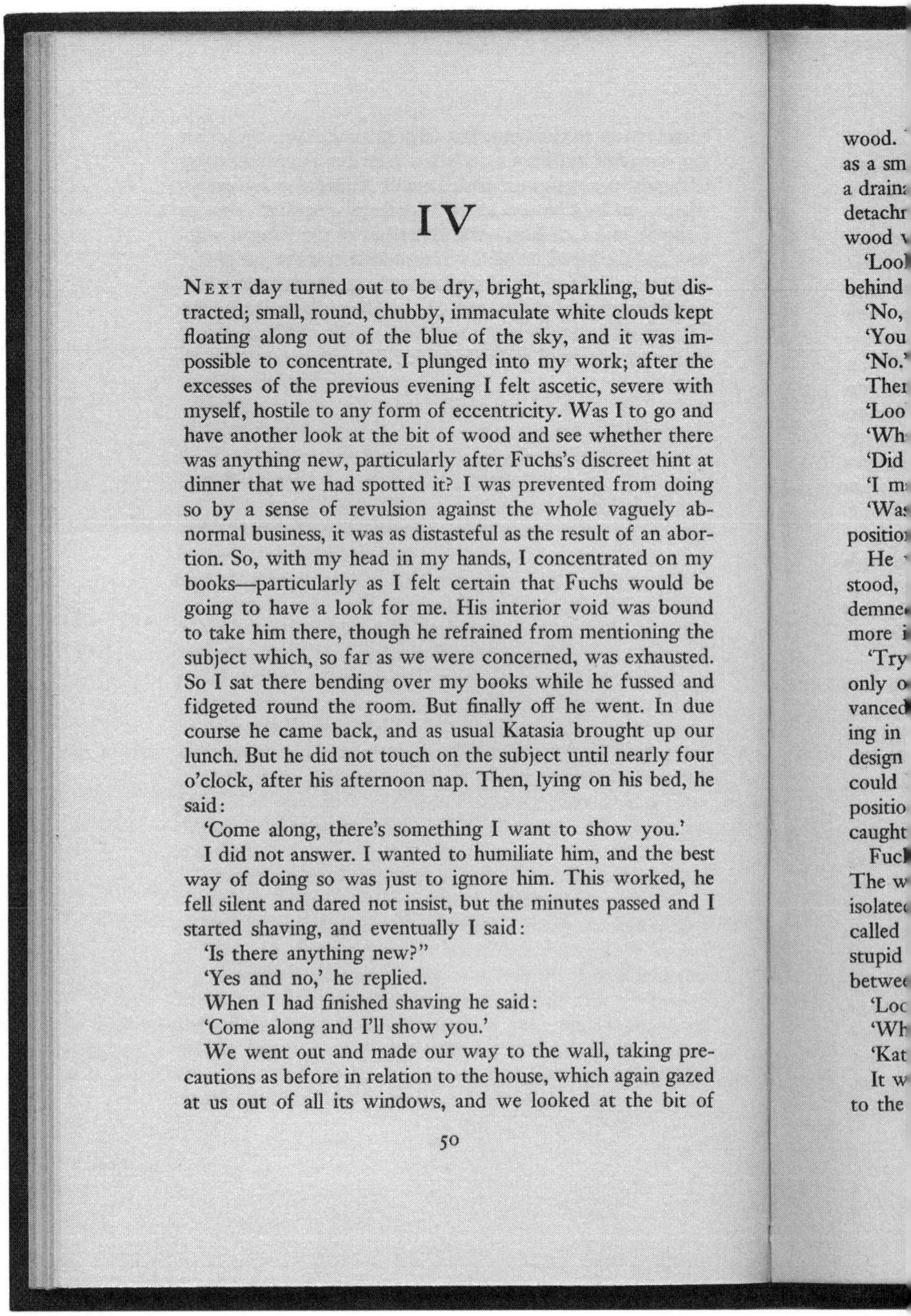

Fig. 38 Page 50 of Witold Gombrowicz's *Cosmos*, published by MacGibbon & Kee in 1967, featuring an exquisite setting of Linotype Janson by the firm of Clarke, Doble & Brendon Ltd of Cattedown, Plymouth. One just now notices two errors: the unligatured f and i ('fidgeted') and the double quotation mark. Reduced from 214 mm deep.

IV

NEXT day turned out to be dry, bright, sparkling, but distracted; small, round, chubby, immaculate white clouds kept floating along out of the blue of the sky, and it was impossible to concentrate. I plunged into my work; after the excesses of the previous evening I felt ascetic, severe with myself, hostile to any form of eccentricity. Was I to go and have another look at the bit of wood and see whether there was anything new, particularly after Fuchs's discreet hint at dinner that we had spotted it? I was prevented from doing so by a sense of revulsion against the whole vaguely abnormal business, it was as distasteful as the result of an abortion. So, with my head in my hands, I concentrated on my books—particularly as I felt certain that Fuchs would be going to have a look for me. His interior void was bound to take him there, though he refrained from mentioning the subject which, so far as we were concerned, was exhausted. So I sat there bending over my books while he fussed and fidgeted round the room. But finally off he went. In due course he came back, and as usual Katasia brought up our lunch. But he did not touch on the subject until nearly four o'clock, after his afternoon nap. Then, lying on his bed, he said:

'Come along, there's something I want to show you.'

I did not answer. I wanted to humiliate him, and the best way of doing so was just to ignore him. This worked, he fell silent and dared not insist, but the minutes passed and I started shaving, and eventually I said:

'Is there anything new?"

'Yes and no,' he replied.

When I had finished shaving he said:

'Come along and I'll show you.'

We went out and made our way to the wall, taking precautions as before in relation to the house, which again gazed at us out of all its windows, and we looked at the bit of

50

Monotype issued a *Janson* (series 1173) in 1986 which is in some ways more faithful to the Stempel type than the Linotype Janson Text is. In some ways less faithful. It lacks some of the charming quirks and queerness of the other designs (it doesn't retain the distinctive squared-up m and n of the italic) but the weight is better for modern printing. The spur of the G is more pronounced than any of the other versions.

The types of *Caslon** (*c.* 1733) are Dutch Old Face types and not of great importance in respect of their design, though the italics are influenced by prevailing styles of British round-hand. In the dreary Victorian epoch dominated by Moderns they were the only Old Face going and so they were put into extensive service by William Pickering and the Whittinghams. The former notably with *The Diary of Lady Willoughby* in 1844, the latter with an edition of Juvenal. The state of British typography had hardly changed when D. H. Lawrence and G. B. Shaw demanded that their books should be set in Caslon (G.B.S. declaring 'I'll stick to Caslon until I die'). A great number of Caslon-based Old Styles were made from 1858 (Miller & Richard) to the turn of the century (Linotype and many others). Monotype produced a few series of Caslon from 1903 to 1915. The original types (of Caslon's foundry) were of varied quality depending on whether great primer or pica (the designs of the letters varied considerably from size to size). The Monotype versions closely resemble the Caslon Old Face from the foundry H. W. Caslon & Co. Ltd which was acquired by Stephenson Blake in 1937. Numerous mutations called Caslon were produced in Britain and America, and a number of these, bearing little resemblance to the eighteenth-century types, exist now in digital versions, but none of the Monotype series has been digitised.

The Caslon design was used however for a very different type, the first important text type of the twentieth century, called *Imprint* (fig. 5). We are jumping ahead of ourselves discussing it here because it is more twentieth than eighteenth-century. The type was designed in 1912 by J. H. Mason and Edward Johnston, with the assistance of Ernest Jackson and Gerald Meynell,† for use in their journal, devoted to 'improving and spreading technical knowledge' in the printing industry, called *The Imprint*. The first issue of January 1913 is set in the Monotype face and it marks the start of the second revival of printing in the modern era (the first being the influence of William Morris's Kelmscott Press) and a turning away from Morris's Arts and Crafts fashion. It is a reformed, regularised Caslon which has none of the oddities or charm. It is larger on the body, has a larger x-height than the Caslons and counters more open – it was designed specially for modern printing (i.e. on dry rather than dampened paper). Stanley Morison says of it:

> The importance of Imprint was that the design had been originated for mechanical composition. It was the first design, not copied or stolen from the typefounders, to establish itself as a standard book-face. Its success as a commercial product proved that in future all types, good or bad, for manual or mechanical composition, would be drawn and pantographically cut by engraving machines.[21]

The Imprint was well received and influential of trends in modern print-

---

* William Caslon I (1692–1766).

† J. H. Mason, the main contributor to the type's design, had worked as Morris's compositor and also for Cobden-Sanderson's Doves Press; Edward Johnston was a calligrapher and designer of the Johnston's Railway Type (1918) used for the London Underground; Ernest Jackson was a master lithographer and an instructor at the Central School of Arts and Crafts in London; Gerald Meynell was the managing director of the Westminster Press. The Monotype Corporation was also instrumental in the design of Imprint. Meynell's technical contribution was negligible. Mason wrote: 'I have read that Meynell claimed to have been jointly responsible with me in the production of the Imprint type. It is true that it was he who sent me the proofs as they were produced, but he had not the long technical experience required, nor had he studied type design sufficiently for that form of creative work.' (Quoted in L. T. Owens, *J. H. Mason* (Muller, 1976), p. 99.)

ing but it shut up shop after only eight issues; the type however proved very successful. It was used at Giovanni Mardersteig's Stamperia Valdònega.

The Miller & Richard Old Styles and the Monotype recutting in the form of Old Style 2 were as thin and anaemic as many of the Victorian Moderns. It is remarkable that the sturdy Imprint in which this fault was completely rectified was later to become just as anaemic itself. Unfortunately the Monotype PostScript version is taken from the design for sizes 9-point and under (but with weight reduced for display settings!). It differs greatly from the design of the larger text sizes (10 to 14 point) of the metal version. In *Typefaces for Books* Sutton and Bartram remark: 'Slightly thinner and less rich, especially in text sizes, than the original hot-metal designs. Looser fit. Italic opened out. General effect more spidery.'[22] Indeed it is that, but I shall say it is worthless as a text type. This deplorable situation occurred when the type was adopted for the Monophoto in the early 1960s; the error, incredibly, was never rectified and the design was also used for the Lasercomp version – although a display version was introduced, which was much lighter (too light for bookwork) but consistent with the original design otherwise. A PostScript display version is not available at present. The digital Linotype version (shown in *Typefaces for Books*) retained the proper design (if anaemically) but without f-ligatures and it is not available as a PostScript type.

The *Fournier* types of a narrow, vertically stressed design, are often described as the first Modern faces. Pierre Simon Fournier (or Fournier-lejeune, 1712–68) was the youngest son of Jean Claude Fournier, who was the manager of the foundry of the widow of the third Guillaume Le Bé. When Jean Claude died in 1730, the eldest son Jean Pierre, aged twenty-three, bought the foundry – and its wealth of ancient punches, matrices, 'roman, italic, civilité, greek, music, vignettes, fleurons', material from 'Augereau, Garamond, Granjon, Hautlin, Danfrie and others'[23] – from the Le Bé III daughters, Angelique and Marie. Pierre Simon was seventeen at the time and Stanley Morison describes him as 'forceful, ambitious, adventurous and quarrelsome, but withal attractive and effective'. He apprenticed in his brother's shop. He produced a prodigious number of 'romans and italics . . . scripts, music type, vignettes and decoration'.* When upon the birth of his elder brother's son he realised that he wouldn't inherit the foundry – he was then twenty-five – he undertook to create an original type adopting certain of the principles which had been recommended by the Académie des Sciences in 1692 for the revision of the typography of the Imprimerie Royale, upon which the *romain du roi Louis XIV* was designed. The principles involved a rationalisation of the letters; they were to be no longer derived from calligraphy but designed 'on a strictly analytical and mathematical basis, using as their norm a rectangle subdivided into 2304 (i.e. 64 times 36) squares' (Steinberg).[24] The royal types were cut in 1693–1702 by Philippe Grandjean (the work was completed by Louis Luce, Fournier's contemporary) and

* 'No man of his time ever accomplished so much as Fournier le jeune.' (*A Tally of Types*, p. 77.) 'Of his tremendous industry (he cut over eighty types in twenty-eight years), and technical brilliance as a punch-cutter and founder, a wealth of evidence remains in his published works.' (Geoffrey Dowding, *An Introduction to the History of Printing Types* (Wace, 1961), p. 61.)

Fig. 39 12-point Monotype Caslon 128 in Herbert Simon's history of The Curwen Press, *Song and Words*, printed at The Curwen Press for George Allen and Unwin in 1973. Swelled rules, adopted by English printers in the late eighteenth century, out of fashion in the early twentieth century, but revived by Stanley Morison and Nonesuch and The Curwen Press, are sadly missing from the typography of contemporary books. Peggy Lang, writing in Oliver Simon's *Signature*, found that the swelled rule 'passes the test of usefulness'. That remark is particularly interesting when one considers current gratuitous and ostentatious use of ornaments etc. 'While its weight achieves emphasis, the tapering ends prevent obtrusiveness, and by its own graduation it brings into harmony varying weights of type.' In his *Introduction to Typography*, Oliver Simon warns: 'As with swash letters, their employment can easily become tiresome if overdone, and their use by unskilled hands can bring as much ugliness to the printed page as a vignette or printer's flowers. . . . The ultra-fat sort invariably annoys the reader and rarely justifies itself for use with text or display types used in books.' But such erring use never occurred at The Curwen Press. Reduced from 245.5 mm deep.

II

APPOINTMENT TO PLAISTOW

THE APPOINTMENT to Stowmarket in 1841 proved to be a piece of geographical good fortune which was to have immense influence in shaping John Curwen's pastoral work. He was only a few miles from Norwich and his friend Andrew Reed and it was not long before a meeting with Sarah Glover and her sister Christiana was arranged.

Miss Glover was then fifty-six years old. She had been experimenting for a long time in making singing easier to learn: it is believed that from about 1812 she began training her choir by a system which was eventually to become known as Tonic Sol-fa. But although John Curwen, through the fame of his *History of Nelly Vanner* and his work in the Sunday schools and Temperance Movement, was probably known to Miss Glover, it is clear that until the meeting in Norwich he knew nothing of the Sol-fa system. An account of his first meeting has fortunately been recorded by Andrew Reed:

I took him to see the Misses Glover in their school, and he was at once riveted by the astonishing results produced by them. He never forgot to allude very honourably to them, so as to give them due credit, but it was himself who saw the general adaptation of the system—who resolved to spread and make it known—who perfected it in many respects, who bore the brunt of the opposition encountered by every novelty—who took the mercantile risks on himself—and who, by his unwearied perseverance and pluck, gave it a place all over the world, wherever music is taught, and exalted it into a scientific notation, which more and more competes with the established notation. Thus he found the chief mission of his life to improve the psalmody of our churches and the singing in our schools, and to make it a delightful medium for the easy culture in homes, schools and churches of harmony wedded to moral and religious poetry.

[7]

ẞt fb fh fj fk ẞt w
J J ȷ Q Q
ẞt fb fh fj fk ẞt
J J Q Q

Alternative roman and italics letters for the digital Monotype Fournier with undescending J for the shortened capitals version and the small capitals, long-tailed Q and a w in the style of Barbou with intersecting strokes.

a royal decree forbade their reproduction. Fournier may have applied the 'logical' theories selectively* but much of his design is essentially the same as the royal types.† It also derives from the condensed romans which J. M. Fleischman cut for Enschedé (1730–68). As Geoffrey Dowding observes, 'although he was technically brilliant he is not to be considered as an innovator of new type designs but rather as a clever adapter of the work of others in that field.'[25] None the less the types used for the Monotype revivals are withal attractive and effective.

The Monotype Fournier series 185 was issued in 1925. It was another successful product, issued only in one weight. It has very little variation of thick and thin. Morison had preferred a different design: the series 178 which was later issued as Barbou (named after Fournier's printer Joseph Barbou). It is very similar (both Monotypes are based on Fournier's *St-Augustin ordinaire* numbers 46 and 47 which were cut before 1742) but slightly heavier, slightly more contrast between thick and thin strokes; the roman has got a splayed capital M and a lower-case w with intersecting strokes, the italic is rather more regularised (f and g rather more temperate, one might say). But the Fournier series 185 was issued owing to Morison's 'absence abroad'.[26] Only one size (14-pt) of Barbou was then produced and it went to the Cambridge University Press where it was used for printing the last three volumes of *The Fleuron*; it was made available in a full range of sizes (8 to 12-pt) only in March 1968, the bicentennial of Fournier's death.‡ 'They are both unmistakably eighteenth-century in cut; neither is conspicuously French, or even markedly continental.'[27]

There was predictably an inclination to use the type for modern settings of French literature. An excellent setting was done by Hazells for the Penguin Classics translation of Laclos's *Les Liaisons Dangereuses* (1961). The type was also used notably for the Penguin editions of La Rochefoucauld and Rimbaud. Other notable examples: Virginia Woolf's *Diary* (The Hogarth Press); the Oxford Goncourt Journal; the Everyman Pepys (fig. 24). A shortened capitals version (series 285) and ligatures as well as an ornaments set are available as digital type – predictably too light but possibly serviceable.

John Baskerville was buried vertically,[28] and indeed he was one of the most vertical men of his era. I am taking Salvador de Madariaga's term from his *Portrait of a Man Standing*, which is among other things a meditation on the vertical and horizontal tendencies of men and nations. Madariaga finds more horizontality than verticality in Englishmen.

The prominence of the herd over the individual has never perhaps been better put both in words and in deeds than by some Englishmen. A Canadian statesman once revealed that during one of his visits to London, Churchill the Great had advised him thus: 'Never stand if you can sit, never sit if you can lie down.' A clear directive from the leader of a horizontal people for whom the vertical position is not natural.[29]

* 'And if he rightly criticized as "pedantic" the application of mathematics to type-faces, as was done in the "Louvre" patterns, he was eager to apply scientific method in the right place, i.e. to type bodies upon which the faces are cast.' (*A Tally of Types*, p. 79.)

† 'His first roman and italic were based on those of Louis Luce – who complained that his ideas had been stolen.' (*An Introduction to the History of Printing Types*, p. 63.)

‡ The type was used for James Moran's *Stanley Morison: 1889–1967* (*The Monotype Recorder*, vol. 43, no. 5 (Autumn 1968)).

The English are not disparaged in this book (quite the contrary! the author speaks of many virtues of the horizontal tendency); the French, at any rate, are seen to be a vertical nation. Most of John Baskerville's equipment and types were sold by his widow for £3,700 to Beaumarchais – who used them for the famous 70-volume Voltaire[30] – and the types enjoyed an esteem in France which they hadn't known in Britain owing mostly to the hegemony of Caslon.

Baskerville had been a writing-master in Birmingham. He was an inscriber of grave-stones. He made a fortune in japanning and set up a printing-office in 1750 when he was 44. Updike quotes from Fournier's *Manuel typographique* (1764–6) the following:

M. Baskerville, a private individual of means, has established at Birmingham, the town where he lives – renowned for its metal manufacturers – a paper-mill, printing offices, and type-foundry. He has spared neither pains nor expense to bring these to the highest perfection. His types are cut with much spirit, his italic being the best in any foundry in England, though the roman characters are a little too broad. He has already published some editions printed from these new types, which, for brilliancy, are real masterpieces. Some are upon hot-pressed paper, and although they are a little fatiguing to the eye, one cannot deny that they are the most beautiful things to be seen for this sort of work.[31]

It is not surprising that Fournier, whose capitals were so narrow, would find the Baskerville letters a little too broad. Indeed the M and T seem quite wide, though they're not so wide as in some of Caslon's types. It is interesting that Updike thought Baskerville's types 'not so good as Caslon's': this was a view which was widely held before the Monotype re-cutting in 1923. He notes that the types 'would drive Caslon's type, for a time, from the field'.

Baskerville's characters had this advantage – they were in line with the tendency toward lighter type-forms which was coming over European printing; and although his fonts never had much vogue in England, they did have an enormous influence on the later development of English type-forms, and on the type-forms of Europe.[32]

The English type-forms being the Miller & Richard Moderns and the type-forms of Europe being those of Didot, Bodoni, Walbaum. But let us look again at the passage from Fournier. He mentions some examples of Baskerville's printing, the 'brilliancy' of them. As novel as Baskerville's types and his undecorated printing, was his use of blacker inks and hot-pressed wove paper. Owing to his perfectionism – a trait not uncommon to printers and typographers – it had taken him seven years (experimenting with type designs and printing methods) to complete his first printing job: his quarto Virgil (1757). Inks, presses, and paper had to be perfected and although he had not trained as a printer he did indeed bring about much perfection of these things. This is from the famous Preface to his royal octavo Milton (1758):

Having been an early admirer of the beauty of Letters, I became insensibly desirous of contributing to the perfection of them. I formed to my self Ideas of greater accuracy than had yet appeared, and have endeavoured to produce a *Sett* of *Types* according to what I conceived to be their true proportion.

The page containing this is reproduced in Updike's *Printing Types* and it is recommended that the student of typography have a look at it. It is evidence of the printer's perfectionism and also a fine example of *modern* printing, such has been his influence.

'His way of printing was so closely connected with the effects of his fonts that they cannot be considered apart from it.'[33] As we have noted, he used wove papers and impressed them much more lightly than was usual. His method of hot-pressing, whereby the moistened printed paper as it came from the press was placed between hot copper, enhanced the contrast of the type against the paper and gave the paper a gloss. The gloss (less than that of many of the papers used nowadays) was much derided by the critics of the day, as were the thin strokes of the type. S. H. Steinberg considered John Baskerville to be 'the greatest type-designer of the post-incunabula age.'[34] Perhaps he was too modern for Updike, who says: 'the fonts appear very perfect, and yet somehow they have none of the homely charm of Caslon's letter' and 'The more we think of Baskerville, the more he appears to be an eclectic, whose types were the result of fashions in calligraphy and whose presswork was an attempt to emulate on paper the finish of japanning'.[35] And: 'He was not among the world's greatest printers, because what he had to say was not in itself great. When we look at his books we think of Baskerville; while to look at the work of Jenson is to think but of its beauty, and almost to forget that it was made by his hands!'[36]

After their use in the Beaumarchais Voltaire the types were bought by various foundries in France and what was left of them existed in obscurity until Bruce Rogers, while at Cambridge as adviser to the Press, 'identified some type from the Fonderie Bertrand as bearing the true Baskerville design and as being mostly cast from original matrices'.* Other than his Greek, which was made in 1758 for the Oxford University Press and still in their possession, there wasn't hide nor hair of Baskerville's types anywhere in England. Most of the types had found their way to Deberny & Peignot (who acquired them from Bertrand in November 1936) and in 1953 the director Charles Peignot made, in the words of S. H. Steinberg, a 'princely gift' of them to the Cambridge University Press.† The Monotype version had not been modelled upon punches or matrices but was made from the Great Primer found in Baskerville's *Comoediae* of Terence of 1772.

Stanley Morison said of it: 'Baskerville cannot be said to be more picturesque than Caslon, but its proportions are better, the face is clearer and the whole design, roman and italic... more efficient for present-day work.'[37] There are a number of interesting if not unique characters: the capital C with arcs almost joined up by the barbs at both ends; the not so wide M and T which none the less seem wide; the W without a middle serif; the italic *h, k, p, z, K, N, Q, R, T, Y, Z*. The Linotype italic (like the model from Bertrand from which it derives)[38] doesn't feature the epigraphic *K, N, T, Y, Z*; alternative italics were supplied for the Monotype version and these included a

* Stanley Morison, *A Tally of Types*, p. 84. Rogers 'made the suggestion that a "Baskerville" might be used at the Press in as distinctive a way as the Fell types were used at Oxford' (James Moran, *Stanley Morison*, p. 45.) The circumstances of the Baskerville project at Monotype are described in Moran's pp. 86–7.

† Brooke Crutchley gives an account of this in his memoir *To Be a Printer* (The Bodley Head, 1980). 'Some of the punches were later replacements or additions, but about the bulk of them, some three thousand in all, there was no question.' (p. 68.)

cap C without the peculiar bottom barb. A specially-made bottom-barbless roman C was used by the Unwin Brothers Greshsam Press.

There are many excellent examples of the type in many different kinds of book. Notable are the *Penguin Dictionary of Science*, printed by Cox & Wyman in 1971 (the Monotype Baskerville was used in a great number of Penguins), *Collins Authors and Printers Dictionary* (Oxford, 1973), Schopenhauer's *Parerga and Paralipomena* (trans. E. F. J. Payne, 2 vols, Oxford, 1974), a fixed-space setting for *Goodbye Baby, and Amen* by David Bailey and Peter Evans (Condé Nast/Corgi, 1969/70), the exquisite two volumes of William Bennett's biography of Baskerville (City of Birmingham School of Printing, 1937).

The type was copied or imitated in the eighteenth century, most notably in a version cut by Isaac Moore in 1766 which came to be known as Fry's Baskerville (Dr Fry was Moore's partner) and this was the name of the Stephenson Blake reproduction (1913) upon which the ATF Baskerville was modelled (also in 1913). A Linotype version was made in 1931 from some of the original matrices which George W. Jones obtained in France.* I agree with Walter Tracy's opinion that this type is 'dull'. The redrawing done by Matthew Carter and John Quaranta and issued by Mergenthaler Linotype (New York) in 1978 is faithful to George Jones's design (or the design supervised by him), if not an improvement of it. Linotype called it Baskerville no. 2 and when ITC acquired it they renamed it New Baskerville; it is available as a digital type (without double-f ligatures). It is a better job than the digital Monotype version which, despite a superior design, is 'bloodless', to use Hans Schmoller's word – even too delicate for John Baskerville's taste – and hardly suitable for ordinary text-setting at sizes under 12 point.

Two types drawn from Baskervillian models (some writers have said the same model) were produced by Linotype (1931) and Monotype (1936). The Monotype, designed by Giovanni Mardersteig and called *Fontana*, is derived from a type of Alexander Wilson's Glasgow Letter-Foundry, called English Roman No. 1, which was first used in an edition of Horace for Foulis in 1760; the Linotype, designed by George W. Jones and called *Georgian*, was also derived from types of Wilson's foundry which were probably made by Richard Austin.

Fontana† was a proprietary type with italics and small caps in a full range of sizes designed for Collins, the Glasgow publishers, by Giovanni Mardersteig when he was employed by them in 1935–6 as an adviser to their Clear-Type Press. It is related by John Dreyfus:

One of his first questions on arrival was 'May I see your clear type'? It was

---

* 'In 1920 Bruce Rogers had persuaded the University Press at Harvard to obtain a font of type cast from matrices struck from the original Baskerville punches which Rogers had discovered to be in Paris. No doubt the Linotype office in New York knew of this, and they must certainly have known of McMurtrie's recommendation of the ATF version and of the Baskerville made by Monotype in Britain. Mergenthaler asked George W. Jones to obtain a supply of the foundry type from Paris, to supervise the production of letter drawings at the Linotype office in north-west England, and to supply copies of them to the New York plant for the making of patterns, punches and matrices. The outcome was a Baskerville remarkably close to the original.' (Walter Tracy, *The Typographic Scene* (Gordon Fraser, 1988), p. 23.) Douglas C. McMurtrie recommended the ATF Baskerville in his *American Type Design in the Twentieth Century* (Chicago, Ballou, 1924), p. 30.

† Named after the Collins fountain device which was designed by Eric Gill in 1936.

Fig. 40 Page 58 of Salvador de Madariaga's *Portrait of a Man Standing* (George Allen & Unwin, 1968), set in 11-point Monotype Baskerville – Unwin's special version with barb or serif missing from the lower arc of capital C. The Fry's Baskerville (a design derived from Baskerville) has got similar Cs (without bottom barbs) but the distinctive top and bottom barbs as found in the ordinary Monotype and Linotype cuttings were a unique feature of Baskerville's type as can be seen in the original specimens. Reduced from 196 mm deep.

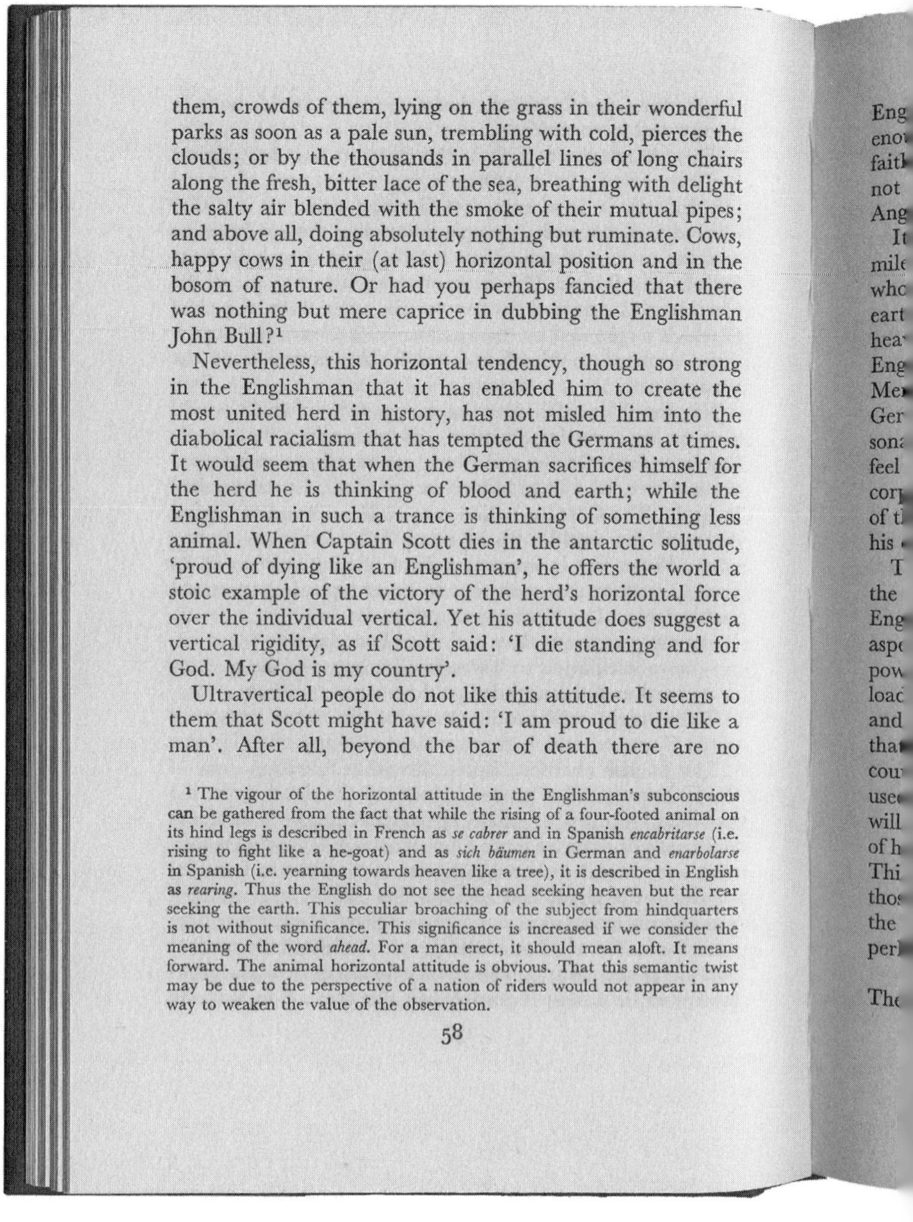

them, crowds of them, lying on the grass in their wonderful parks as soon as a pale sun, trembling with cold, pierces the clouds; or by the thousands in parallel lines of long chairs along the fresh, bitter lace of the sea, breathing with delight the salty air blended with the smoke of their mutual pipes; and above all, doing absolutely nothing but ruminate. Cows, happy cows in their (at last) horizontal position and in the bosom of nature. Or had you perhaps fancied that there was nothing but mere caprice in dubbing the Englishman John Bull?[1]

Nevertheless, this horizontal tendency, though so strong in the Englishman that it has enabled him to create the most united herd in history, has not misled him into the diabolical racialism that has tempted the Germans at times. It would seem that when the German sacrifices himself for the herd he is thinking of blood and earth; while the Englishman in such a trance is thinking of something less animal. When Captain Scott dies in the antarctic solitude, 'proud of dying like an Englishman', he offers the world a stoic example of the victory of the herd's horizontal force over the individual vertical. Yet his attitude does suggest a vertical rigidity, as if Scott said: 'I die standing and for God. My God is my country'.

Ultravertical people do not like this attitude. It seems to them that Scott might have said: 'I am proud to die like a man'. After all, beyond the bar of death there are no

[1] The vigour of the horizontal attitude in the Englishman's subconscious can be gathered from the fact that while the rising of a four-footed animal on its hind legs is described in French as *se cabrer* and in Spanish *encabritarse* (i.e. rising to fight like a he-goat) and as *sich bäumen* in German and *enarbolarse* in Spanish (i.e. yearning towards heaven like a tree), it is described in English as *rearing*. Thus the English do not see the head seeking heaven but the rear seeking the earth. This peculiar broaching of the subject from hindquarters is not without significance. This significance is increased if we consider the meaning of the word *ahead*. For a man erect, it should mean aloft. It means forward. The animal horizontal attitude is obvious. That this semantic twist may be due to the perspective of a nation of riders would not appear in any way to weaken the value of the observation.

58

explained to him that no such type existed, although all their types were in fact clear. This did not satisfy Mardersteig who suggested that if they called themselves a Cleartype Press, they ought to have a type which would distinguish them from other printers.[39]

In Harry Carter's assessment of it, in *Signature* in 1936, he notes: 'The design is not original: it is taken from a fount cut for Wilson's foundry, near

Glasgow, about 1760. Fontana may, I hope without offence, fairly be called an accurate reproduction of Wilson's type; it is as near the original as Monotype Bell, and nearer than the previously cut Baskerville or Bodoni.'[40] In the specimen of Wilson's English Roman No. 1 which is reproduced in Harry Carter's article, it can be seen that the type was copied scrupulously. There are certain aspects of it, peculiarities of the lower-case g, which are rather similar to Mardersteig's design for Dante, even though it is a type of a different species. I think Dante is a much nicer design; there is much awkwardness in Fontana, historically interesting but irksome to twentieth-century readers; and when one compares original specimen sheets one sees that Baskerville's types were quite superior to Wilson's. At the end of his article, Harry Carter notes: 'The proprietors do not normally print for outside customers, but it is understood that they would be willing to undertake work in Fontana if it had a special typographic interest.' Collins allowed Dr Mardersteig to use the type for an edition of Walter Savage Landor's *Imaginary Conversations*, which he designed and printed in 1936 for The Limited Editions Club of New York. The type was released for general use in 1961, but it was used rarely. It has not been issued in a digital form.

I agree with Walter Tracy that George W. Jones's *Georgian* is a much better type than his Baskerville (even though the Baskerville may have more faithfully followed its model). If Granjon is rather overpraised I think Georgian is underpraised.* It was used now and again in Penguins but one doesn't find many examples of it. Hugh Williamson attributes its design to a specimen of Alexander Wilson's from 1772.[41] The type is very light with an excellent letterfit; the lower-case gs are especially fine (they seem rather large, which was Wilson's style; they are very similar to the Fontana gs but the loop is a little less flat); the j and f are expertly drawn – I think they're a better job than the Granjon j and f (a set of f-ligatures such as were devised for Granjon were also made for Georgian and also seldom used); the capitals are smaller and more consonant with the lower-case than they are in Baskerville's type; there is the slightest curve to the tail of Georgian R. Both Georgian and Fontana have got a capital C with a barbed lower arc but not as pronounced as Baskerville's. I think the roman was a better job than the italic. There was a semi-bold called Victorian. It is a pity that no digital version of this type was ever made, but then perhaps – until a better technique for producing digital types is employed – it's just as well.

The *Bell* types, which were cut in 1788 by the greatest of English punchcutters Richard Austin, suffered a similar fate to Baskerville's types which had been their main influence – which is to say they were lost and forgotten. John Bell (1746–1831) was, in eighteenth-century style, an educationist and publisher (notably of cheap editions of the classics, including a 109-volume *Poets of Great Britain from Chaucer to Churchill* (1777–92)), proprietor of newspapers and periodicals (*The Morning Post*, published from 1772 until 1937, *The World, The Oracle, Bell's Weekly Messenger*), his own letterfounder (The British Letter Foundry), the second proprietor of the first

---

* I am surprised that Ian Rogerson, author of *George W. Jones: Master of Master Printers 1860–1942* (Manchester Metropolitan University Library, 1993), calls this type 'unexceptional' (p. 52).

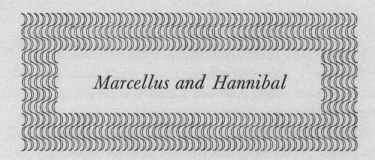

Marcellus and Hannibal

*Claudius Marcellus, the conqueror of Sicily, was killed
in a skirmish with Hannibal's troops in 208 B.C.
Hannibal said of him that he was a good
soldier but a bad general.*

HANNIBAL. Could a Numidian horseman ride no faster?
Marcellus! ho! Marcellus! He moves not . . . he is dead. Did
he not stir his fingers? Stand wide, soldiers . . . wide, forty
paces . . . give him air . . . bring water . . . halt! Gather those
broad leaves, and all the rest, growing under the brushwood . . . unbrace his armor. Loose the helmet first . . . his
breast rises. I fancied his eyes were fixed on me . . . they have
rolled back again. Who presumed to touch my shoulder?
This horse? It was surely the horse of Marcellus! Let no
man mount him. Ha! ha! the Romans too sink into lux-
ury: here is gold about the charger.

GAULISH CHIEFTAIN. Execrable thief! The golden chain
of our king under a beast's grinders! The vengeance of the
gods has overtaken the impure . . .

HANNIBAL. We will talk about vengeance when we have
entered Rome, and about purity among the priests, if they
will hear us. Sound for the surgeon. That arrow may be
extracted from the side, deep as it is . . . The conqueror of
Syracuse lies before me . . . Send a vessel off to Carthage.
Say Hannibal is at the gates of Rome . . . Marcellus, who
stood alone between us, fallen. Brave man! I would rejoice
and can not . . . How awfully serene a countenance! Such

15

TE PALINURE PETENS 89

'Aimer et haïr, ce n'est qu'éprouver avec une passion singulière l'être d'un être.'

'Quand l'univers considère avec indifférence l'être que nous aimons, qui est dans la vérité?' – JOUHANDEAU.

We think we recognize someone in passing. A mistake, but a moment later we run into them. This pre-view was our arrival on their wavelength, within their magnetic orbit.

Like the glow-worm; dowdy, minute, passive, yet full of mystery to the poet and erotic significance to its fellows; so everything and everybody eternally radiate a dim light for those who care to seek. The strawberry hidden under the last leaf cries, 'Pick me'; the forgotten book, in the forgotten bookshop, screams to be discovered. The old house hidden in the hollow agitates itself violently at the approach of its predestined admirer. Dead authors cry 'Read me'; dead friends say 'Remember me'; dead ancestors whisper, 'Unearth me'; dead places, 'Revisit me'; and sympathetic spirits, living and dead, are continually trying to enter into communion. Physical or intellectual attraction between two people is a constant communication. Underneath the rational and voluntary world lies the involuntary, impulsive, integrated world, the world of Relation in which everything is one; where sympathy and antipathy are engrossed in their selective tug-of-war.

We learn a new word for the first time. Then it turns up within the next hour. Why? Because words are living organisms impelled by a crystallizing process

U.G.–5

[9]

L'Éducation Sentimentale
(1844–5)

FLAUBERT returned home from Vernon to Rouen on New Year's Day 1844, but left for Deauville immediately, where the family had been thinking of building a villa, and it was on the road been Pont l'Évêque and Rouen, when driving with his brother Achille, while he himself was holding the reins, that he had his first seizure – whatever it may have been, epilepsy or some other nervous ailment. He fell to the ground; his brother carried him to the nearest house and bled him, fearing that he was dead. After repeated bleedings he seemed to recover and he was brought home to Rouen, where he came under his father's treatment. So terrible was this treatment that it seems to us marvellous today that he did not, in fact, succumb to it. A seton was put on his neck to draw off the blood, fastened permanently in position, and he was kept on a very low diet, with little meat and no wine or tobacco, although he had always enjoyed these pleasures. Writing to Chevalier he said:[1]

My dear old Ernest, without knowing it you've almost had to mourn the death of the honest man who is writing you these lines. Yes, old fellow; yes young man; I almost departed to see Pluto, Rhadamanthus and Minos. I'm still in bed, with a seton on my neck, which is a stiff collar less yielding than that of an officer of the national guard; with masses of pills, tisanes, and especially with that spectre, a thousand times more terrible than all the illnesses in the world, a diet. You must know, my dear friend, that I've had a congestion of the brain, which is something like a miniature attack of apoplexy, accompanied by aching nerves, which I still have because it is fashionable. I almost croaked in the hands of my family. . . . They bled me three times all at once, and, at last, I opened my eyes. My father wants to keep me here

Fig. 41 (opposite) A rare example of Fontana. This is Giovanni Mardersteig's 12/14 setting for W. S. Landor's *Imaginary Conversations* which was printed in 1936 for the Limited Editions Club of New York at the Officina Bodoni, Verona, and shown in Monotype's publication, *The Work of Giovanni Mardersteig with 'Monotype' Faces* (Salfords, 1967), also printed at Verona (at the Stamperia Valdònega). Reduced from 257 mm deep.

Fig. 42 Linotype Georgian in Hazells' setting for the 1967 Penguin edition of *The Unquiet Grave* by Palinurus, also called Cyril Connolly. It has got too much line-spacing: the *Flaubert* looks better.

Fig. 43 A page of *Flaubert* by Enid Starkie (Penguin, 1971). Printed by Cox & Wyman. Note the É in the fourth line which is shortened to conform to the Linotype parameters. Monotype Bell with distinctive square brackets is used to very good effect for chapter heads. It is one of my favourite Penguins.

Both reduced from 180 mm deep.

London lending library, The British Library, and a few other things. The design for his type was informed by French designs; Stanley Morison writes: 'although Bell did not engage in typefounding until twenty years after the death of Pierre Simon Fournier, it is extremely probable that he was acquainted with his specimens and with those of others, like François Ambroise Didot, who followed the proportions of Fournier's letters. Bell himself says he "examined and compared the Types of every Foundry in Europe".' [42] His type is called 'transitional' and also the 'first British modern'. There are many remarkable aspects of it: the sharpness of the serifs which was in Morison's view 'the greatest development of "finish" that had occurred since Aldus substituted his bracketed for Jenson's flat serif', the elimination of the long ſ, ranging figures (1234567890), both of which were done to aid the ordinary reader,* more contrast between main strokes and thin strokes, many attractive curves and terminal blobs (k, K, R, f, g, j, y), the square brackets [ ]. Morison observes that 'Bell's use of paper and ink, and his recourse to Paris for the illustrations of his editions, prove that he had learned much from Baskerville'; his 'daily newspaper *The Oracle* (1787) ranks as the most elegant sheet ever published.' [43] For one reason or another he failed to produce a bourgeois (9-point) as his competitors were using for their advertising matter (he had got long primer to paragon – 10 to 20-point) and this, in 1794, cost him *The Oracle* and three years later his Foundry – his type, 'the first modern type forgotten, not to be seen again in England until 1930'.

The types did survive in England (they were acquired by Stephenson, Blake and Company) but obscurely, anonymously, neglectedly. They were, however, widely used in America, 'seen in Massachusetts in 1792, Pennsylvania in 1795, and their use can be traced in New York in 1800'. [44] In 1864 Henry Oscar Houghton, the publisher of the Riverside Press at Cambridge, Massachusetts, bought a set of the types (newly cast) from Stephenson Blake, and these were admired by Daniel Updike when he was employed there in the 1880s, and then by his successor, Bruce Rogers. The type was then called Brimmer (after one of the press's popular authors, Martin Brimmer); Updike had some founts made from the Stephenson Blake matrices for his own use which he called 'Mountjoye'. It was 'the first type experimented with' [45] by Bruce Rogers; there 'were two cases of each size' and he bought them from Riverside and later sold them back. [46] In January 1925, while doing research into a different matter at the Bibliothèque Nationale, Stanley Morison came across a copy of 'Address to the World by Mr Bell, British-Library, Strand, London' and straight away recognised the types which he knew as Brimmer. He thereupon marked Updike's card for him; [47] in 1930 he published a handsome full-length study: *John Bell, 1745–1831* (Cambridge) and the Monotype facsimile was cut in the following year.

It is an admirable typeface but not as adaptable as Baskerville, Fournier, Bembo and most of the other Monotype revivals. It was however used very nicely in an Oxford edition of Boswell's *Life of Johnson* printed by Geoffrey

* 'His *English Chronicle* in 1786 and his *The World* in 1787 banned from the newspaper world the long "ſ" which Bell had first dispensed with in his *Shakespere* [*sic*] edition of 1785. Bell was the first printer to realize that a newspaper is read at a speed and for purposes different from the reading of a book; and he drew the typographical conclusions.' (S. H. Steinberg, *Five Hundred Years of Printing*, p. 230.)

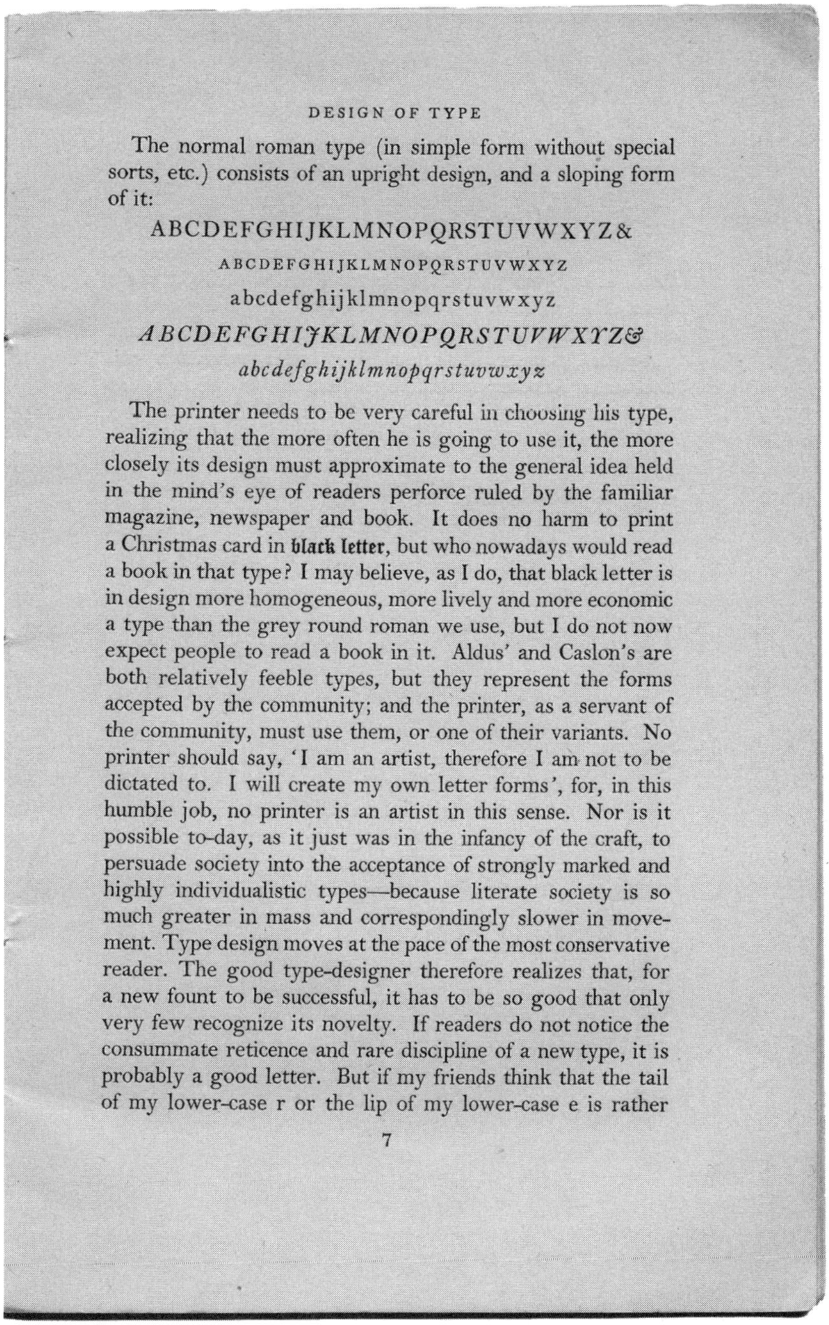

Fig. 44 Stanley Morison's *First Principles of Typography*, set 11/12½ Monotype Bell and printed at the Cambridge University Press for the Cambridge Authors' and Printers' Guides in 1951. The alphabet shows an alternative roman K and R and alternative italic J, K, R. Reduced from 215 mm deep.

DESIGN OF TYPE

The normal roman type (in simple form without special sorts, etc.) consists of an upright design, and a sloping form of it:

ABCDEFGHIJKLMNOPQRSTUVWXYZ&

ABCDEFGHIJKLMNOPQRSTUVWXYZ

abcdefghijklmnopqrstuvwxyz

ABCDEFGHIJKLMNOPQRSTUVWXYZ&

abcdefghijklmnopqrstuvwxyz

The printer needs to be very careful in choosing his type, realizing that the more often he is going to use it, the more closely its design must approximate to the general idea held in the mind's eye of readers perforce ruled by the familiar magazine, newspaper and book. It does no harm to print a Christmas card in 𝔟𝔩𝔞𝔠𝔨 𝔩𝔢𝔱𝔱𝔢𝔯, but who nowadays would read a book in that type? I may believe, as I do, that black letter is in design more homogeneous, more lively and more economic a type than the grey round roman we use, but I do not now expect people to read a book in it. Aldus' and Caslon's are both relatively feeble types, but they represent the forms accepted by the community; and the printer, as a servant of the community, must use them, or one of their variants. No printer should say, 'I am an artist, therefore I am not to be dictated to. I will create my own letter forms', for, in this humble job, no printer is an artist in this sense. Nor is it possible to-day, as it just was in the infancy of the craft, to persuade society into the acceptance of strongly marked and highly individualistic types—because literate society is so much greater in mass and correspondingly slower in movement. Type design moves at the pace of the most conservative reader. The good type-designer therefore realizes that, for a new fount to be successful, it has to be so good that only very few recognize its novelty. If readers do not notice the consummate reticence and rare discipline of a new type, it is probably a good letter. But if my friends think that the tail of my lower-case r or the lip of my lower-case e is rather

7

Cumberlege in 1953; Siegfried Sassoon's *Diaries* (Faber, 1981–5); a bit less well in Gilbert Ryle's *Dilemmas* (Cambridge, 1954). It does not usually look well under 10-point; it was never to my knowledge used by Penguin. The Monotype digital version features most of the alternative characters, one bar through the £ rather than two as there used to be.

I'll just briefly mention Bodoni (Giambattista), fascinating a figure as his is, interesting as his typography is, for the *Bodoni* types designed for machine

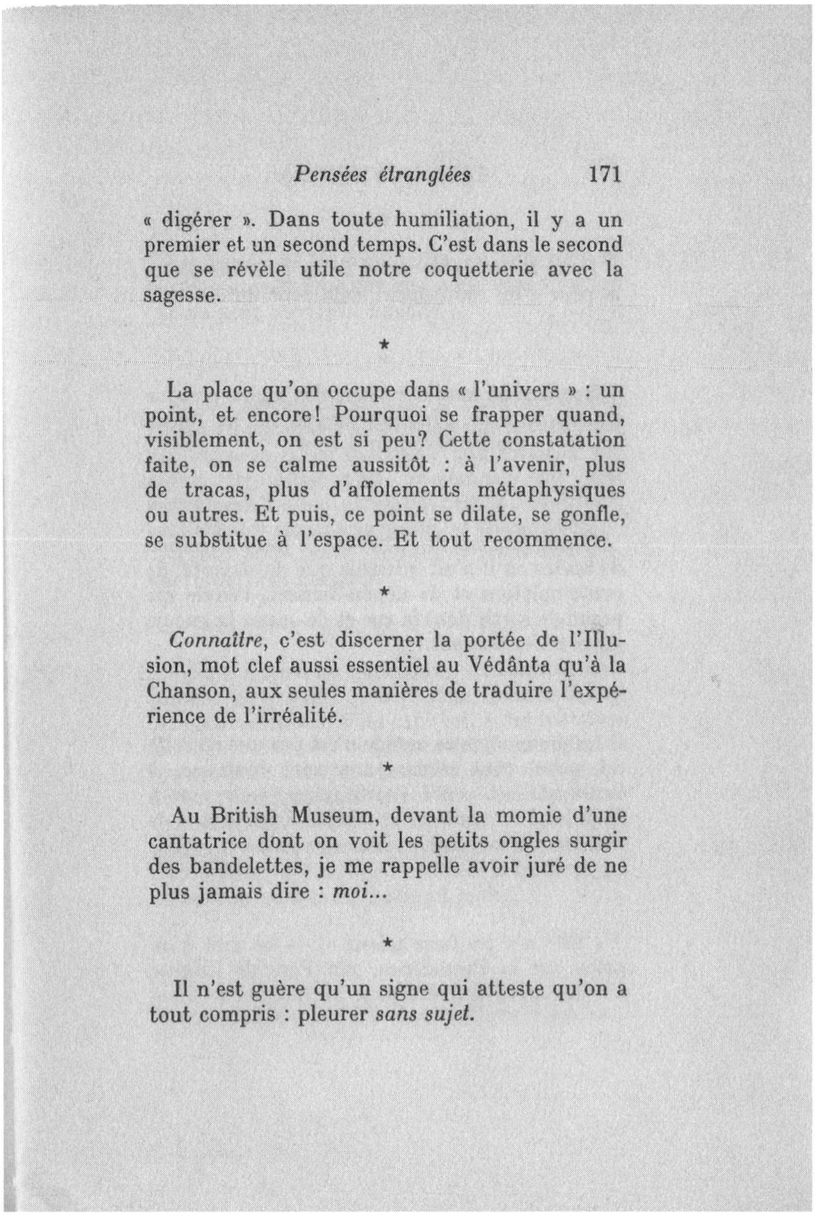

Fig. 45 A page from *Le mauvais démiurge* by E. M. Cioran (Gallimard, 1969). Bodoni and Didot are still very popular in France. The original Didot punches descended to Deberny & Peignot. This example shows a Monotype variation of Firmin Didot's type of *c.* 1784, called Neo Didot (series 65), which, though Hugh Williamson may have thought it a travesty, is quite more readable than the Ludwig & Mayer facsimiles or the revival designed by Adrian Frutiger for Linotype in 1992. It is more pleasing than the modern versions of Bodoni (ATF, Monotype, Bauer, Berthold) which Seán Jennett finds 'inhuman and cold and rather perfect … ultimately unsympathetic and exhausting'. Reduced from 203 mm deep.

Pensées étranglées   171

« digérer ». Dans toute humiliation, il y a un premier et un second temps. C'est dans le second que se révèle utile notre coquetterie avec la sagesse.

*

La place qu'on occupe dans « l'univers » : un point, et encore! Pourquoi se frapper quand, visiblement, on est si peu? Cette constatation faite, on se calme aussitôt : à l'avenir, plus de tracas, plus d'affolements métaphysiques ou autres. Et puis, ce point se dilate, se gonfle, se substitue à l'espace. Et tout recommence.

*

Connaître, c'est discerner la portée de l'Illusion, mot clef aussi essentiel au Védânta qu'à la Chanson, aux seules manières de traduire l'expérience de l'irréalité.

*

Au British Museum, devant la momie d'une cantatrice dont on voit les petits ongles surgir des bandelettes, je me rappelle avoir juré de ne plus jamais dire : *moi…*

*

Il n'est guère qu'un signe qui atteste qu'on a tout compris : pleurer *sans sujet*.

composition, though they proved immensely popular for use in magazines, brochures, ephemeral printing, have never found much favour among book designers in England (more favour in America, it seems). Examples can be found in Alan Bartram's *Making Books*: Monotype Bodoni 135 in a design by Anthony Froshaug for Alain-Fournier's *The Wanderer* (*Le Grand Meaulnes*) (Paul Elek, 1947) and a design for Rimbaud's *A Season in Hell* with French and English translation parallel texts for John Lehmann (1949), and the shortcomings of the type are conspicuous. Bodoni was much influenced by Fournier and the contrast and brilliance of his letters and presswork were owed to Baskerville. His designs were derived mainly from the Didot letters, *c*. 1784; he cut many variants (and many variants for foundry and machine composition were produced) but he was not a printer of books for reading and he was more concerned with objects to please the eye than legibility. Seán Jennett finds the type 'inhuman and cold and rather perfect ... ultimately unsympathetic and exhausting'.[48] Curiously this type which exploits contrast and brilliance more than any other design appears rather jejune in books of the present age, especially when set at smaller sizes (ordinary text sizes), but of course it was never intended for its current employment. Bodoni is often used in French printing in lieu of Didot (a digital Didot for desktop publishing was produced by Linotype (Frankfurt) in 1993). I have got a few books, recently published, with Bauer Bodoni – the most delicate, least suitable version* – printed execrably on art paper.

The 1784 type of Firmin Didot, whose letters were more readable than Bodoni's – 'admirably clear and open, and by no means deserved to be travestied as they have been' (Hugh Williamson)[49] – was travestied a good deal and I think one of the greater travesties, an early Monotype Neo Didot variation which was widely used in France, quite often by Gallimard, was a rather good design. The Didots were also adopted or copied in Germany where the black-letter was seen as a hindrance to the reformist and neo-classical trends. A particularly interesting and attractive *Antiqua* was produced from 1803 to 1828 by J. G. Justus Erich Walbaum, *Schriftgießer und Stempelschneider* (typefounder and punch-cutter), of Goslar and later of Weimar. In his early days as an apprentice confectioner making his own confectionary moulds, he taught himself engraving. Whence he became an engraver of sheet music, and thence a typefounder. His typefoundry at Goslar (1796–1802) was highly successful and his Weimar typefoundry (1803–36) 'became the most famous of its kind throughout Germany'.† It was sold to the Leipzig typefounders and printers Brockhaus and was acquired in 1918 by H. Berthold.

The type was brought to England by Oliver Simon for use at The Curwen Press.

During the period when I was editing *The Fleuron*, several books printed in Walbaum by Poeschel & Trepte, of Leipzig, had come to my notice and in 1925 we bought a complete range from the Berlin foundry of Berthold who held the original punches and matrices. ... This type was not looked upon too favourably by some experts, and it certainly possesses some letters, notably the capital R, which are rather disturbing. It has, however, many merits. Its general appearance on the printed page is one of excellence and crispness owing in part to the vertical stress of the shading and the fineness of the serifs. For The Curwen Press it had at the time two special advantages. By chance, this type was for many years exclusive to the Press and this enabled us, in those perhaps too type-conscious years, to obtain many clients amongst the *cognoscenti* ... Further, there is an unusual difference in the emphasis of weight between the larger sizes and the small so that we could use the large sizes for display purposes in a variety of jobbing work.[50]

The last sentence is interesting because this peculiar book face which has an unmistakable cast of its era found more work in the twentieth century in

J. G. JUSTUS ERICH WALBAUM

---

* Designed by Heinrich Jost and issued in 1926.

† Karl G. Bruchmann, 'Walbaum's Early Years in Goslar and Weimar', *The Monotype Recorder*, vol. 41, no. 4 (1959), p. 10.

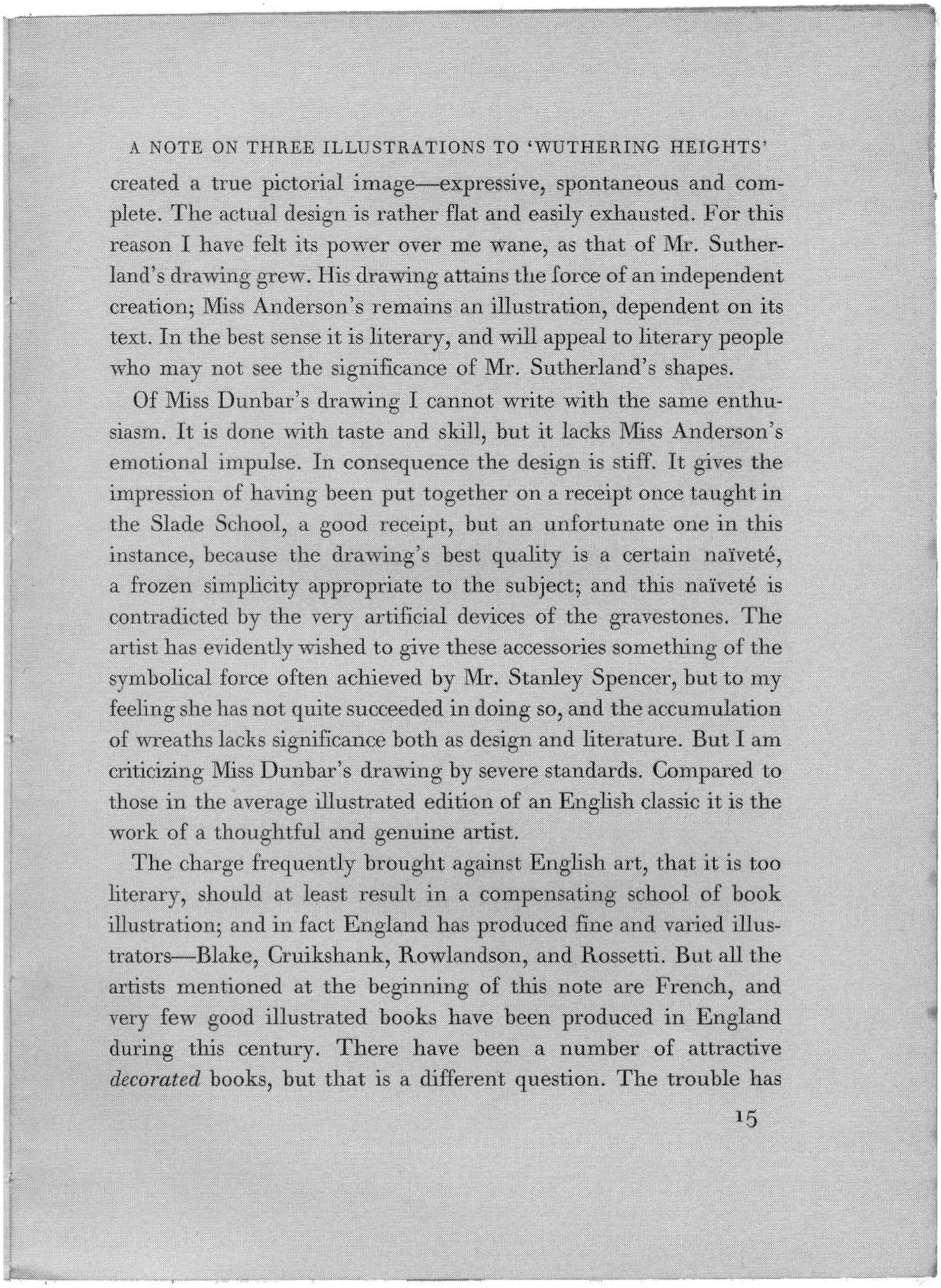

A NOTE ON THREE ILLUSTRATIONS TO 'WUTHERING HEIGHTS'

created a true pictorial image—expressive, spontaneous and complete. The actual design is rather flat and easily exhausted. For this reason I have felt its power over me wane, as that of Mr. Sutherland's drawing grew. His drawing attains the force of an independent creation; Miss Anderson's remains an illustration, dependent on its text. In the best sense it is literary, and will appeal to literary people who may not see the significance of Mr. Sutherland's shapes.

Of Miss Dunbar's drawing I cannot write with the same enthusiasm. It is done with taste and skill, but it lacks Miss Anderson's emotional impulse. In consequence the design is stiff. It gives the impression of having been put together on a receipt once taught in the Slade School, a good receipt, but an unfortunate one in this instance, because the drawing's best quality is a certain naïveté, a frozen simplicity appropriate to the subject; and this naïveté is contradicted by the very artificial devices of the gravestones. The artist has evidently wished to give these accessories something of the symbolical force often achieved by Mr. Stanley Spencer, but to my feeling she has not quite succeeded in doing so, and the accumulation of wreaths lacks significance both as design and literature. But I am criticizing Miss Dunbar's drawing by severe standards. Compared to those in the average illustrated edition of an English classic it is the work of a thoughtful and genuine artist.

The charge frequently brought against English art, that it is too literary, should at least result in a compensating school of book illustration; and in fact England has produced fine and varied illustrators—Blake, Cruikshank, Rowlandson, and Rossetti. But all the artists mentioned at the beginning of this note are French, and very few good illustrated books have been produced in England during this century. There have been a number of attractive *decorated* books, but that is a different question. The trouble has

15

Fig. 46 Monotype Walbaum used to splendid effect in Oliver Simon's quadrimestrial and quintessential *Signature*, no. 4 (November 1936) printed at The Curwen Press. Reduced from 247 mm deep.

commercial contexts than book publishing. And it is also interesting to note that it was employed in such work soon as it arrived in England, for at The Curwen Press 'Harold Curwen abolished class distinction between the printing of books and miscellaneous printing'.* Their typography, illustration and presswork were as excellent in their work for the Southern Railway, the Westminster Bank, Twinings – with drawings or engravings by Edward Bawden, Paul Nash and John Nash – as their limited editions.

Among the experts who did not look too favourably upon the type was Stanley Morison whose interest in producing a Monotype version (1933/59) was apparently more to do with the reputation it had acquired at The Curwen Press and its prospect of success in the German market than with his own tastes.[51] Non-lining figures and small capitals were added.

The German Linotype (1960) and Berthold (1975, 1979) both produced modified designs (with subdued Rs), the Bertholds done by the redoubtable G. G. Lange. The digital Monotype version, taken from the 10-Didot design, is faithful to the original model.

In the late 1780s George Nicol, bookseller to King George III, and John Boydell, a publisher of engravings who possessed a collection of paintings illustrating the works of Shakespeare, conceived and undertook to publish 'a magnificent national edition of Shakspeare',[52] and in March 1790 they engaged the printer William Bulmer who established the Shakspeare Printing-Office in Cleveland Row, St James's, and there set up an ink factory and a foundry. The types to be used were those which had been designed and cut under Nicol's supervision by the punch-cutter William Martin, younger brother of Robert Martin who was Baskerville's foreman and successor.[53] Nicol specified that the types take as models 'the sharp and fine letter used by the French and Italian printers'.[54] They were otherwise – and to a much greater extent – influenced by Baskerville's types.† The first number of the Shakespeare (*Richard III* and *Much Ado About Nothing*) was published in January 1791 to much acclaim.[55] The exuberant Dr Dibdin wrote: 'No work of equal magnitude (I speak of the typographical part) ever presented such complete accuracy and uniform excellence of execution. There is scarcely one perceptible shade of variation, from the first page of the 1st volume to the very last page of the work; either in the colour of the ink, the hue of the paper, or the clearness and sharpness of the types.'[56]

Here is some of William Bulmer's prolix Advertisement to his *Poems by Goldsmith and Parnell* (Shakspeare Printing-Office, 1795):

To raise the Art of Printing in this country from the neglected state in which it had long been suffered to continue, and to remove the opprobrium which had but too justly been attached to the late productions of the English press, much has been done within the last few years; and the warm emulation which has discovered itself amongst the Printers of the present day, as well in the remote parts of the kingdom as in the metropolis, has been highly patronized by the public in general. The present volume, in addition to the SHAKSPEARE, the MILTON, and many other valuable works of elegance, which have already been given to the world, through the

---

* Holbrook Jackson, *The Printing of Books* (Cassell, 1938), p. 243.
† Hansard thought them 'A decided imitation of Baskerville' (*Typographia* (Baldwin, Cradock & Joy, 1825), p. 360).

medium of the Shakspeare Press, are particularly meant to combine the various beauties of PRINTING, TYPE-FOUNDING, ENGRAVING, and PAPER-MAKING; as well with a view to ascertain the near approach to perfection which those arts have attained in this country, as to invite a fair competition with the best Typographical Productions of other nations. How far the different Artists, who have contributed their exertions to this great object, have succeeded in the attempt, the Public will now be fully able to judge. Much pains have been bestowed on the present publication, to render it a complete Specimen of the Arts of Type and Block-printing.

The whole of the Types, with which this work has been printed, are executed by Mr. William Martin, . . . a very ingenious young Artist, . . . who is at this time forming a Foundry, by which he will shortly be enabled to offer to the world a Specimen of Types, that will, in a very eminent degree, unite utility, elegance, and beauty.

The ornaments are all engraved on blocks of wood, by two of my earliest acquaintances, Messrs. Bewicks, of Newcastle upon Tyne and London, ... They have been executed with great care, . . . they form the most extraordinary effort of the art of engraving upon wood, that ever was produced in any age, or any country. Indeed it seems impossible that such delicate efforts could be obtained from blocks of wood.

Of the Paper it is only necessary to say, that it comes from the manufactory of Mr. Whatman.[57]

Prolixious but worth quoting. We can appreciate the considerable pride which this great printer rightly took in his work, his employees and associates. The excellence of Thomas Bewick's wood-engravings is matched by Bulmer's typography and presswork. Bulmer, who was a commercial printer, was none the less as fastidious in the matters of inking and paper as Baskerville and Bodoni had been. A facsimile of the Bulmer type, expertly made by M. F. Benton, was issued in 1928 by ATF; the Monotype version, cut specially for the Nonesuch Dickens in 1937 and later issued in 1967 in 8, 10, 11 and 12-point, is taken from the same model from which the ATF version was taken and there are scarcely any differences between them. The Bulmer type is heavier than Bell and Baskerville and has got a smaller x-height than the former; it has got nearly as many queer characters as Bell: the curly-tailed R, the scythe-tailed Q, the backwards-leaning g. The Monotype version was supplied with two sets of ranging figures – one of cap-height and the other of three-quarters height (like the figures of Bell). Non-lining figures were also supplied and five display sizes were added in 1969. The digitised Monotype Bulmer (1995) is supplied with the three kinds of figures and bold and display forms.

The art of printing in England which was raised by Bulmer and Bensley to such high standards would upon the shutting-up of Bulmer's shop fall into a neglected state again. As Francis Meynell put it: 'English printing lost its light in the early 19th century.'*

The printer became the servant of a competitive business-man, the bookseller-publisher. In France the Didots, publishers as well as printers, had been able to consult their own tastes; in Italy Bodoni had been subsidised. In England piece-work rates for fine work were three times those for ordinary; or perhaps the juster emphasis would be in the statement that careless printing could be had at one-third the price of careful.

The typefaces which followed Bulmer's were careless designs, much execrated by twentieth-century writers. Three types from the dismal epoch[58]

Fig. 47 A rook from p. 71 of Thomas Bewick's *A History of British Birds* (*Land Birds*), published at Newcastle in 1797. This example, scanned from a reproduction of a reproduction and reduced (from the original size of 63 × 85 mm), can scarcely convey the exquisite detail of the original. 'Wood-engraving received its first honours at the hands of Thomas Bewick late in the eighteenth century. Although it was known before Bewick's time it was little practised, and he enlivened it by the introduction of a fresh technique and a consummate mastery of the medium. . . . He was, perhaps, the first artist of note to become specifically a book illustrator.' (Seán Jennett, *The Making of Books*, p. 125.)

* *English Printed Books* (Collins, 1947), p. 26.

Fig. 48 Monotype Bulmer (with short ranging figures) from Mackays' 'unrivalled type specimen book', *Type for Books: A Designer's Manual* (advised by John Ryder and Hugh Williamson, printed and bound at the works of W & J Mackay Ltd at Lordswood, Chatham, on Basingwerk Parchment by Grosvenor Chater, and published by The Bodley Head in 1976). The type was used for the 25-volume Nonesuch Dickens (printed by R. & R. Clark) and it is described in the publisher's Prospectus to the edition (1937) as 'a vivid but wholly unaffected letter-design. . . . The utilities of this letter-design . . . are immediately obvious. Of conscious "beauty" it is happily free. Affectation, mannerisms, or even strongly marked character, in themselves sometimes desirable, would be wholly inappropriate in any long body of work, more especially in a Dickens. In Dickens the style is the man; the type must be neutral, lest it alter the accents of the man. Dickens lived in the Darkest Age of printing, and the improvement of these last few years in type-design and the modern technique of casting and impression have never yet been used to do him honour.' Reduced from 245 mm deep.

Abbreviations for metric and imperial measurements do not take a full point, e.g. m (metre), mm (millimetre), kg (kilogramme), km/h (kilometre per hour). Also use kW (kilowatt), kWh (kilowatt-hour), kV (kilovolt), kVA (kilovolt-ampere).

Degrees, decorations, etc, after names will be set in small capitals, with points, each decoration preceded by a comma.

The following abbreviations do not take s in the plural—lb, cm, cwt, dwt, gr, gm, in (inches), min (minutes), mm, oz, but tons, yds, qrs. In descriptive matter, per cent (no point) will be used; in tables %.

Where the Greek characters μ for micro, and Ω for ohm are required, the upright series 90 and not Porson, will be used.

Degrees of angle will be spelt out, but degrees of temperature will be printed, e.g. 57°C.

5. *Nautical Terms*

Oxford spelling will be followed, e.g. draught, mizen, trysail (not draft, mizzen, trisail): jib (n.) for the sail, gybe (v.) for the action. The following will be used: bermudan, genoa (without capitals).

In setting the names of ships, prefixes and possessives will be in roman, the name of the ship in italic; e.g. the *Aquitania*'s hull, H.M.S. *Victory*. S.S. will be used for steamship, s.s. for screw-steamer.

F. will be used for force when it is the force of the wind. A1 will be set with a 2-unit space between and without a full point.

Points of the compass will carry only one full point i.e. N. NE. NNE.

6. *Capital Letters*

Unnecessary capitalization will be avoided. Capitals will be used to begin nouns, verbs, and adjectives in the titles of books, etc, in headlines and in display set in upper and lower case or

[xiii]

have been produced continuously (from epoch to epoch) and are available currently from Adobe or Monotype: Old Style 2, Modern Extended 7, Scotch Roman 46.* The first of these (which was the second type cut for the Monotype machine: in 1901) is and always has been an irredeemably bad design (derived from Miller and Richard) and its survival appears to be owed to its having a great range of special sorts for foreign languages (therefore invaluable to textbook publishers); the second and third were taken from types originally cut by Richard Austin (who had made the Bell types) for Wilson's in Glasgow and William Miller & Co. in Edinburgh. Their designs were much influenced by the Didot and Bodoni types; they have got certain merits but more defects. Neither is very readable and they are seldom seen in modern books. The Modern 7 featured a range of over 600 mathematical sorts and so it survived; the Scotch Roman had certain peculiarities which lent it some charm† and so conveyed it into the present age, but it is of interest here only because it figures in the design of an excellent type called Linotype *Caledonia*.

Linotype Caledonia was designed by W. A. Dwiggins and issued in 1939. It was his second design for a text type, his first being the successful but cold, monotonic, Electra. W. A. Dwiggins, born at Martinsville, Ohio, in 1880, went to Chicago at the age of nineteen to study illustration at the Frank Holme School of Art and there made the acquaintance of the design and lettering tutor F. W. Goudy. In 1903 he opened a jobbing-printing office in Cambridge, Ohio, but business was poor. When Goudy removed his press from Chicago to Hingham, Massachusetts, in 1904, he invited Dwiggins and his wife to join him; they did and Dwiggins lived there until his death in 1956. Goudy found himself out of sympathy with Boston society and removed again to New York in 1906; Dwiggins stayed on and worked at Hingham and Boston for nearly twenty years as an advertising artist – illustrator and lettering artist – but he became disatisfied with advertising and so set hand to designing and illustrating books. In 1923 he had the good fortune of meeting Alfred Knopf and obtained work from him in 1928. He designed and illustrated nearly three hundred books for Knopf and established the Borzoi style. He designed eight books for the Limited Editions Club. Perhaps his most famous job was his design for a Random House edition of Wells's *The Time Machine* (1931) which featured stencilled vignettes, aptly described by Ruari McLean as 'highly idiosyncratic and unconventional'.

His illustrations and book design are mainly very competent exercises of the *art deco* sort of decoration which was fashionable in the 1930s but soon to be as dated as Victorian design. His ideas for a sans serif 'gothic' type – or rather his complaint that 'no good Gothic capitals' existed – which he expressed in his *Layout in Advertising* (Harpers, 1928) came to the notice of Harry L. Gage at Mergenthaler Linotype who invited him to design such a type. The Metro type (1929–30) of a Germanic 'geometric' Kabel/Erbar style was a success; Linotype offered him a contract and his association with

* A Linotype Scotch Roman, called Scotch 2 in England, was issued in 1902. A digital version of it is currently available from Linotype.

† Seán Jennett's appraisal that it 'pointed forward into the slough of the nineteenth century' (*The Making of Books*, p. 266) notwithstanding.

them (he designed twelve types for them) continued until his death. At Hingham he built a marionette theatre, made the puppets (which were perhaps creations of greater merit than his book designs), wrote and performed the plays. Or rather they were written by his Doppelgänger, Dr Hermann Püterschein. One is tempted to look for a theatrical element in his illustration if not in his type designs. He developed some interesting working methods in which calligraphy (or lettering) was combined with templates and stencils cut out of celluloid; he made his drawings at 12-point enlarged ten times (or at 1/156,000 inch = 10 inches).[59] A facsimile of his letter in hand-drawn roman and italic letters to Rudolph Ruzicka, explaining his working methods, was published as *WAD to RR : a letter about designing type* (Cambridge, Mass., Harvard College Library, 1940). Walter Tracy devotes a chapter of *Letters of Credit* to Dwiggins. He considers Electra to be 'one of the best text types designed in this century' (the last century), but he says very little about Caledonia.

I suppose I like Caledonia because of its oddities (as I like other types also for their oddities), perhaps such oddities as would be deemed unacceptable flaws by Walter Tracy and others, but I might be prejudiced because I only really took notice of the type recently in one of my favourite books, a collection of Geoffrey Grigson called *The Contrary View* (fig. 49), and then in another book which I enjoyed : R.A. Hewitt's *Style for Print*. The latter contains the type's own fractions which are very nice (I don't know whether or not designed by Dwiggins).

I have got a copy of the Linotype prospectus, a little hardbound book designed and written by Mr Dwiggins and Dr Püterschein.* I would scan it if it weren't so fragile. The designer's note begins:

The effort that matured into Caledonia started with a strong liking for the Scotch Modern face. That sound, workable type has served the printing craft for a hundred years. But there are a few features about it that are not quite happy.

It then describes the attempts to resolve or modify 'those features' and how they did not prove satisfactory. 'It appears that Scotch is Scotch, and doesn't stay Scotch if you sweat the fat off it. The results were pinched and mean and lacked both color and action.' (pp. viii–ix.) Further designs involved 'attempts to blend' Baskerville and Scotch Roman, Didot and Scotch Roman (or 'Scotch Modern' as Dwiggins calls it). But 'One was not trying for a revival, one wanted something modern and individual.' (p. x.) Finally a design combining elements or styles of Scotch Roman and Bulmer was developed. The type was 'christened . . . Caledonia because the project was inspired in the first instance by the work of Scotch typefounders.' (p. xii.)

The face as it emerges is not at all like Bulmer's Martin nor like Wilson's Scotch, but it has touches of both of them in spots. Also it has something of that simple, hard-working, feet-on-the-ground quality that has kept Scotch Modern in service for so many years.

At first I thought the setting of *The Contrary View* a rather poor job; the type seemed to want leading (it is 11-point on a 12-point body but with long

---

* *Caledonia : a new printing type designed for Mergenthaler Linotype* ('With a note on the face by the designer and a note on the designer by Hermann Püterschein'), Brooklyn, Mergenthaler Linotype, 1939.

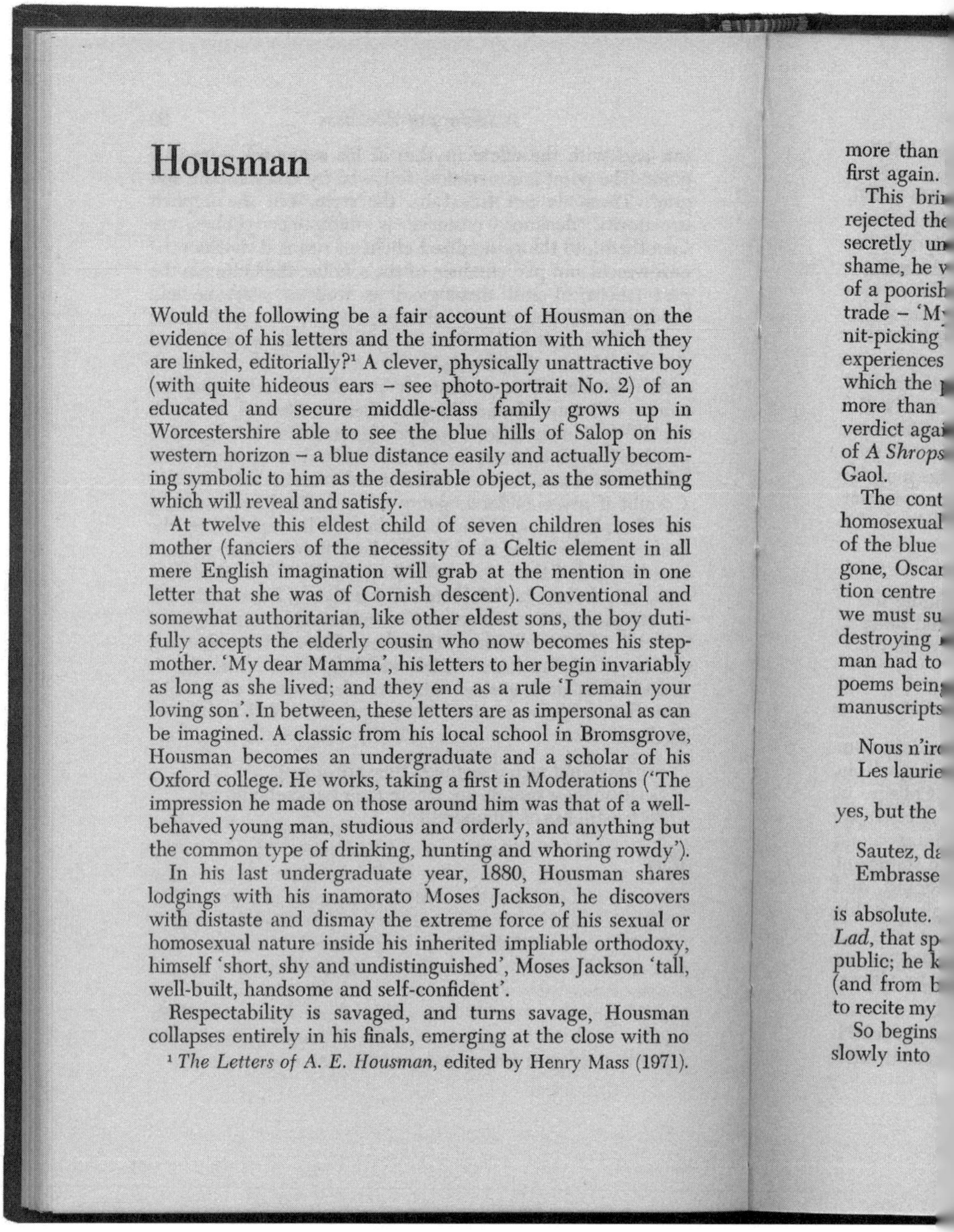

Housman

Would the following be a fair account of Housman on the evidence of his letters and the information with which they are linked, editorially?[1] A clever, physically unattractive boy (with quite hideous ears – see photo-portrait No. 2) of an educated and secure middle-class family grows up in Worcestershire able to see the blue hills of Salop on his western horizon – a blue distance easily and actually becoming symbolic to him as the desirable object, as the something which will reveal and satisfy.

At twelve this eldest child of seven children loses his mother (fanciers of the necessity of a Celtic element in all mere English imagination will grab at the mention in one letter that she was of Cornish descent). Conventional and somewhat authoritarian, like other eldest sons, the boy dutifully accepts the elderly cousin who now becomes his stepmother. 'My dear Mamma', his letters to her begin invariably as long as she lived; and they end as a rule 'I remain your loving son'. In between, these letters are as impersonal as can be imagined. A classic from his local school in Bromsgrove, Housman becomes an undergraduate and a scholar of his Oxford college. He works, taking a first in Moderations ('The impression he made on those around him was that of a well-behaved young man, studious and orderly, and anything but the common type of drinking, hunting and whoring rowdy').

In his last undergraduate year, 1880, Housman shares lodgings with his inamorato Moses Jackson, he discovers with distaste and dismay the extreme force of his sexual or homosexual nature inside his inherited impliable orthodoxy, himself 'short, shy and undistinguished', Moses Jackson 'tall, well-built, handsome and self-confident'.

Respectability is savaged, and turns savage, Housman collapses entirely in his finals, emerging at the close with no

[1] *The Letters of A. E. Housman*, edited by Henry Mass (1971).

more than
first again.
    This bri
rejected the
secretly un
shame, he v
of a poorish
trade – 'M
nit-picking
experiences
which the
more than
verdict aga
of *A Shrops*
Gaol.
    The cont
homosexual
of the blue
gone, Oscar
tion centre
we must su
destroying
man had to
poems bein
manuscripts

    Nous n'ir
    Les laurie

yes, but the

    Sautez, d
    Embrasse

is absolute.
Lad, that sp
public; he k
(and from b
to recite my
    So begins
slowly into

Fig. 49 Geoffrey Grigson's *The Contrary View* (Macmillan, 1974), set in Linotype Caledonia by Western Printing Services, Bristol. A less than perfect example. The long gs are used in this book but quite a few short gs pop up like little gremlins (note 'emerging' in the penultimate line). Reduced from 245 mm deep.

descenders almost touching subjacent ascenders; *Style for Print* is 11/13¾), the thick and thin contrast and close line-spacing had a slightly dazzling effect. Or rather a poorer job than I now think it is. I noticed also a good deal of bouncing of characters and then the two gs (one short and two long in 'slogging' on p. 131 of *The Contrary View*).* This was not so much to do with shortcomings of the type (but the bouncing is partly owed to design: the n is shorter than the a; the round characters appear larger) as with the particular job of composition (many misalignments). But all those odd things – the apostrophes and quote marks much too small, the blending of disparate forms, the deformed j, J, f (owing to the Linotype constraints) compressed or condensed so agonisingly and incongruously mixed in with grand Rs and Gs – give this type the character and comeliness which the Electra type so conspicuously lacks.†

Caledonia was not supplied with 'old-style' figures originally and I have not been able to determine when they were supplied. They're not shown in Western Printing Service's specimen book (1960) or *Book Types from Clowes* (1965) but they're found in the Mergenthaler Linotype specimen book of 1958. *Typefaces for Books* shows a sample of the digitised Caledonia – with very short descenders – supplied for the Linotron 202 and Linotronics. New Caledonia, the redrawing done by Matthew Carter and John Quaranta in 1979, follows the long descenders design of the original. The type's serviceability is demonstrated in Hewitt's *Style for Print*.

[2]

We now come to three types of Eric Gill – one of the great sacred monsters of England and certainly the greatest type-designer of the twentieth century. He fancied Fabianism, contrariwise causes (D.H.Lawrence, in a review of Gill's *Art-Nonsense, and Other Essays*, found him 'maddening, like a tiresome uneducated workman arguing in a pub – 'argefying' would describe it better – and banging his fist'[60]), Ananda Coomaraswamy ('The artist is not a special kind of man, but every man is a special kind of artist'[61]), Catholicism ('pre-Tridentine', pro-Dominican, anti-Jesuit). He didn't fancy trousers, he didn't fancy pants: he fashioned for himself a smock-frock or monk's

---

* 'When the American Linotype company adopted the principle of standard alignment about 1913 each size was given its own baseline position to which all their subsequent type faces conformed. Unfortunately, the taste of the time being what it was, the standard alignments were fixed too low for the kind of descenders which came to be desired by book designers in the 1920s and 30s, when types of the past were being studied, appreciated and revived. Linotype therefore found it necessary to produce alternative 'long' descender characters (which really means descenders of better proportion than the regular sort) in such classic types as Garamond and Janson, and also in Dwiggins's Electra and Caledonia. George W. Jones who was responsible for the English Linotype company's Granjon, Georgian and other distinguished revivals, would have nothing to do with the standard alignments, and insisted that the baseline in his types should be so placed as to ensure that the descenders were of satisfactory length.' (Walter Tracy, *Letters of Credit*, p. 49.)

† I believe that some of the success of this design is owed to turning the Linotype deficiencies or deformities into advantages; there is a charming quality to the f which doesn't attempt to hide its deformity.

habit which he wore habitually.* A fascinating picture of his froward character and his extraordinary sexual tastes is found in Fiona MacCarthy's biography (Faber, 1989). But quite more interesting is the way in which his passions and demons and his considerable learning and sensibility, and indeed his probity, came together in his work. One of the best pictures of him in this regard was given by David Kindersley, who as a young man of eighteen was apprenticed to Mr Gill at his stone-carving workshop at Pigotts at Hughenden near High Wycombe, in Buckinghamshire.† And here we also find a more likeable fellow than might be known by his own contrariwise version of himself.‡

Much of his artwork – his drawings or stone carvings of human figures – leaves me cold. His types are another matter. He considered himself, in any case, 'a letter-cutter and monumental mason', in that order. He attended the Central School of Arts and Crafts and was much influenced by the master calligrapher Edward Johnston, but he wasn't as keen on calligraphy as he was on 'lettering in stone'; he acquired a knowledge of Latin inscription and in his earliest inscriptional work you can see much of his Perpetua and his other types (the g and the R particularly).[62] '*Perpetua* is undoubtedly the finest classical alphabet evolved in this country between the eras of *Caslon* and *Baskerville* and our own time, with the possible exception of *Bell*.' (Robert Harling.)[63] It was the first original book type to be designed for Monotype, if you don't count Imprint as an original design. 'What was wanted was a design that, while being new, was of general utility and in no respect unusual.' (Stanley Morison.)[64] Gill was fond of fellow-Catholic Morison and so he was persuaded despite other commitments (to Robert Gibbings's Golden Cockerel Press for which he was designing another roman type), the ongoing stone-carving work and (from 1928) his involvement at the printing office he set up at Pigotts with his son-in-law, René Hague, and contrariwise attitudes as regards modern commercial industry (of which Monotype was an exponent). He affected to be unsure of himself. But he was pleased none the less: he wrote to Desmond Chute: 'I'm now a salaried official at the Lanston Monotype Corpn. What ho! This means advice in 'type faces'. Salary v. handsome too & I like typography don't you know.'[65] And to Stanley Morison: 'But you will remember that when I made you these drawings of alphabets I expressly disclaimed the suggestion that I was type designing. . . . However I am coming round by degrees to consider myself capable of designing a fount of type, so its [*sic*] all right & all the difficulties

R g R g R g

Eric Gill's *Gill Sans* (1927), *Perpetua* (1929), *Joanna* (1930; Monotype, 1957), shown at 30-pt.

---

* 'The garment he wore came down to his bare knees, below which were gartered stockings and ordinary black, laced shoes.' (Rayner Heppenstall, *Four Absentees* (Barrie & Rockliff, 1960), p. 55.)

'Towards the end of his life he received many honours. . . . but his A.R.A. might justifiably have been refused by him because he had on one occasion been denied entry to a Royal Academy dinner due to his attire, he was wearing his own kind of smart evening smock.' (David Kindersley, *Eric Gill: Further Thoughts by an Apprentice* (The Wynkyn de Worde Society, 1982), p. v.)

† 'Mr Gill made a great master and a perfect teacher. He never seemed to get angry or worried if we made any mistake or even worse broke a stone or two. He used to put great trust in us!' (Laurence Cribb in a letter to Robert Harling in Robert Harling's *The Letter Forms and Type Designs of Eric Gill* (Eva Svensson, 1978), p. 20.)

‡ 'Despite his oddities, Gill was very popular. Burch, as well as Morison and Beatrice, enjoyed his company, and so did everyone else at the Monotype organization.' (Nicolas Barker, *Stanley Morison*, p. 236.)

can be got over.'[66] Morison, just three years at his job and still a long way from attaining his clout, anticipated resistance at Monotype (in the form of Frank Pierpont, imperious works manager supported by diplomatic managing director William Burch) and so at his own expense he arranged for the punch-cutter Charles Malin in Paris to cut a set of 12-Didot romans, caps and lower-case, and a set of accompanying titling capitals. Morison was successful but there followed many complications, twists and turns and the job took seven years to complete.[67] Upon seeing the type cast from Malin's punches Gill suggested a number of changes:

> I think a very nice fount can be made from these letters, but I agree with you in thinking that several details must be altered before it can be passed, and certainly before I should like to see my name attached to it. Not that I think it is unworthy of me, but simply that it makes me shy at present.
>
> (i) The y must be altered – the blob removed . . .
> (ii) The tail of the "g" is rather heavy. You see it all over the page . . .
> (iii) I think the bow of the lower case "r" is too heavy.
> (iv) I agree the space between the letters is too great.
> (v) I agree that the capitals are too short . . .
>
> Apart from these details which, if corrected, would I think make the page effect very much better, I agree in thinking that a nice useful type can be made. Will it be for sale to all and sundry?[68]

Morison was concerned to 'preserve absolutely the chiselled quality'[69] of Gill's letters and so the patterns produced at the Monotype drawing office were taken from the matrices and types made from Malin's punches rather than photographic enlargements. In August 1928, 'The first specimen was a private print of the English translation, made for the Purpose by Walter Shewring, of *The Passion of Perpetua and Felicity* who were martyred at Carthage in the year 203.'[70]

The original accompanying italic, or rather 'sloped roman', was called *Felicity*. Morison was keen to apply his idea of 'sloped romans' (as he had set out in an article, 'Towards an Ideal Italic', in *The Fleuron*, vol. 5, 1926) which he deemed more agreeable for use with roman letters (for book titles, emphasis, etc.) than the common chancery style which originally hadn't been an auxiliary to roman but used independently, and Gill who was more romanly inclined than italically inclined was amenable to this idea. It did not win the management's approval, however, and a more italic sort of sloped roman was designed. The Perpetua and Felicity (as it was still named) were finally issued in 1932.* Comparing it to the Monotype revivals, Robert Harling wrote:

> Apart from its other considerable merits, *Perpetua* was distinguished from these types by its originality, which had nothing in common with the self-conscious, self-indulgent oddities of other contemporary would-be classic faces such as *Pastonchi* or some of Frederic Goudy's types. *Perpetua* is clearly a disciplined design that derives from Gill's earlier experience and experiments.[71]

Pastonchi (designed by Eduardo Cotti of Turin for the poet Francesco

---

* First used commercially in Gill's *Art-Nonsense*, published by Cassell in December 1929. The italic was not yet completed and so 'the author's emphasis is expressed by underlining, a desperate (and unique) device which is at least preferable to the German habit of spacing lower-case letters' (Stanley Morison, *A Tally of Types*, pp. 101–2). A 13-pt fount of the original Felicity went to Hazell Watson & Viney in January 1931.

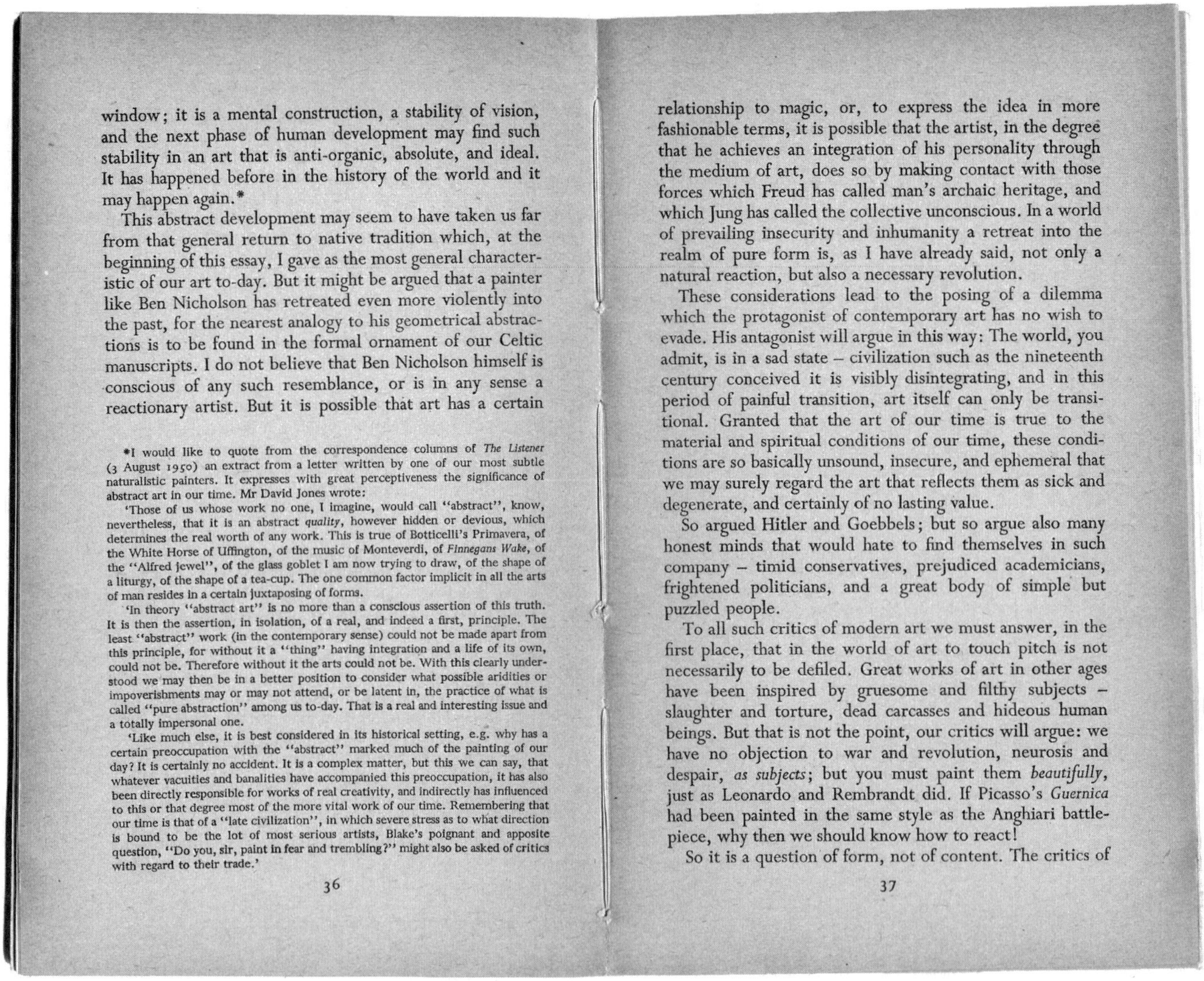

window; it is a mental construction, a stability of vision, and the next phase of human development may find such stability in an art that is anti-organic, absolute, and ideal. It has happened before in the history of the world and it may happen again.*

This abstract development may seem to have taken us far from that general return to native tradition which, at the beginning of this essay, I gave as the most general characteristic of our art to-day. But it might be argued that a painter like Ben Nicholson has retreated even more violently into the past, for the nearest analogy to his geometrical abstractions is to be found in the formal ornament of our Celtic manuscripts. I do not believe that Ben Nicholson himself is conscious of any such resemblance, or is in any sense a reactionary artist. But it is possible that art has a certain

*I would like to quote from the correspondence columns of *The Listener* (3 August 1950) an extract from a letter written by one of our most subtle naturalistic painters. It expresses with great perceptiveness the significance of abstract art in our time. Mr David Jones wrote:

'Those of us whose work no one, I imagine, would call "abstract", know, nevertheless, that it is an abstract *quality*, however hidden or devious, which determines the real worth of any work. This is true of Botticelli's Primavera, of the White Horse of Uffington, of the music of Monteverdi, of *Finnegans Wake*, of the "Alfred Jewel", of the glass goblet I am now trying to draw, of the shape of a liturgy, of the shape of a tea-cup. The one common factor implicit in all the arts of man resides in a certain juxtaposing of forms.

'In theory "abstract art" is no more than a conscious assertion of this truth. It is then the assertion, in isolation, of a real, and indeed a first, principle. The least "abstract" work (in the contemporary sense) could not be made apart from this principle, for without it a "thing" having integration and a life of its own, could not be. Therefore without it the arts could not be. With this clearly understood we may then be in a better position to consider what possible aridities or impoverishments may or may not attend, or be latent in, the practice of what is called "pure abstraction" among us to-day. That is a real and interesting issue and a totally impersonal one.

'Like much else, it is best considered in its historical setting, e.g. why has a certain preoccupation with the "abstract" marked much of the painting of our day? It is certainly no accident. It is a complex matter, but this we can say, that whatever vacuities and banalities have accompanied this preoccupation, it has also been directly responsible for works of real creativity, and indirectly has influenced to this or that degree most of the more vital work of our time. Remembering that our time is that of a "late civilization", in which severe stress as to what direction is bound to be the lot of most serious artists, Blake's poignant and apposite question, "Do you, sir, paint in fear and trembling?" might also be asked of critics with regard to their trade.'

36

relationship to magic, or, to express the idea in more fashionable terms, it is possible that the artist, in the degree that he achieves an integration of his personality through the medium of art, does so by making contact with those forces which Freud has called man's archaic heritage, and which Jung has called the collective unconscious. In a world of prevailing insecurity and inhumanity a retreat into the realm of pure form is, as I have already said, not only a natural reaction, but also a necessary revolution.

These considerations lead to the posing of a dilemma which the protagonist of contemporary art has no wish to evade. His antagonist will argue in this way: The world, you admit, is in a sad state – civilization such as the nineteenth century conceived it is visibly disintegrating, and in this period of painful transition, art itself can only be transitional. Granted that the art of our time is true to the material and spiritual conditions of our time, these conditions are so basically unsound, insecure, and ephemeral that we may surely regard the art that reflects them as sick and degenerate, and certainly of no lasting value.

So argued Hitler and Goebbels; but so argue also many honest minds that would hate to find themselves in such company – timid conservatives, prejudiced academicians, frightened politicians, and a great body of simple but puzzled people.

To all such critics of modern art we must answer, in the first place, that in the world of art to touch pitch is not necessarily to be defiled. Great works of art in other ages have been inspired by gruesome and filthy subjects – slaughter and torture, dead carcasses and hideous human beings. But that is not the point, our critics will argue: we have no objection to war and revolution, neurosis and despair, *as subjects*; but you must paint them *beautifully*, just as Leonardo and Rembrandt did. If Picasso's *Guernica* had been painted in the same style as the Anghiari battlepiece, why then we should know how to react!

So it is a question of form, not of content. The critics of

37

Fig. 50 Herbert Read's *Contemporary British Art* (Penguin, 1951), set in 9-pt Perpetua by Hunt, Barnard & Co.

Fig. 51 (opposite) *At Swim-Two-Birds* by Flann O'Brien (Penguin, 1968), set in Monotype Joanna by Cox & Wyman. The length of descenders is not compromised at

smaller sizes in this type. A lot of ink-squash but for word-spacing and other finer points one of the best jobs for a Penguin I've ever seen. Compare this to the larger Joanna in fig. 20 (J. Bronowski, *The Ascent of Man*).

Both reduced from 180 mm deep.

bottles, fondling and opening them and pouring dusky libations into medhers of old thick pewter.

Don't be all day, said the Good Fairy from the mantelpiece.

By the way, said the Pooka carelessly, could I see you alone for a moment?

Me? said Orlick. Certainly.

Excellent, said the Pooka. Let us go out into the passage for a moment.

He linked an arm in polite friendship and walked towards the door, endeavouring to match his club-step to the footstep.

Don't be too long now, said Casey, the drink is cooling.

The door closed. And for a long time the limping beat of the Pooka's club could be heard, and the low hum of his fine talk as they paced the passage, the Pooka and his Orlick. Conclusion of the foregoing.

Biographical reminiscence, part the eighth: While I was engaged in the spare-time literary activities of which the preceding and following pages may be cited as more or less typical examples, I was leading a life of a dull but not uncomfortable character. The following approximate schedule of my quotidian activities may be of some interest to the lay reader.

Nature of daily regime or curriculum: Nine thirty a.m. rise, wash, shave and proceed to breakfast; this on the insistence of my uncle, who was accustomed to regard himself as the sun of his household, recalling all things to wakefulness on his own rising.

10.30. Return to bedroom.

12.00. Go, weather permitting, to College, there conducting light conversation on diverse topics with friends, or with acquaintances of a casual character.

2.00 p.m. Go home for lunch.

3.00. Return to bedroom. Engage in spare-time literary activity, or read.

6.00. Have tea in company with my uncle, attending in a perfunctory manner to the replies required by his talk.

7.00. Return to bedroom and rest in darkness.

8.00. Continue resting or meet acquaintances in open thoroughfares or places of public resort.

148

11.00. Return to bedroom.

Minutiae: No. of cigarettes smoked, average 8·3; glasses of stout or other comparable intoxicant, av. 1·2; times to stool, av. 2·65; hours of study, av. 1·4; spare-time or recreative pursuits, 6·63 circulating.

Comparable description of how a day may be spent, being an extract from 'A Conspectus of the Arts and Natural Sciences,' from the hand of Mr Cowper. Serial volume the seventeenth: I am obliged to you for the interest you take in my welfare, and for your inquiring so particularly after the manner in which time passes here. As to amusements, I mean what the world call such, we have none; but the place swarms with them, and cards and dancing are the professed business of almost all the gentle inhabitants of Huntingdon. We refuse to take part in them; or to be accessories to this way of murthering our time, and by so doing have acquired the name of Methodists. Having told you how we do not spend our time, I will next say how we do. We breakfast commonly between eight and nine; till eleven, we read either the Scripture, or the Sermons of some faithful preacher of these holy mysteries; at eleven, we attend Divine Service, which is performed here twice every day, and from twelve to three we separate, and amuse ourselves as we please. During that interval I either read in my own apartment, or walk, or ride, or work in the garden. We seldom sit an hour after dinner, but if the weather permits, adjourn to the garden, where with Mrs Unwin, and her son, I have generally the pleasure of religious conversation till tea time. If it rains, or is too windy for walking, we either converse within doors, or sing some hymns of Martin's collection, and by the help of Mrs Unwin's harpsichord make up a tolerable concert, in which our hearts, I hope, are the best and the most musical performers. After tea, we sally forth to walk in good earnest. Mrs Unwin is a good walker, and we have generally travelled about four miles before we see home again. When the days are short, we make this excursion in the former part of the day, between church-time and dinner. At night, we read and converse as before, till supper, and commonly finish the evening with either hymns, or a sermon, and last of all the family are called to prayers. Conclusion of the foregoing.

Comparable further description of how a day may be spent, being a day from the

149

Pastonchi for use in an edition of the Italian classics, and produced by Monotype in 1926 in the quest for a programme of new faces which included Perpetua) was quite the ugliest type Monotype ever produced, worse even than those self-indulgent Goudy types. What is particularly interesting is how dated those types look and how Perpetua doesn't show its age. Yet Perpetua is scarcely seen nowadays.[72] I have a volume of Frances Partridge's diaries (*Life Regained*, Weidenfeld & Nicolson, 1998) in which it is used (but with too much leading) and Penguin used it for a while (until around 1960) but I suspect that at such small sizes they found it unsatisfactory. It is not awfully readable at small sizes and this was recognised by Stanley Morison.*

The capital R in sizes below 30-point (or below 24-point in Stephenson

---

* *A Tally of Types*, pp. 103–4.

Rg Rg

The original 30-pt design and the currently available digital Perpetua

1234567890

1234567890

Perpetua and Joanna figures

Blake Perpetua) was quite a different R (the design of the smaller R, shown left, was used originally, with adjustments, for 8 to 24 point); the digitised version appears to derive from the original 10-point letters. The original alternative characters – italic gy, a long-tailed Qu, straight-tailed y, non-descending J, and footless U – are not available for the digital version at present.[73]

Gill's figures are particularly fine – he'd got a lot of practice in as an in-scriber of memorials and head-stones. I think his *Joanna* type was a better job than Perpetua. It was designed for use at the Hague & Gill printing office and was cut by H.W.Caslon & Co. Ltd in September 1930 and used notably in Gill's *Essay on Typography*, the fourth piece of printing done at Pigotts (published by Sheed & Ward in June 1931; reprinted with revisions 1936). The *Essay* was set in the Hague & Gill house style in 12-point unjustified (left-ranged), leaded 4 points, with captions set solid; ampersands and abbreviations were used to adjust line-lengths etc., and many words were shortened by setting their final letters in 8-point raised to align with the 12-point caps; opening quotes were dropped to the mean-line. The foundry Joanna had got large capitals lining with the lower-case ascending letters which were used in the *Essay* as initials where new paragraphs were indicated with paragraph marks (also lining with the large caps) rather than indentions; the normal caps were slightly shorter.

The type, named after Gill's youngest daughter Joan (married to René Hague in 1930), was as unusual as the Pigotts settings: it had got slab-serifs but nothing otherwise in common with Clarendons or Egyptians, very little thick and thin contrast, large but only somewhat narrow letters. 'Gill taught his pupils, especially latterly, to reduce the emphasis between thick and thin to a minimum. What Gill learned in the disciplines of chisel and stone he was apt to impart to alphabetical experiments in other media.' (Robert Harling.)[74] The italic is in Robert Harling's view 'without a doubt, Gill's most successful version of the sloped roman.... No other alphabet of this century has managed to make typographical affectation so readable.... He had obviously marked, learned and digested Stanley Morison's notes concerning the requirements for a "sloped roman" rather than the more pronounced slope of the conventional italic form.'[75] The slope is only three degrees but the letters are of a very different, much more narrow design than the romans. The caps and figures are hardly different to the roman and were only added later.

The printing office at Pigotts did not fare well (and reference is made in David Kindersley's memoir to the resentment among the stone masons in the workshop at the opposite end of the Pigotts farm who felt that Mr Gill was squandering money on the Press 'whilst we had little to comfort us materially'[76]). In 1936 J.M.Dent & Sons acquired a part-interest and removed the printing office to High Wycombe; in 1937 they obtained the rights to the type and commissioned Monotype to cut an 11-pt version for machine composition. The Dent settings were conventionally justified and indented. The Joanna type was issued to the public in 1958. It is now available in pleasing digital versions of semi-bold, bold and extra-bold for both romans and italics, as well as a version of the original which is rather thin, even as Monotype themselves acknowledged when it was issued in 1990:

It is doubtful if Gill would have been quite so enthusiastic about its mechanical

G

Galitzianer

Pronounced *goll-itz-ee-*ON-*er*, to rhyme with 'doll itsy on her.'

A Jew from Galicia, a province of Poland/Austria. (When Poland was partitioned in 1772, Austria grabbed Galicia.)

Galicia, heavily populated by Jews (in the early twentieth century, they comprised over ten per cent of the population) was a seat of Talmudic learning; it had several important *yeshivas* which produced prominent rabbis and scholars. The Jewish population of Galicia benefited from Emperor Joseph II's decree of 1780, making education compulsory for his subjects.

The *Galitzianer* and the *Litvak* were often at odds, each claiming superiority over, and looking with a certain disdain upon, the other. The respective chauvinists viewed a marriage between a *Litvak* and a *Galitzianer* as almost exogamous, and wedding guests were fond of predicting that no good could come of such a strange misalliance.

My parents spoke with a certain prissiness about both *Galitzianers* and *Litvaks*. We were *Poylish* (Polish) – and were no doubt regarded, in turn, as *infra dig* by such *Galitzianers* and *Litvaks* as put on airs.

And Russian Jews, especially of the *intelligentsia*, looked down with cool impartiality upon all the rest. Among *Galitzianers*, a *Deutsch* or German Jew, was regarded as modernized, probably unreligious, and certainly one who wore no beard, *payess*, hat. As for German Jews – ! A self-appointed elite, they clearly disliked, snubbed or despised non-German *Jehudim*; and they were (if one must generalize) heartily disliked – and envied

galut [125]

– by the poorer, less assimilated, much more religious kin to their east.

The *familiengefiel* (family feeling) of a common heritage, shared values, common problems, common threats, misfortunes and persecutions, was nevertheless exceedingly strong among European Jewry.

In the United States, the social-prestige scale was sensitive and exact: first-generation Jews envied second-generation Jews; and German Jewish families – Kuhns, Warburgs, Seligmans, Kahns, Schiffs, Lehmanns, Loebs, Ochses – became an elite of remarkable influence and social cohesiveness. The 'pecking order' of this Establishment, its pride, philanthropy, snobbery, and Pecksniffian patronage of Russian and Polish Jews – all this is described by Stephen Birmingham in *Our Crowd: The Great Jewish Families of New York*.* San Francisco's Jews became a distinguished, conspicuously civic-minded group of descendants of settlers dating back to the Gold Rush.†

See LITVAK.

galut
galus

Pronounced GOLL-*us*, to rhyme with 'call us.' Hebrew: 'exile.'

1. Exile; the Diaspora; the dispersion of the Jews among the lands outside of Israel.

* Harper & Row, 1967.

† For an illuminating inquiry into the identification patterns, social hierarchy, practices, values and conflicts within the conglomerate Jewish communities in America, see Nathan Glazer's excellent *American Judaism* in the Chicago History of American Civilization series, Daniel Boorstin, editor. University of Chicago Press, 1957; also Moses Rischin's *The Promised Land: New York's Jews 1870-1914*. Corinth Books, 1964; also, the articles by Nathan Glazer, Simon Kuznets, and Jacob Lestschinsky in *The Jews: Their History, Culture and Religion*, Vol. II, third edition, Louis Finkelstein, editor. Harper, 1960; and *The Jews; Social Patterns of an American Group*, Marshall Sklare, editor. The Free Press, 1960.

Fig. 52 Leo Rosten's *The Joys of Yiddish* (Penguin, 1970), set and printed by Cox & Wyman in Linotype Pilgrim with shoulder-heads in Monotype Bell, initials in Monotype Castellar (designed by John Peters; issued in 1957). Note the folio in brackets. In the *Penrose Annual* in 1953, Robert Harling remarked that 'in *Pilgrim* we have all the recognisable and admirable Gill qualities. His touch is in every curve and line. Here is yet another example of his felicitous essays in the unending quest for the perfect alphabet. The ceaseless and never monotonous preoccupation with the curve of the tail to the upper-case "R", the distribution of solid and void in the lower-case "a" and "g", and so on.'

virtues if he could see filmset Joanna printed by offset, yet even in this skinny form it remains a notably attractive and distinguished face.[77]

An example of it printed on coated paper is shown in fig. 20 (*The Ascent of Man*); fig. 52 shows a rare use of Joanna in a Penguin and with much ink squash; among the best examples is the setting in Robert Harling's *The Letter Forms and Type Designs of Eric Gill* (Eva Svensson, 1978).

In 1936 Hague & Gill printed an edition of Sterne's *A Sentimental Journey* for the Limited Editions Club (New York) in a new type which Gill called Bunyan. There was no italic and so Perpetua italic was used. Robert Harling says that the type 'may be considered as a careful balance between the *Golden Cockerel* type and *Joanna*'; it also bears much resemblance to Perpetua. Gill was not as interested in developing new types as refining certain forms which he derived from Latin inscription on the one hand and Edward Johnston's calligraphy on the other. As Harling observed: 'His pleasure lay in refining, not in reshaping the classical alphabet, in varying the distribution of weight, the curve of serif, the careful balance of ascender and descender.' In 1950 Gill's widow sold the rights to the design to Linotype who issued the type in 8 to 14 point as *Pilgrim* in 1953. An italic was based upon some trial drawings which Gill made for a sloped roman. An accompanying display type (18 to 36 point in roman, italic and bold) was designed by Reynolds Stone and issued in 1955 as Minerva.

The type was very successful in England and particularly favoured for paperbacks. There are many fine examples of it in Penguins and Fontanas; it was used notably in the 1960s for the Cape Editions which were designed by Germano Facetti and printed by Clays. The lower-case b is flat at the bottom; the a has a flat seriffed foot.* A digital version for the Linotronic 300 was produced by the German Linotype office in Frankfurt, but the technology did not allow for special characters and so the double-f ligatures were forsaken; non-lining figures and small capitals were also omitted.

James Sutton and Alan Bartram in *An Atlas of Typeforms* say of Joanna: 'Like Perpetua, it still retains too much stone-carved form for it to be really satisfactory as a type, which has a special need of rhythm and smoothness over long passages of text.' Pilgrim, they say, 'is perhaps Gill's most satisfactory text type'.[78]

I don't agree with Messrs Sutton's and Bartram's judgment of Perpetua and Joanna: Gill's types are quite satisfactory and pass the test of fitness for purpose if the composition and printing are carried out with some care (appropriate size, measure, paper, inking, etc.). I believe the examples I've referred to are proof of that. There is considerable difference however between Gill's types and those of Jan van Krimpen. Self-effacing does not mean refined or beautiful, nor does it mean undistinguished or lacklustre; fitness for purpose does not mean all-purpose (such types do not exist, much as some people

* Such as he had originally drawn for Perpetua but changed upon seeing Malin's proofs. 'It was Gill, writing to Morison on September 1, 1928, who suggested that the lower case "a" with its serifed foot – a shape derived from his own stonecut letter – had a "clumsy heaviness" as it stood. It would be better, he thought (illustrating his ideas with a sketch) if a curved stroke were substituted. It was one of several occasions on which he was to learn the limitations placed on the designer by reduction in scale.' (James Mosely, 'Eric Gill's Perpetua Type', *Fine Print*, vol. 8, no. 3 (July 1982), p. 94.)

may try to prove otherwise). Three of the text types Van Krimpen designed during his thirty-five years at Joh. Enschedé en Zonen were adopted by Monotype for machine composition: *Lutetia, Romulus, Spectrum*. The first of these was designed for Enschedé in 1924 and recut by Monotype in 1930. It featured all the peculiar forms which Van Krimpen was to use but with slight variation in his other type designs: wide pen-drawn letters (a Jensonian sloped e-bar for Lutetia but not the other types), light in colour (thick strokes being very thin), fine serifs, a razor sharpness which can have only been accomplished by an expert punch-cutter such as P. H. Rädisch (who cut all of Van Krimpen's types, their best collaborations being the titling versions Lutetia Open and Romulus Open). Monotype's promotional literature acknowledges the shortcomings of these first two types.* Of the first they say: 'Lutetia is the least versatile of the original designs of Van Krimpen available on "Monotype" machines. Its consciously decorative qualities limit its use, and it is perhaps most suitable for such work as ceremonial printing, poetry, limited editions and books with restricted continuous reading.' It has too much the mark of the perfectionist. Sem Hartz, Van Krimpen's colleague and successor at Enschedé, believed 'the first cutting of Lutetia after van Krimpen's drawings, but without his personal supervision during the making of the punches, is more successful than the later version.'

The punchcutter, in his unhampered rendering of the designer's drawings, seems to have interpreted rather than followed them, producing a happy looking typeface. The designer, however, insisted on a recutting of the type and although it certainly is flawless in its final form it has a slightly stilted look which is absent from the first version.[79]

Of the sloped roman of Romulus (Monotype, 1936) Monotype wrote: 'in spite of the undoubted success of the sloped roman as an independent face, as a partner to the roman it lacks the distinctive quality necessary to draw attention to the single italicised word.'[80] The sloped roman was an application of Morison's theory ('a sloped roman type, sufficiently inclined to be differentiated from the primary type, yet following its design as closely as possible'[81]). A. F. Johnson, reviewing Romulus in *Signature* no. 13 (1940), wrote: 'This may be logical, but results in a stiff and monotonous letter', and Van Krimpen himself regarded the sloped roman as a failure. A script type, called Cancelleresca Bastarda, with many swash characters, was later designed but it did not render the type more suitable for bookwork. It was other things, however – the defects which Walter Tracy identified (oddly formed letters, incongruity of characters, characters too wide among characters too narrow) – which impaired the types. None the less, Van Krimpen's types were well received at Enschedé (the design for Lutetia won him his job there) and at Monotype,† and the designer was always held in highest esteem. Spectrum is his only serviceable text type and, as Walter Tracy has carefully argued, it suffers also from defects which 'diminished its chance of

---

* Published after Stanley Morison's death but while his successor John Dreyfus, Van Krimpen's great champion, was still at Monotype.

† 'Nevertheless, the Lutetia is so handsomely proportioned and finely fashioned, possesses so happily that combination of originality and familiarity necessary to reading (lacking in the ninety-and-nine other original types at hand) that it may be fairly described as the best independent type design made for a score of years.' (Morison in the catalogue for the Enschedé exhibition held in London in 1929, quoted in Moran, pp. 141–2.)

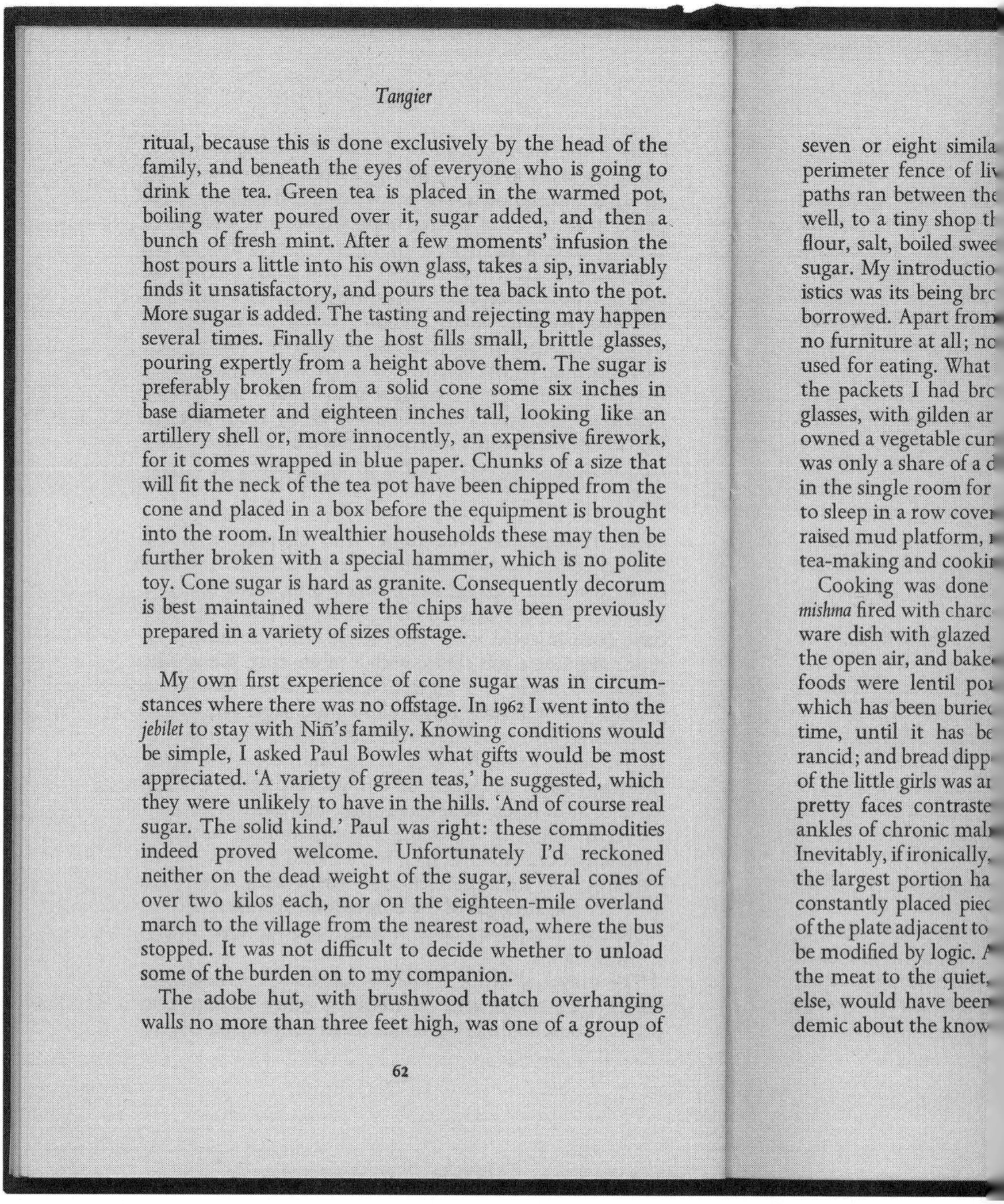

Tangier

ritual, because this is done exclusively by the head of the family, and beneath the eyes of everyone who is going to drink the tea. Green tea is placed in the warmed pot, boiling water poured over it, sugar added, and then a bunch of fresh mint. After a few moments' infusion the host pours a little into his own glass, takes a sip, invariably finds it unsatisfactory, and pours the tea back into the pot. More sugar is added. The tasting and rejecting may happen several times. Finally the host fills small, brittle glasses, pouring expertly from a height above them. The sugar is preferably broken from a solid cone some six inches in base diameter and eighteen inches tall, looking like an artillery shell or, more innocently, an expensive firework, for it comes wrapped in blue paper. Chunks of a size that will fit the neck of the tea pot have been chipped from the cone and placed in a box before the equipment is brought into the room. In wealthier households these may then be further broken with a special hammer, which is no polite toy. Cone sugar is hard as granite. Consequently decorum is best maintained where the chips have been previously prepared in a variety of sizes offstage.

My own first experience of cone sugar was in circumstances where there was no offstage. In 1962 I went into the *jebilet* to stay with Niñ's family. Knowing conditions would be simple, I asked Paul Bowles what gifts would be most appreciated. 'A variety of green teas,' he suggested, which they were unlikely to have in the hills. 'And of course real sugar. The solid kind.' Paul was right: these commodities indeed proved welcome. Unfortunately I'd reckoned neither on the dead weight of the sugar, several cones of over two kilos each, nor on the eighteen-mile overland march to the village from the nearest road, where the bus stopped. It was not difficult to decide whether to unload some of the burden on to my companion.

The adobe hut, with brushwood thatch overhanging walls no more than three feet high, was one of a group of

62

Fig. 53 Angus Stewart's *Tangier: A Writer's Notebook* (Hutchinson, 1977), set in Monotype Spectrum and printed by The Anchor Press Ltd, Tiptree, Essex. A particularly successful setting owing to judicious inking and choice of paper. Note the minuscular 1962 in the second line of the second paragraph. Reduced from 215 mm.

unqualified welcome into the printer's typographic resources'.[82] It is only just serviceable. The worst of its faults are the non-ranging figures which 'are hard to take – cramped and diminished, looking as though they belong to a type two sizes smaller' (Tracy). It was originally intended for a small folio bible to be produced for the Spectrum Publishing Company of Utrecht but the plans to publish such a bible were abandoned. It is a variation of the theme of Lutetia and all his other types, though featuring a greater x-height and a darker colour (both great improvements). The chancery italic is quite narrow but the letterfit for both roman and italic is very good. It is not only its curiously small numerals but other sad and strange errors mostly arising from its over-refinement by which it fails the test of fitness for purpose as a book type.

Walter Tracy said that 'Van Krimpen thought like an artist, not like a designer. He worked from an inner vision, not from a broad view of practical realities and requirements.' He did not want to make concessions.

On the evidence of the types themselves it seems reasonable to suppose that, in spite of his presence in a great printing house, his considerable knowledge of historical type faces, and his experience as a book designer, Van Krimpen was not ruled by the designer's sense of 'fitness for purpose' when he was designing a type.[83]

Sem Hartz said that 'the steadfast character of van Krimpen, coupled with his focalized talent, made it impossible for him to accept with wise resignation things he despised. He would always retaliate if he had the feeling that book typography was harmed in any way. For he was – and this is often forgotten by those who opposed him – a specialist with all the inhibitions of specialization.'

Sem Hartz designed a semi-bold for Spectrum in 1972. Digital versions of the type are produced by Monotype.

Giovanni Mardersteig's *Dante* is also an original design (as Gill's and Van Krimpen's were) but considerably more informed by a particular influence: the letters of Francesco Griffo. It was his third Aldine type, his first being the Griffo (1929) and Zeno (1935–6) types, and it was also cut (between 1947 and 1954) by the Parisian punch-cutter Charles Malin. Writing about his Zeno type which was 'inspired by the noble handwritten roman letter of Lodovico degli Arrighi', Dr Mardersteig said: 'a type must renounce all personal character and be inconspicuously at the disposal of the public'. The success of his designs owes much to that belief but in each of his types, as in any type which is not designed by committee, the designer's persona is readily cognisable. The shape of Mardersteig's capital C is more Giovanni than Francesco and it is quite as distinct as Eric Gill's R. Unlike his Griffo, Mardersteig's Dante derives more loosely from Francesco Griffo's type.

The Dante type was first used in 10 and 12 Didot to print Boccaccio's *Trattatello in laude di Dante* at the Officina Bodoni, Verona, in 1955. Mardersteig credited its success to Charles Malin: 'Despite the many corrections I made after the first cutting, he always patiently helped me to achieve the balance and harmony I was looking for and he showed keen pleasure in the many improvements brought about by minor changes.'[84] 49 of the 198 editions printed on the handpress at the Officina Bodoni were set in Dante.

Mardersteig, who had been pleased with Monotype's production of his

Fontana type, agreed to Stanley Morison's suggestion to produce a version of Dante for machine composition (according to John Dreyfus, 'about a year before the handcut version was first seen by the public in 1955'[85]).* He was, however, not very interested in adding a semi-bold version – or, more exactly, in taking part in the project: Malin had died in 1956 and Mardersteig said: 'When the inventive powers of Malin came to an end, so did my pleasure in type designing.'[86] In his short history of the type† John Dreyfus tells how the designer was none the less persuaded to assist the Monotype staff and the young punch-cutter (just 23 years old), Matthew Carter, and how he (Mardersteig) participated, suggesting 'comparatively minor' changes:

Comparatively minor they may have been, but none the less Mardersteig's first group of suggestions alone affected a total of seventeen characters. Many different factors were involved. In a few letters, he spotted irregularities of weight – the top serif in *N* was too light, and so was the extremity of the foot of *R*. A few other letters had been made too wide for his liking, in an attempt to use up available unit values. Occasionally he saw ways to improve on his original designs as cut by Malin, so he set about providing new italic drawings for *B* and *r*. Later, as sizes never cut by Malin were added to the Monotype range, he perceived through photographic enlargements that a simple proportional increase from a smaller size would produce too coarse a result, so that a great many letters had to be modified.[87]

Dante is also a very refined type but infinitely more readable than the other refined types of the twentieth century. It has none of the faults of Van Krimpen's types and not the rigidness and coldness of Jan Tschichold's Sabon (see below).‡ It is certainly one of the most beautiful type-faces ever designed. One is pleased to see a rather good digital version (created by Monotype in 1991). A bold was added (designed by Ron Carpenter) and the semi-bold was renamed 'Medium'; the titling fount is included as well as the original *g* (as an 'alternative'), two italic double-g's (*gg*, *gg*), *zy* and the original *z*. Before the digital Dante was issued John Dreyfus wrote:

Dante having been designed with the express intention of impressing its letters into and not onto paper, Mardersteig was opposed to its being adapted for photo-composition and offset printing. But since his death, a few craftsmen have become as skilled at modifying metal types into new forms suitable for the new computer technology, as Malin was skilled at converting large two-dimensional drawings into much smaller three-dimensional punches.[88]

For sundry reasons – time and loci of technological transitions, connections and disconnections between the offices in New York, London, Frankfurt; mergers and close-downs – certain Linotype types were never digitised. Particularly those of the British Linotype such as Georgian, Jubilee, Juliana. There was a digitised Pilgrim, as we have noted, which was included in the 'Library' supplied with the Linotronic 300 (as it was included among the

g g gg gg zz , ; ;

The original italic g and z, comma and semi-colon, which are now alternative characters, and those of the standard character-set of the digital Monotype Dante italic.

---

* One might also mention Mardersteig's and Morison's friendship of thirty years and Mardersteig's regular use of Monotype types – Centaur, Poliphilus, Bembo, Garamond, Baskerville, Imprint, Times New Roman – at the Stamperia Valdonega which he established in 1949 for machine composition and printing.

† 'The Dante Type', *Fine Print*, vol. 11, no. 4 (October 1985), pp. 219–21.

‡ 'Compared with the smooth perfection of Sabon, it is slightly more rugged, but therefore perhaps easier to live with.' (Hans Schmoller, *Two Titans: Mardersteig and Tschichold* (New York, The Typophiles, 1990), p. 73.)

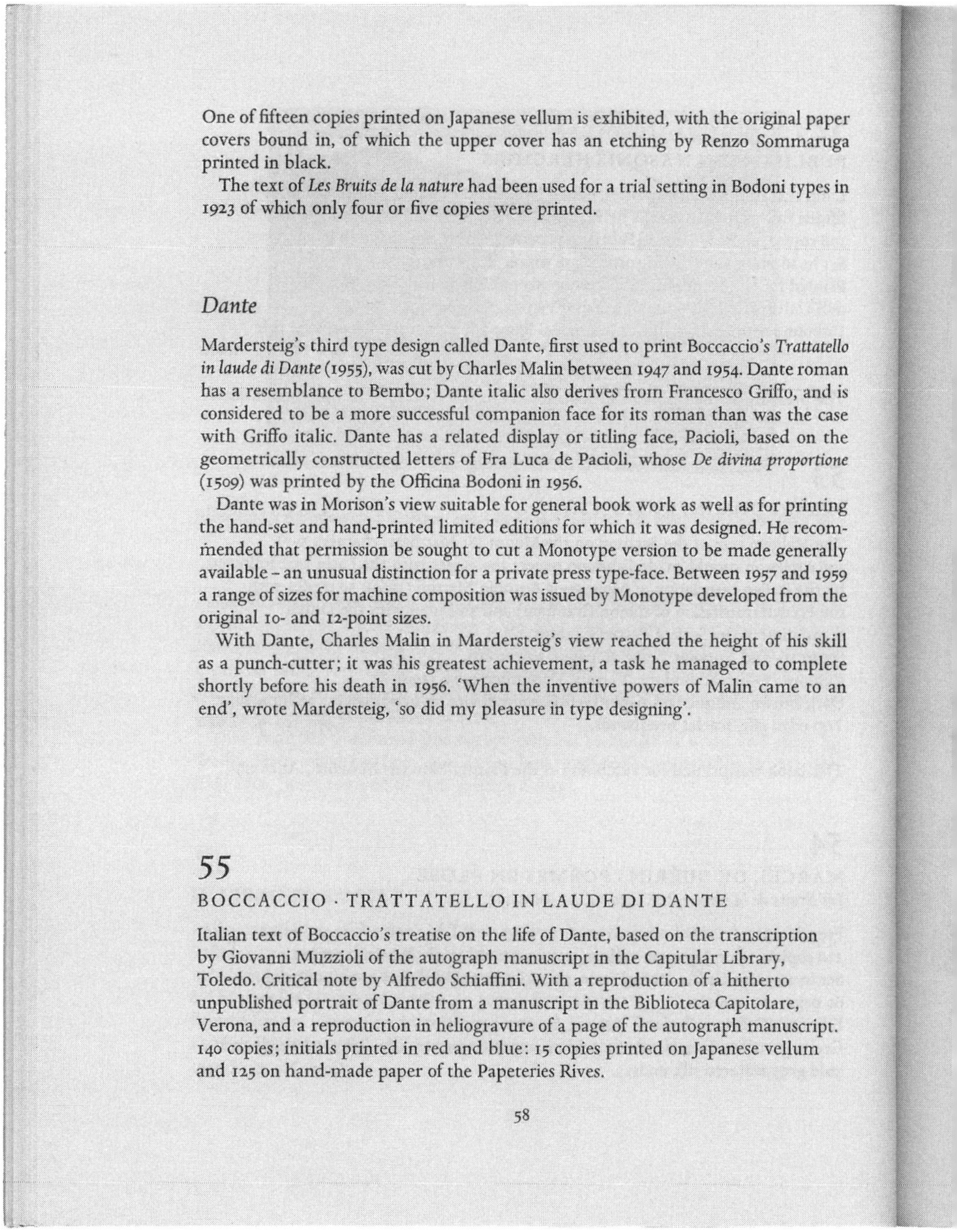

Fig. 54 John Barr, *The Officina Bodoni* (The British Library, 1978), designed by Sebastian Carter, set in Monotype Dante, printed by The Curwen Press, Plaistow. Reduced from 246 mm deep.

One of fifteen copies printed on Japanese vellum is exhibited, with the original paper covers bound in, of which the upper cover has an etching by Renzo Sommaruga printed in black.

The text of *Les Bruits de la nature* had been used for a trial setting in Bodoni types in 1923 of which only four or five copies were printed.

Dante

Mardersteig's third type design called Dante, first used to print Boccaccio's *Trattatello in laude di Dante* (1955), was cut by Charles Malin between 1947 and 1954. Dante roman has a resemblance to Bembo; Dante italic also derives from Francesco Griffo, and is considered to be a more successful companion face for its roman than was the case with Griffo italic. Dante has a related display or titling face, Pacioli, based on the geometrically constructed letters of Fra Luca de Pacioli, whose *De divina proportione* (1509) was printed by the Officina Bodoni in 1956.

Dante was in Morison's view suitable for general book work as well as for printing the hand-set and hand-printed limited editions for which it was designed. He recommended that permission be sought to cut a Monotype version to be made generally available – an unusual distinction for a private press type-face. Between 1957 and 1959 a range of sizes for machine composition was issued by Monotype developed from the original 10- and 12-point sizes.

With Dante, Charles Malin in Mardersteig's view reached the height of his skill as a punch-cutter; it was his greatest achievement, a task he managed to complete shortly before his death in 1956. 'When the inventive powers of Malin came to an end', wrote Mardersteig, 'so did my pleasure in type designing'.

55

BOCCACCIO · TRATTATELLO IN LAUDE DI DANTE

Italian text of Boccaccio's treatise on the life of Dante, based on the transcription by Giovanni Muzzioli of the autograph manuscript in the Capitular Library, Toledo. Critical note by Alfredo Schiaffini. With a reproduction of a hitherto unpublished portrait of Dante from a manuscript in the Biblioteca Capitolare, Verona, and a reproduction in heliogravure of a page of the autograph manuscript. 140 copies; initials printed in red and blue: 15 copies printed on Japanese vellum and 125 on hand-made paper of the Papeteries Rives.

58

Linotype faces removed from New York to Frankfurt), but it has not since been made available to desktop users.[89] Georgian, Jubilee and Juliana don't look like being digitised. That is a pity but then one expects that they'd have stood little chance of being converted to digital form properly; that at Linotype they would either have their letters regularised – as Mergenthaler-

Linotype have done for Baskerville, Caledonia, Century Schoolbook, Janson – or not provided with small capitals, f-ligatures ('expert' sets such as Monotype have produced for most of their text types but which Linotype haven't offered). There is nothing necessarily unethical in modifying the design of a metal type to be adopted for digital setting. Indeed, a degree of modification may be necessary to render the digital *effectively* closer to the metal type. I don't think the 'New' Linotypes as drawn by Matthew Carter, John Quaranta, Adrian Frutiger, since the late 1970s, are poor jobs: unlike the abominations called 'Caslon', 'Baskerville', produced at H. Berthold by the hand or under the supervision of Gerhard Günter Lange, they are mostly careful and reasonable renditions.* Monotype have not taken this course with their own types (though, of course, like the Linotypes, they are mainly revivals themselves). Rather, they've made more conservatively adjusted copies of their metal types (though many by way of Monophoto versions), and that, as we have seen, has yielded disadvantages: namely insufficient weight at ordinary text sizes. Yet, the thought of modifying the designs of the famous Monotype faces which are described in this chapter as Linotype have done is quite unthinkable. Such modifications, at any rate, if done to compensate for digital shortcomings, are to do with technology at hand and one anticipates happier solutions: adjustments which can be made to a fount† specially designed for 11-point, for example, for printing conditions (paper etc.) to *emulate* the superior effect of metal typography and letterpress printing. If such circumstances were to occur I should be extremely pleased to see a digital recutting of such an exquisite type as *Juliana*.

Sem Hartz, in early days a featherweight boxer, later the designer of Linotype Juliana and Van Krimpen's successor at Enschedé, was an engraver and the creator of many fine postage stamps which Enschedé printed for the Netherlands post office. In 1951 he was introduced by the printer James Shand to Walter Tracy, the manager of typeface development at Linotype & Machinery Ltd, who commissioned him to design a new book type. In a recollection published in 1969 on the occasion of an exhibition of Hartz's graphic work in Brussels,‡ Tracy recalled that work, which commenced in the autumn of 1952, went slowly, owing partly to preference being given to other designs in progress, but also to the fact that Sem Hartz was new to the methods practised at Linotype: 'Sem's long experience as an engraver had made him expert in working at "final size"; to draw letters 6 or 7 cm high for a 12-pt type was, at that time, a new task for him.' The type, which was named after the queen of the Netherlands, was presented in *Penrose Annual*, vol. 52 (1958). Its design was influenced by sixteenth-century Italian letters but in some ways it is reminiscent of Gill's types and this is partly owed to its being the work of engraver rather than calligrapher. It is as excellent a type as Gill's Perpetua and Joanna and Mardersteig's Dante – or perhaps superior for being more adaptable. It is handsomer than Gill's Pilgrim. It featured a long descenders version and italic small capitals. Its narrowness made it

* The post-metal versions feature normalised f-curves.
† I use the older spelling here because I am not speaking of a general roman or italic form of a type but a particular *size* of a particular type.
‡ 'The Juliana Type Design', *S. L. Hartz in de grafische wereld* (Brussels, Bibliotheek Albert I, 1969), pp. 45–6. This book is set not in Hartz's Juliana but in Jan van Krimpen's Lutetia (the version with horizontal e-bars).

Corrigan Mrs Stewart had met mainly on the racecourse, but her encounters with the painters and writers had been in the Paris cafés and her stories about them always ended with her saying: 'And there they were, my dear, staggering about just like you and the rest of the young fellows are doing today.'

She was unlike other old ladies in that she never spoke of the past from a personal angle, so nobody was told what she herself had been doing in Paris at this period. Nina Hamnett, who was better at painting old people than she was with the young, did a superb portrait of her, which for some time after she died hung above the spot where for so long she'd sat, though I don't know what happened to it in the end.

The death of Mrs Stewart—in the late Forties or early Fifties—marked, as writers of memoirs are fond of saying, the passing of an epoch, and it might have pleased her to know that she'd become a symbolic figure to a whole generation now no longer young: for there are few former Wheatsheaf habitués whose eyes fail to light up in memory of her name.

Regulars, Wits and Bums
Alan Ross, then a junior naval officer on leave, used to come round, among others, about this time. As a promising young poet he had been discovered by John Lehmann, whom he was later to succeed as editor of *The London Magazine*, and Lehmann had also printed in *New Writing and Daylight* portions of a novel which alternated brilliantly scenes of civilian and naval life but was never completed.

Ross in the navy had served with the triple murderer Ronald Chesney but he did not know that yet, since Chesney so far had murdered only once: his own mother, for which he'd been tried and acquitted at the age of 17 under his real name of John Donald Merrett.

Ross was very young and ingenuous in manner: clean shaven in those days with a dark complexion and black sleek hair which showed up handsomely against his blue and gold uniform, and he had brown eyes which peered with un-abashed interest at everybody and everything and took in a

158

very great deal: as was revealed when h
memory, with remarkable precision except f
voice allotted to me, the complete Wheat:
London Magazine editorial last year.

He described of course an evening on
everyone was there but the point was, as he sa
that such an evening *could* and indeed son
place.

But there were other figures whom he did
possibly did not notice, without whom
wouldn't really have been complete: they n
ground and the unsung chorus and occasic
night, the entire cast.

These fell roughly into three categories
and Bums.

Regulars, of whom Mrs Stewart was the
the old Home Guard who though extremel
tunic medal ribbons of more campaigns th
possibly have served in: it was thought tha
ribbons had been handed down to him by hi
I was using him as a model for the old sv
Guard film which Dylan and myself were
Then there was the Central European sp
relegated to the middle of the counter from
so easy to get a drink; the orange-faced wo
cause of the many layers of make-up which s
made it impossible to assess her age), whose p
made it sound like the parrot house in the
reputed to have green silk sheets on her be
was brave enough to investigate the rumou
the tart who was more respectable than n
customers: she mostly moved in a no-ma
public and saloon bars and patronized both

Sister Ann was short and wholesome-lo
wore russet-brown tweeds and a round ru
shape like a schoolgirl's. She used no make
round red spots on her round apple cheek

Fig. 55 *Memoirs of the Forties* by Julian Mac-laren-Ross (Alan Ross, 1965), set in Linotype Juliana and printed at the Shenval Press at Hertford. Reduced from 197 mm deep.

attractive for use in paperbacks and first-rate examples of it can be found in many Penguins. Walter Tracy:

> The Juliana type seems to me to be one of the most elegant designs of this century; its italic is particularly original and charming. But perhaps I am not sufficiently detached. Stanley Morison decidedly *was*. He wrote: 'I like very much the type by S. H. I see in Penrose; well designed, practical, economic and bound to be successful.'[90]

At the very end of the days of metal typography (in 1960) a group of German master printers conceived the idea of a new type to be produced in identical form for mechanical composition – single-letter and line-casting (Monotype and Linotype) – and hand-composition (Stempel). The sizes were to be 6 to 12 point for the Linotype and Monotype and 6 to 48 point for the foundry type.[91] According to John Dreyfus, the master printers 'recorded a distinct preference for something in the manner of Garamond, but modified to suit contemporary taste and needs.'*

> The new type was to correspond as closely as possible with the weight and x-height of 'Monotype' Garamond, but it was to be drawn approximately 5% narrower in its proportions for reasons of economy.

The job was given to Jan Tschichold, who based his design on the *S. Augustin* roman and the *Litera Currens Ciceroniana* italic attributed to Claude Garamond and Robert Granjon in the 'Egenolff–Berner' specimen of 1592. At Stanley Morison's suggestion the type was named after Jacques Sabon, assistant to the widow Egenolff, and later the Egenolff foundry's proprietor (1572–80). It was certainly not an easy job: Tschichold's type had to conform to the parameters of three different technologies: the 18-unit Monotype system; the Linotype roman and italic duplexed matrix and its inability to cast kerned letters; and the German Standard Line, established for black letter and used for foundry type, which allowed little room for descenders. There was also some consideration given to adapting the type for photocomposition. That this can have been done at all and result as it did in such a comely type is proof of the designer's great talent and skill, but it would seem the technical constraints together with the designer's tastes rendered the type rather more rigid, less graceful, than its sixteenth century models. The italics are particularly awkward (many of the lower-case letters appearing abnormally wide owing mainly to torturous constraints of the Linotype), but it is not an impression of ungainliness one receives: on the contrary, one finds the type perhaps too polished and there is something strangely rather dull about its adamantine perfection. Comparing the style of Tschichold's working methods with Mardersteig's – or really, their personalities – Hans Schmoller remarked that while Dr Mardersteig made careful but tentative drawings for the punch-cutter to work from, Tschichold made 'highly finished drawings on a very large scale, and immensely detailed comments on the typefounder's proofs. No manual punch-cutting was involved. Everything was done pantographically.'[92] Nothing left to chance.

Sabon is a German type which conforms to German standards. Its connection to Salfords is negligible. There are no concessions to English tastes. This is significant because although the primary market was in Germany

---

* 'Sabon: the first "harmonized" type', *Penrose Annual*, vol. 61 (1968), p. 63.

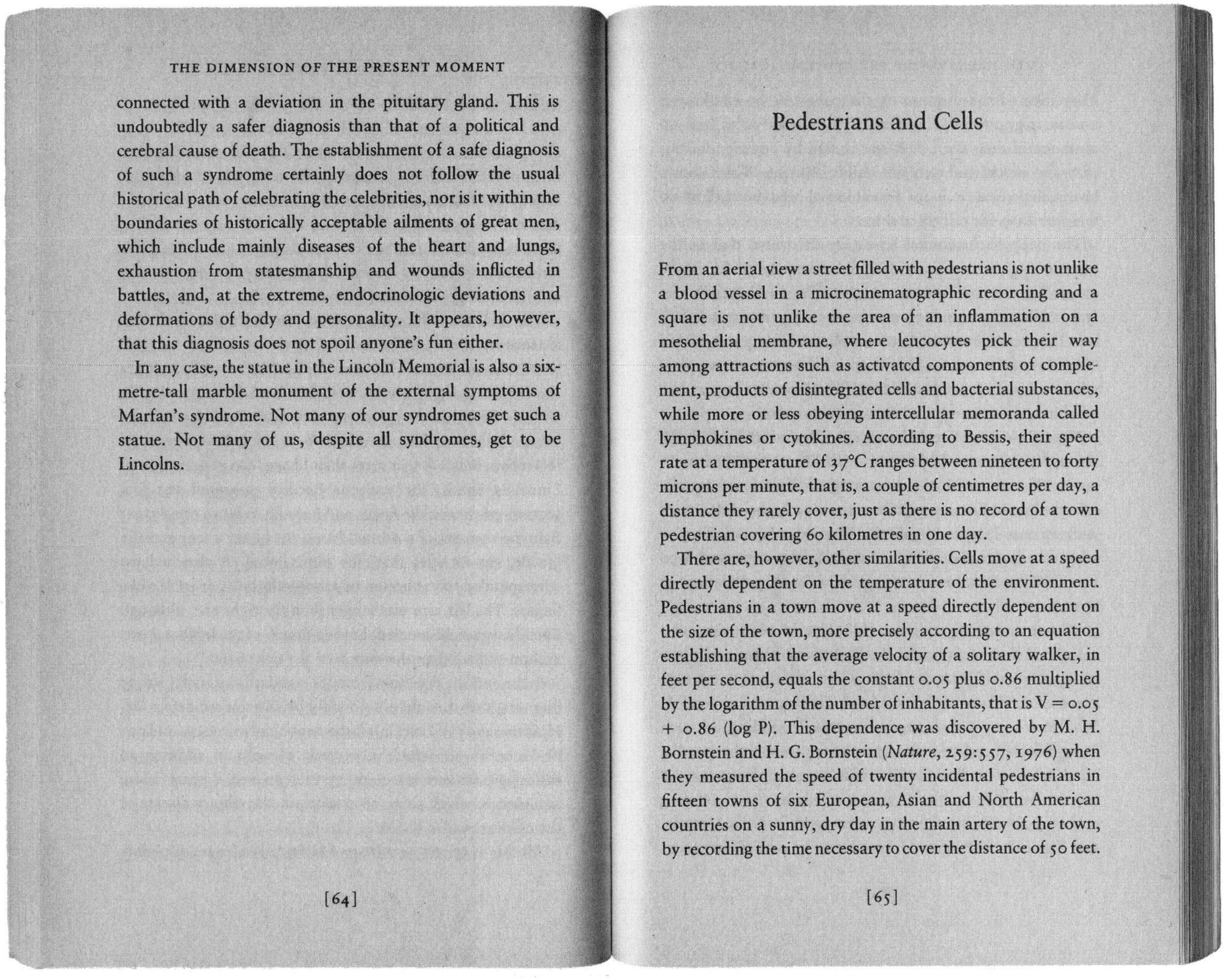

connected with a deviation in the pituitary gland. This is undoubtedly a safer diagnosis than that of a political and cerebral cause of death. The establishment of a safe diagnosis of such a syndrome certainly does not follow the usual historical path of celebrating the celebrities, nor is it within the boundaries of historically acceptable ailments of great men, which include mainly diseases of the heart and lungs, exhaustion from statesmanship and wounds inflicted in battles, and, at the extreme, endocrinologic deviations and deformations of body and personality. It appears, however, that this diagnosis does not spoil anyone's fun either.

In any case, the statue in the Lincoln Memorial is also a six-metre-tall marble monument of the external symptoms of Marfan's syndrome. Not many of our syndromes get such a statue. Not many of us, despite all syndromes, get to be Lincolns.

[64]

Pedestrians and Cells

From an aerial view a street filled with pedestrians is not unlike a blood vessel in a microcinematographic recording and a square is not unlike the area of an inflammation on a mesothelial membrane, where leucocytes pick their way among attractions such as activated components of complement, products of disintegrated cells and bacterial substances, while more or less obeying intercellular memoranda called lymphokines or cytokines. According to Bessis, their speed rate at a temperature of 37°C ranges between nineteen to forty microns per minute, that is, a couple of centimetres per day, a distance they rarely cover, just as there is no record of a town pedestrian covering 60 kilometres in one day.

There are, however, other similarities. Cells move at a speed directly dependent on the temperature of the environment. Pedestrians in a town move at a speed directly dependent on the size of the town, more precisely according to an equation establishing that the average velocity of a solitary walker, in feet per second, equals the constant 0.05 plus 0.86 multiplied by the logarithm of the number of inhabitants, that is $V = 0.05 + 0.86 \,(\log P)$. This dependence was discovered by M. H. Bornstein and H. G. Bornstein (*Nature*, 259:557, 1976) when they measured the speed of twenty incidental pedestrians in fifteen towns of six European, Asian and North American countries on a sunny, dry day in the main artery of the town, by recording the time necessary to cover the distance of 50 feet.

[65]

Fig. 56 C'est Sabon? *The Dimension of the Present Moment* by Miroslav Holub, edited by David Young (Faber, 1990), photoset in Sabon by Wilmaset, Birkenhead, Wirral, in Fabers' house style and printed by Richard Clay Ltd at Bungay, Suffolk. A carefully designed but dull and stiff-looking page. Too much leading, and I expect Jan Tschichold would have taken a poor view of the word-spacing. A cold, rather stand-offish face made more chilly by rigid page design. But there it is. Reduced from 197 mm deep.

there was from the beginning the intention of selling the type to British, American and other non-German printers.

The Germanism of Sabon is particularly distinguishable by its lower-case f. The type was supplied (as were most German foundry and machine-cast types) with ff, fi, fl, ß and an ft ligature. As the f-ligature is used in German composition for some words but not for others (e.g. hinausfliegen but not unbegreiflich)[93] and as the combinations fb, fh, fk, and words with umlauts such as fährt, förmlich, für, are common, the German f was normally designed with a narrow curve.* Indeed the f-curve of most German types is so slight that the ligature seems extravagant. Never mind necessary (an f-ligature being a means of protecting the projection of the kern). The effs of the double f-ligatures supplied with Sabon were joined only at the bar (the difference of curve between first f and second is scarcely perceptible). That is well, the design is pleasing, but the fi then sticks out like a sore thumb (the fl (both roman and italic) is happier).[94] Some of Tschichold's drawings are shown with John Dreyfus's article (in pages 66–7 of the *Penrose Annual*, vol. 61) and in these we find f-ligatures with connecting effs which are consonant with the design of the fi.† The final version of the double-f might have been to do with an anticipation of their non-use in German filmsetting machines. In any event, no expert set for desktop users is available. The italic *f* is uncurved at the bottom as is the italic *j* (originally its end was like that of the *f* but it has since been tapered slightly) so as to stay within the Linotype confines.‡ The italic *Q* is misshaped (as the Linotype Granjon italic *Q* is) for the same reason. The roman figures, however, are particularly admirable.

1234567890

Despite its shortcomings the type has proved rather popular: it was used by Ron Costley at Fabers for a great number of their non-fiction titles (Faber works of fiction were set in Palatino, as directed by Gerald Cinamon). Linotype now offer a new Sabon, called Sabon Next (designed by Jean-François Porchez, issued in 2002), with most of the oddities reformed – those which are mentioned above as well as the uncomfortable design of its italics. But so many corrections and modifications were made that some of the type's precious little charm has been diminished.

While many felicitous examples of the master calligrapher and book designer Hermann Zapf's *Aldus* can be found among the artefacts of German printing, the type tends to look rather lacklustre even in the most carefully composed and well designed British or American books. This is, of course, a matter of my particular experience but I should have been inclined to under-praise the type had I not seen it used so nicely in its first appearances in *Imprimatur* and in the Linotype specimen books. Can this be explained by the peculiarities of prevailing national styles or is it to do with special qualities of the German language? The Aldus type was designed in 1953 specially for the Linotype: it is a narrower, book-weight version of the designer's much-esteemeed Palatino (Stempel, 1950) and it is a better type for text-setting

---

* This may have proved a factor of Linotype's success in Germany where the kerned f of the Monotype faces conversely proved a disadvantage.

† Trump-Mediäval (designed by Georg Trump for Weber, 1954) also features such a conspicuous fi but it is less problematic for being consonant with the design the type's double-f.

‡ The italic f of the filmsetting and digital versions takes its design from the Stempel (foundry) type; the machine-cast italics featured Linotype's ungainly crochet-hook.

than the common form of Palatino (designed for photo-composition) which seems to have been more favoured than Aldus in the UK and US.[95] The type's scribal character is derived from Renaissance models and a few calligraphic caprices[96]; it has a satisfactory weight in its digital form and this is certainly much in its favour, but it has also lost, as has nearly every type converted from metal to digital, something of its crispness, its punch.* The metal version was produced in 6 to 12 point Didot sizes; the digital version is larger than most of the Monotype types and it tends to seem rather restless at sizes over 11 point (this paragraph is set in 10½/13). *The italics, which were drawn to the set-widths of the roman letters, are mostly unchanged in the digital version.* The double-f, ft, ch, ck of the metal version were omitted from the digital character-set, but the omission of the double-f in English-language settings is mitigated by the design of the non-kerning f.

Trump-Mediäval is a type of as much a German mould as Aldus or Palatino – but less lacking in lustre. Indeed it is one of the most attractive German *Antiquas* and I believe it is better suited to English texts and non-German tastes than Aldus, Stempel Garamond, *et al*. It was issued in roman, italic, bold, extra-bold and bold condensed forms by the C. E. Weber foundry of Stuttgart in 1954 (the same year as the issue of Aldus) with Linotype matrices for the roman and italic in 6 to 10 point (Didot). It was marketed rather successfully to advertising typographers in the US where it was called Trump Imperial. Its designer was Professor Georg Trump, director of the Meisterschüle für Deutschlands Buchdrucker at Munich.[97] There is a very fine specimen in *Imprimatur*.† It is as scribal as Zapf's Palatino and Aldus, but it is quite different otherwise and equally distinctive in its general design. It is informed of many of the ideas which inform the designer's Schadow, Delphin and Codex.[98] The italics are, save for the *a*, *e*, *f*, sloped roman. It is a larger type than Aldus: this paragraph is set 9½/12½. It is a pity that its double-f, which was supplied with the Monotype Lasercomp version, is not to be found in the present digital version. It is unfortunate that no digital version of the Trump-Gravur letters exists.

Fig. 57 Cover of the Weber foundry's specimen of Trump-Gravur, printed at Stuttgart, 1960. Reduced from 297 mm.

There are now a good number of new types (designed and issued *c*. 1990 and after) which can be recommended for bookwork. As regards fitness for purpose – the suitability of their designs at normal text sizes – they are mostly superior to the earlier digital versions of old metal types. Many designs of merit have lately been produced in the Netherlands (among them, Lexicon, Quadraat, Renard and Documenta).‡ This paragraph is set in a type of an unusual and particularly attractive cast called *Scala*, which was designed by Martin Majoor in the late 1980s as a proprietary type for the Vredenburg Music Centre in Utrecht.§ An earlier type of Dutch origin, Linotype Lectura (fig. 58), which was designed by Dick Dooijes and issued originally by Tetterode in 1969 and supplied in a digital version for the Linotron 202 and Linotronic 300, is unfortunately not currently available.

* Perhaps the lack of lustre I've noted was owed to the examples being non-metal settings.
† 'Aus den Philosophischen Tagebüchern des Leonardo da Vinci', *Imprimatur*, new series, vol. 4 (1964), between pages 156 and 157.
‡ Lexicon (Enschedé, 1992) was designed by Bram de Does; Quadraat (FontShop International, 1992) and Renard (Enschedé, 2000) were designed by Fred Smeijers; Documenta (Dutch Type Library, 1993) was designed by Frank Blokland.
§ Issued in 1991 by FontShop International. The paragraph is set in 10/13.

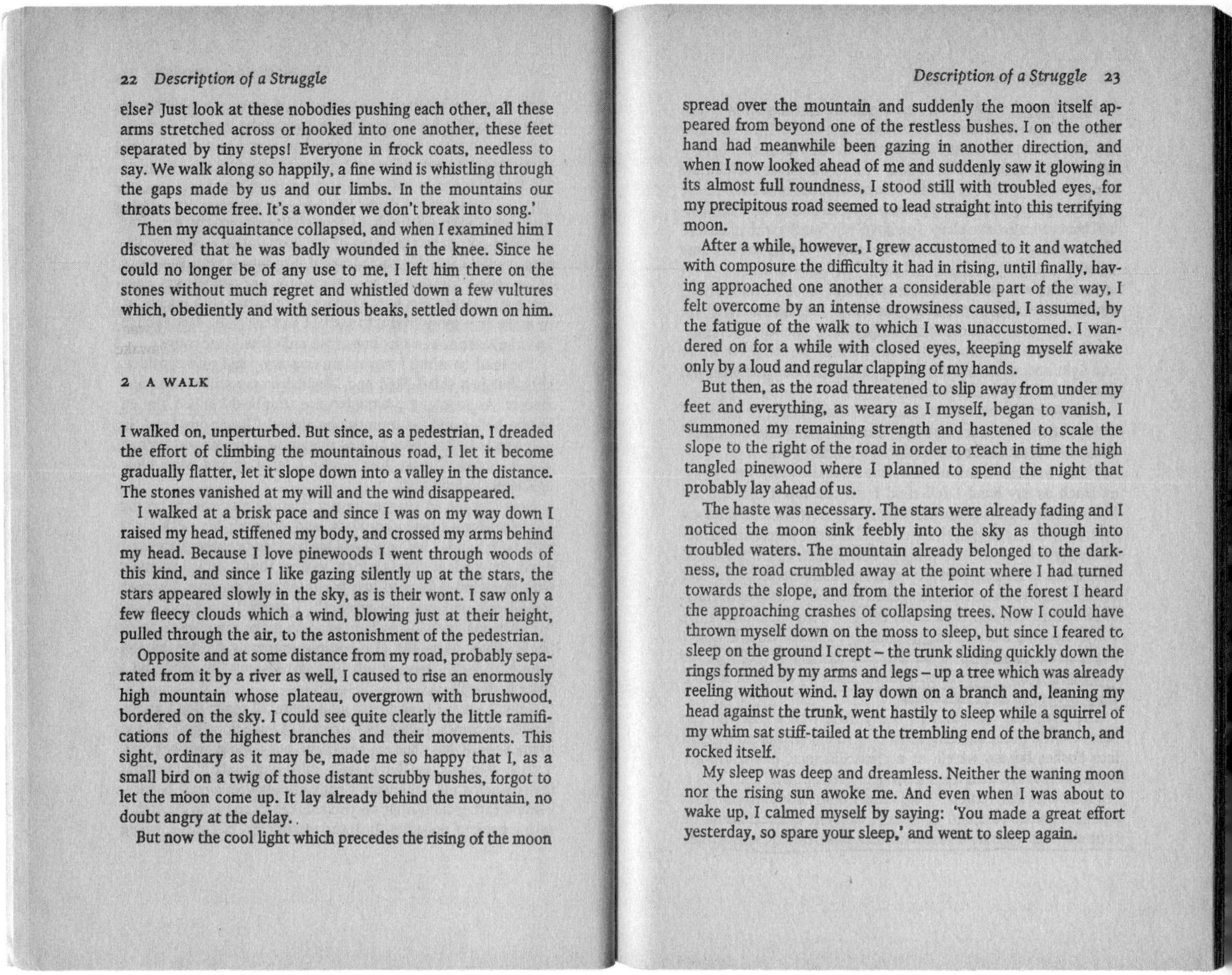

else? Just look at these nobodies pushing each other, all these arms stretched across or hooked into one another, these feet separated by tiny steps! Everyone in frock coats, needless to say. We walk along so happily, a fine wind is whistling through the gaps made by us and our limbs. In the mountains our throats become free. It's a wonder we don't break into song.'

Then my acquaintance collapsed, and when I examined him I discovered that he was badly wounded in the knee. Since he could no longer be of any use to me, I left him there on the stones without much regret and whistled down a few vultures which, obediently and with serious beaks, settled down on him.

2 A WALK

I walked on, unperturbed. But since, as a pedestrian, I dreaded the effort of climbing the mountainous road, I let it become gradually flatter, let it slope down into a valley in the distance. The stones vanished at my will and the wind disappeared.

I walked at a brisk pace and since I was on my way down I raised my head, stiffened my body, and crossed my arms behind my head. Because I love pinewoods I went through woods of this kind, and since I like gazing silently up at the stars, the stars appeared slowly in the sky, as is their wont. I saw only a few fleecy clouds which a wind, blowing just at their height, pulled through the air, to the astonishment of the pedestrian.

Opposite and at some distance from my road, probably separated from it by a river as well, I caused to rise an enormously high mountain whose plateau, overgrown with brushwood, bordered on the sky. I could see quite clearly the little ramifications of the highest branches and their movements. This sight, ordinary as it may be, made me so happy that I, as a small bird on a twig of those distant scrubby bushes, forgot to let the moon come up. It lay already behind the mountain, no doubt angry at the delay.

But now the cool light which precedes the rising of the moon

spread over the mountain and suddenly the moon itself appeared from beyond one of the restless bushes. I on the other hand had meanwhile been gazing in another direction, and when I now looked ahead of me and suddenly saw it glowing in its almost full roundness, I stood still with troubled eyes, for my precipitous road seemed to lead straight into this terrifying moon.

After a while, however, I grew accustomed to it and watched with composure the difficulty it had in rising, until finally, having approached one another a considerable part of the way, I felt overcome by an intense drowsiness caused, I assumed, by the fatigue of the walk to which I was unaccustomed. I wandered on for a while with closed eyes, keeping myself awake only by a loud and regular clapping of my hands.

But then, as the road threatened to slip away from under my feet and everything, as weary as I myself, began to vanish, I summoned my remaining strength and hastened to scale the slope to the right of the road in order to reach in time the high tangled pinewood where I planned to spend the night that probably lay ahead of us.

The haste was necessary. The stars were already fading and I noticed the moon sink feebly into the sky as though into troubled waters. The mountain already belonged to the darkness, the road crumbled away at the point where I had turned towards the slope, and from the interior of the forest I heard the approaching crashes of collapsing trees. Now I could have thrown myself down on the moss to sleep, but since I feared to sleep on the ground I crept – the trunk sliding quickly down the rings formed by my arms and legs – up a tree which was already reeling without wind. I lay down on a branch and, leaning my head against the trunk, went hastily to sleep while a squirrel of my whim sat stiff-tailed at the trembling end of the branch, and rocked itself.

My sleep was deep and dreamless. Neither the waning moon nor the rising sun awoke me. And even when I was about to wake up, I calmed myself by saying: 'You made a great effort yesterday, so spare your sleep,' and went to sleep again.

Fig. 58 Franz Kafka, *Description of a
Struggle and Other Stories*, translated by
Willa and Edwin Muir, Malcolm Pasley,
Tania and James Stern (Penguin, 1979), set
in Linotype Lectura, printed by Hazells.
Reduced from 197 mm deep.

Notes

1 **The school of close spacing** (*pages 9–29*)

1 Geoffrey Dowding, *Finer Points in the Spacing and Arrangement of Type* (Wace, 1954), p. 3.

2 'Hans Schmoller 1916–85', *The Monotype Recorder*, new series no. 6 (April 1987), p. 10.
According to Schmoller himself, Tschichold's 'two-and-a-half years at Penguin were without doubt the culmination of his career. What he found was a mess resulting from long neglect and incompetence. He soon made Penguins the envy of the world, not only for their editorial vitality and acumen – but also for their elegance inside, and outside on the covers. In the face of every conceivable difficulty – initial antagonism to the "foreign expert", lack of adequate assistance, problems with expressing himself in English – he enforced the Tschicholdian laws, he codified and criticized, he cajoled and demanded, and in the main he got what he wanted.' (*Two Titans: Mardersteig and Tschichold* (New York, The Typophiles, 1990), p. 57.)
Also in the Schmoller number is this, by Nicolas Barker: 'Tschichold was a very difficult man. I remember that Hazell's used to tell me that they always used to pull twelve, not six, proofs of every title page for which he sent them a layout. They would send off six at first, and, sure enough, back would come one covered with minute adjustments to the letter- and line-space. They would then wait for a fortnight, and send the second six, and always alleged that they would get one back passed for press. I don't know if that is true but no one would have needed – or dared – to try that trick on Hans. He knew what he wanted and was able to communicate it in a way that generally produced it first time around: he also had the benefit of the discipline that Tschichold had instilled in getting printers to follow layouts and instructions accurately. But on this foundation he so built up the 'Penguin style' that it became a byword for good design. ('Hans Schmoller: a Valediction', p. 63.)

3 The *Penguin Composition Rules* are reproduced in Ruari McLean, *Jan Tschichold: Typographer* (Lund Humphries, 1976), pp. 94–5.

4 Lawrence W. Wallis, 'Typecorrosion', *MacPublishing*, vol. 1, no. 4; reprinted in his collected essays, *Typomania* (Severnside, 1993), p. 102.
See *Seybold Report on Desktop Publishing*, vol. 4, no. 10 (June 1990), pp. 3–23, and vol. 8, no. 1 (September 1993):
'*Quark fixes H&J in 3·2*. In comparing the features of PageMaker 5·0 and Xpress 3·2, we failed to notice that Quark had improved its default H&J settings. To our further chagrin, Quark has adopted exactly the settings that Seybold had recommended in Vol. 4, No. 10.
'The new settings . . . increase the spread between minimum and maximum wordspacing, open up the optimum spacing slightly, and drastically limit the amount of letterspacing. We think that users will now get better results "out of the box". (As always, knowledgeable users could change the default settings themselves at any time.) The change also affects the composition-quality advantage that we gave PageMaker in last month's comparison, although there still are some differences between the two programs.'

5 'In Depth: Text and Typography' (San Jose, California, Adobe Systems Inc., 2002), p. 22.

6 Olav Martin Kvern and David Blatner, *Real World Adobe InDesign 2* (Berkeley, California, Peachpit Press, 2003), p. 240.
   Similar advice is imparted by Sandee Cohen in her book, *InDesign 2 for Macintosh and Windows* (Peachpit, 2002). On p. 295: 'I also prefer a minimum of three letters before the hyphen and three after. This avoids breaking words as *un-excited* or *reluctant-ly*.'

7 'In Depth: Text and Typography', p. 2.

8 ibid. p. 5.

9 ibid. p. 4.

10 *Editor's Manual of Penguin House Style* (Harmondsworth, Penguin, 1973), p. 102. The passage appears under 'Typographical Considerations'; under 'Word Division at the End of the Line', the eighth rule reads: 'Avoid breaks in more than two successive lines' (p. 58) but a footnote is added which says: 'To save correction costs, Penguin sometimes ignores this rule.'

11 Ronald McIntosh, *Hyphenation* (Bradford, Computer Hyphenation, 1990). The passages quoted in this book were taken from the html version at www.hyphenologist.co.uk/book/BOOK-ED3.HTM.

12 *Hart's Rules for Compositors and Readers*, 39th edn, 1983.

13 Americans seem to favour rather rigid policies. John W. Clark, in his 'Chapter on American Practice', in Eric Partridge's *You Have a Point There* (Hamish Hamilton, 1953), writes on p. 220: 'American printing offices and handbooks (which generally follow them in such purely typographical matters) are very fussy and uniform and unbending about syllabification (both in dividing words at the end of a line and in indicating the pronunciation of words in dictionaries and the like). Generally, they would never allow *div-i-sion* or *di-vis-ion*, but would insist on *di-vi-sion*; never *sy-llabification*, but *syl-labification*. And in dividing words at the end of a line, American printers frequently will not break before the third letter, though American typists will: the printer, i.e., if he were breaking for the end of a line and not in order to indicate pronunciation, would avoid *di-vision* and would try for *divi-sion*.'

14 Eric Gill, *An Essay on Typography*, 2nd edn (Sheed & Ward, 1936), p. 92.

15 Geoffrey Dowding, *Finer Points in the Spacing and Arrangement of Type*, p. 19.

16 Geoffrey Dowding, *Factors in the Choice of Type Faces* (Wace, 1957), pp. vii–viii.

17 'In Depth: Text and Typography', p. 15.

18 David Kindersley, 'Optical letter spacing', *Penrose Annual*, vol. 62 (1969), p. 167.

19 ibid. p. 170.

20 Walter Tracy, *Letters of Credit* (Gordon Fraser, 1986), p. 78.

21 David Kindersley, *Optical Letter Spacing for the New Printing Systems* (Lund Humphries, 1976), p. 36.

22 Tracy, p. 79. The *Linotype-Schriftenreigen* (Frankfurt am Main, 1962) shows 28 logotypes for such letter combinations as Ta, Va, Wa, etc., including a rather uncomfortably closed-up T and i, and occluded ch and ck such as are favoured by German tastes (from Fraktur ch and ck), for their Baskerville, Bodoni Book, Garamond, Janson, Palatino and Walbaum roman and italic types.

23 Bruce Rogers, *Paragraphs on Printing* (New York, William E. Rudge's Sons, 1943), p. 94. The passage is quoted by Tracy in *Letters of Credit*, p. 79.

24 'In Depth: Text and Typography', p. 14.

25 The US Patent for Adobe's 'Pointsize-variable character spacing' (10th August

1999) contains references to nine other patents for methods or devices described as: 'Method and apparatus for automatically spacing characters during composition' (Gerber Scientific Products Inc., 1986); 'Method and apparatus for generating aesthetically alterable character designs' (Vital Lasertype Inc., 1990); 'Method and apparatus for minimizing the visual degradation of digital typefaces' (Sun Microsystems Inc., 1994); 'Character processing apparatus capable of automatic kerning' (Canon Kabushiki Kaisha, 1995); 'Process for preparation of characters' ('Verfahren zur Zurichtung von Schriften', URW, 1995); 'Apparatus and method for adjusting character spacing' (Omron Corporation, 1996); 'Methods and apparatus for hinting a font for controlling stem width as font size and resolution of output device may vary' (Microsoft, 1997); 'System and method for automatically spacing characters' (Macromedia, 1997); 'Algorithmic character-space adjustment computed from character-sequence-based constants and font size' (Lathrop, 1998).

26 'In Depth: Text and Typography', p. 14.

27 A dim view of the word 'robust' is taken by the type manufacturers P22 who say it is a 'buzz word'.

28 'In Depth: Text and Typography', p. 7.

29 Hermann Zapf, 'About micro-typography and the *hz*-program', *Electronic Publishing*, vol. 6, no. 3 (September 1993), p. 288.

30 Andrew Bluhm, *Photosetting* (Pergamon Press, 1968), p. 94. 'A book printer's experience with a computer', by Richard Clay IV, was published in *Graphic Technology*, vol. 18 (1966).

31 'The design of faces for "Monophoto" Film Matrices', *The Monotype Recorder*, vol. 42, no. 2 (Spring 1961), pp. 15–23.
    'When photo-composition became a reality in the 1950s the manufacturers of typesetting machines had to make an important decision: whether or not to carry forward into the new system the principle of optical compensation, when the plain and tempting fact was that the photographic part of the system was capable of producing a considerable range of type sizes from just one font. To abandon the principle altogether was to risk forfeiting a substantial part of a reputation for typographic quality. The manufacturers faced the problem by compromise. American Linotype produced film replicas of both the 8 and 12 point versions of text types, and of the 18 point where display sizes existed.... Some [manufacturers] apparently thought that increasing the x-height of the faces would be an acceptable alternative. It is not. Although it assists the legibility of the small sizes it vulgarises the larger ones.... Too much concern for the look of the display sizes may mean that the art-work size chosen, say the 12 point, produces a cramped result at 6 and 8 point.... The Bembo face, an admirable example of optical compensation by the Monotype drawing office, demonstrates the point.' (Walter Tracy, *Letters of Credit*, pp. 54–5.)

32 Robin Kinross, 'What is a Typeface?', *Baseline*, no. 7 (1986), p. 18.

33 The first Monotype Lasercomps (the Mark 1), introduced in 1976, used a separate master (or pre-sized bitmaps) for every point-size, but this was owed to the design of the technology rather than to an interest in preserving the different original designs for different point-sizes. Other imagesetters had employed similar technologies.
    'Fonts were digitized for a specific output point size range. One "master"-sized character could be used to produce a variety of character heights (by lengthening or shortening the writing strokes) and a variety of widths (by spacing the writing strokes closer together or farther apart). There was, naturally, a limit to how far you could stretch or shrink any given digitized character, so most digital CRT machines used a series of "master sizes" to cover the full range of sizes.

For example, the Autologic APS-4, introduced in 1971, used 10-, 20-, 40- and 80-point masters to cover the full range of sizes from 5-point to 96-point.' (Jonathan Seybold, from the *Seybold Report on Desktop Publishing*, vol. 4, no. 2 (16th October 1989), presented at http://www.seyboldreports.com/SRDP/dp4/DP04-02.htm.)

The Lasercomp Sprint, 'deploying digital fonts encoded as outlines, instead of as pre-sized bitmaps', was introduced in 1983. 'The characters were expressed as vectored outlines. Included in the machine controller was computer logic for dynamically sizing characters on the fly.' ('Monotype Chronicles' at agfamonotype.co.uk.) Writing in 1983, Lawrence Wallis explained that on the Mark 1 'Jobs must be passed through the computer logic twice: the first to compile a bit map of the page and the second to expose images.' With the Sprint 'a single character master can be utilised to span an output size range of 6 to 96 point by electronic scaling dynamically' ('Pixelated Future for Typesetting: or a RIPping yarn for printers', *Typomania*, p. 135).

34 'In practice, users have been disappointed over the years. One key reason is the poor support in page layout programs, including QuarkXPress, Adobe Page-Maker, and, the final insult, Adobe's own InDesign. Other problems have been apparent in the actual designs. The optical scaling capabilities, for example, never came up to user expectations. . . . Although Adobe's implementation had near-fatal aesthetic and technological flaws, it represented the best effort yet to regain the superior aesthetic qualities and readability of the finest metal-era typefaces. Those began to disappear in the 1960s and are now used by only a handful of dedicated, ultra high quality printers. Multiple Masters had the (unrealized) potential to offer a great deal of that quality to the desktop users, without even asking them to think about it. . . . Was it necessary for Multiple Masters to die? Probably not. Several factors contributed: inexpert and uninteresting designs; a purportedly "open" technology that was in fact proprietary; and inadequate interface support early on to Aldus, Quark and Macromedia.' (Bill Troop, 'A giant step backwards for Adobe?', *Macobserver.com*, 6th October 1999.)

35 *OpenType User Guide for Adobe Fonts* (San Jose, California, Adobe Systems Inc., 2002), p. 2.

2 Mise-en-page etc. (*pages 31–52*)

1 Hugh Williamson, *Methods of Book Design*, 2nd edn (Oxford, 1966), p. 24.

2 There is a good piece, all very positive, on Richard Hollis in Kinross's *Unjustified Texts* (Hyphen, 2002), pp. 81–6.

Another example of Richard Hollis's work for Whitechapel – pages 8 and 9 of *David Hockney : Paintings, Print and Drawings* – done ten years before the Baselitz job, is shown on page 32 of James Sutton's and Alan Bartram's *Typefaces for Books* (The British Library, 1999). The style is much the same: text chopped up by great blocks of white (but the Hockney job doesn't feature the extreme line-lengths of the Baselitz job). Both designs use Berthold Block Schwer for titling ('slightly redrawn by Hollis and used as a "house" letter for the gallery' (Robin Kinross, *Modern Typography*, p. 170)); both are exceedingly poor jobs of composition: an interviewer's questions are set in a left-ranged egyptian (Monotype Rockwell) and the artist's answers are set left-ranged and larger in Monotype Grotesque 215 with lower-case ells used execrably for figure-ones. Sutton and Bartram say that 'the design mirrors the informality and simplicity of the text, and even suggests the physical presence of two people seated opposite each other'.

3 Stanley Morison, *First Principles of Typography* (Cambridge, 1951), p. 15.

4 Seán Jennett, *The Making of Books*, 4th edn (Faber, 1967), pp. 293–4.

5 Jennett, p. 282.

'Quotations become more telling if isolated by white lines, and quotation marks, which are fidgety, may by this means often be dispensed with. Such isolation is a far more logical treatment than the irritating inverted commas and apostrophes.' (J. H. Mason, 'Printing', in *Fifteen Craftsmen on Their Crafts*, edited by in John Farleigh (Sylvan Press, 1945), p. 56.)

6 *Paragraphs on Printing, elicited from Bruce Rogers in talks with James Hendrickson on the Functions of the Book Designer* (New York, William E. Rudge's Sons, 1943; reprinted New York, Dover, 1979), p. 57.

7 Jennett, p. 292.

8 *Chambers English Dictionary* (W. & R. Chambers, 1988), p. 968.

3 On book design and typographic style (*pages 53–64*)

1 Richard Hendel, *On Book Design* (Yale University Press, 1998), p. 33.

2 ibid. p. 79.

3 ibid.

4 ibid.

5 Letter to the author from Richard Hendel, 2nd July 2001.

6 Letter to the author, 27th July 2001.

7 Letter to the author, 2nd August 2001.

8 John R. Biggs, *An Approach to Type*, 2nd edn (Blandford, 1961), p. 136.

9 'I normally begin the design with the text spread and the choice of typeface(s). Everything else evolves from these selections. The initial decisions are based on my intuitive reactions to the content of the book and to suggestions offered by publisher and author.' (David Bullen quoted in *On Book Design*, p. 92.)

10 Robert Bringhurst, *The Elements of Typographic Style*, 2nd edn (Point Roberts, Washington, Hartley & Marks, 1996), p. 9.

11 Alan Bartram, *Making Books* (The British Library, 1999), p. 67.

12 Bringhurst, p. 9.

13 ibid. p. 115.

14 ibid. p. 113.

15 ibid. pp. 89–90.

16 ibid. p. 142.

17 Rudolph Ruzicka (1883–1978), the designer of Mergenthaler-Linotype Fairfield, who immigrated to the United States in 1894, or Rudolf Růžička (b. 1941), the Czech composer? Zuzana Licko has told me that she does not use the diacritical mark (called *mäkčeň* in Slovak) with her name.

A *háček* (meaning 'little hook' in Czech) is an inverted circumflex modifying a *c*, *e*, *n*, *r*, *s*, *z* (see p. 76 and note); the term is used by American printers but it is also called a 'wedge' or a 'caron'. 'Caron' is used by Robert Bringhurst in his 'Appendix A: Sorts & Characters' (*The Elements of Typographic Style*, p. 274). J. C. Wells, of the Department of Phonetics and Linguistics, University College London, writes: 'The term "caron", however, is wrapped in mystery. Incredibly, it seems to appear in no current dictionary of English, not even the OED. Yet it is the term used without discussion for this diacritic in as authoritative and influential a source as The Unicode Standard (1991, 2000).' (J. C. Wells, 'Orthographic diacritics and multilingual computing' (*Language Problems and Language Planning*, vol. 24, no. 3 (2001); http://www.phon.ucl.ac.uk/home/wells/dia/diacritics-revised.htm.) Nor is it in my *Chambers*.

18 Bringhurst, p. 134.

19 ibid. p. 49.

20 ibid.

21 Bringhurst, p. 48.

22 *Tact in Typographical Design* (Cambridge, Rampant Lions Press, 1962), p. 5.

4 Points of style (*pages 65–77*)

1 G. V. Carey, *Punctuation* (Cambridge, 1957), p. vi.

2 Mackays of Chatham, *Type for Books: a Designer's Manual* (The Bodley Head, 1976), p. xii.

3 *Lund Humphries Desk Book*, 5th edn (Lund Humphries, 1971), unpaginated ('house rule' no. 10).

4 Herbert Rees, *Rules of Printed English* (Darton, Longman & Todd, 1970), unpaginated (rule 265).
'There are some who follow the rule laid down in *Modern English Usage* but admit one exception, that of inserting a full-stop when the abbreviation is itself a prounceable word: e.g. "Cpl" and "Bt", but "Bart." (there is, indeed, something to be said for making a Coy. Commander distinguishable from a Coy Commander).' (G. V. Carey, *Mind the Stop* (Penguin, 1971), pp. 32–3.)

5 R. M. Ritter, *The Oxford Guide to Style* (Oxford, 2002), p. 63.

6 C. A. Hurst and F. R. Lawrence, *Letterpress: Composition and Machine-work* (Ernest Benn, 1963), p. 83.

7 *Oxford Guide to Style*, pp. 64–5.

8 James Sutton and Alan Bartram, *Typefaces for Books* (The British Library, 1990), p. 282.

9 ibid. p. 283.

10 David Jury, *About Face* (RotoVision, 2000), p. 46. *The Oxford Guide to Style* advises against the decimal: 'Use a full point in decimals. (Decimal currencies were formerly considered a special case, with their point set in the medial position – £1·17 – but this convention is rarely maintained now.)' (p. 168); 'This style has long been out of favour, especially as it may be confused with a medial-dot multiplication symbol, and should not be used unless reproducing a facsimile' (p. 171).

11 *Rules of Printed English*, nos. 66–9.
Herbert Rees gives five interesting examples of 'Miscellaneous uses of dashes' in *Monotype Newsletter*, no. 88 (February 1971), p. 17 – one of which shows en-dash and em-dash used together.
'The dash can be used to prolong the sound of a particular letter, as in the case of a stutter. In this context, an en rule is sufficient, but note the em rule after the "growl" in the following:
'Gr–r–r—there go, my heart's
abhorrence!
Water your damned flower-pots, do!'
This is better than his examples in *Rules of Printed English*.

12 Flann O'Brien, *The Hard Life* (Macgibbon & Kee, 1961), p. 127. In this, the British edition (set in Monotype Fournier by Messrs Taylor Garnett Evans & Co. Ltd of Manchester), en-dashes (followed by word-space) are used in the dialogue as our example shows, while unspaced em-dashes are used for parenthetical matter; the American edition (Pantheon, 1962; designed by Vincent Torre; set in Linotype Electra) uses unspaced em-dashes for both dialogue and parenthetical matter.

13 *The Elements of Typographic Style*, p. 80.

14 *Monotype Newsletter*, no. 88, p. 17.

15 Richard Hendel, *On Book Design*, p. 44.

16 *Finer Points*, p. 25.

17 ibid.

18 ibid. p. 20.

19 ibid. p. 21.

20 *Letters of Credit*, pp. 76–7.

21 *Introduction to Typography*, p. 7.

5 Types for books (*pages 79–132*)

1 *A Tally of Types* (Cambridge, 1953), p. 44.

2 *An Approach to Type*, 2nd edn (Blandford, 1961), p. 76.

3 *Methods of Book Design*, 3rd edn, p. 108. His view was modified from his sec-ond edition where he writes: 'In the founts below 12-point the design is not seen at its best, since the letters are small and light; the grace of the individual let-ters is more evident in the larger sizes' (Oxford, 1966, p. 80).

4 Bruce Rogers, *The Centaur Types* (Chicago, October House, 1949), p. 13.

5 *A Tally of Types*, p. 56.

6 James Moran, *Stanley Morison* (Lund Humphries, 1971), p. 139.

7 ibid, p. 140. The Poliphilus type also featured a small question mark which is retained in the digital version; no alternative was ever produced.

8 From the essay to the *De Aetna* (Officina Bodoni, 1969) translated by John Barr in *Officina Bodoni* (The British Library, 1978), p. 43.

9 *A Tally of Types* (introduction to the 1973 edition, edited by Brooke Crutch-ley), p. 32.

10 Moran, p. 79.

11 *Letters of Credit* (Gordon Fraser, 1986), p. 40. The Linotype works were locat-ed at Altrincham.

12 'Its most distinctive peculiarity is the long downward tail to the italic k – criti-cized by all who disliked any tendency to flourish.' (*A Psychological Study of Typography*, p. 37.) This particular flourish is owed to necessary accommoda-tion of the Linotype technology which limited the widths of letters.

13 *A Tally of Types* (1953), p. 23.

14 *The Making of Books*, p. 260.

15 ibid. p. 209.

16 Netty Hoeflake, 'Van Dijck', *A Tally of Types* (1973), p. 113.

17 'Monotype Van Dijck and Christoffel Van Dyck', *Signature*, no. 6 (1937), p. 46.

18 In his article in the appendix of the 1973 edition of *A Tally of Types*, p. 118.

19 *Methods of Book Design*, 3rd edn, p. 120.

20 *Fine Print*, vol. 10, no. 1 (January 1984), p. 30.

21 *A Tally of Types*, p. 21. The first issue of *The Imprint* contained an advertise-ment inserted by the editors for 'the services of a young man of good education and preferably of some experience in publishing and advertising' to which Stan-ley Morison, aged twenty-three, unhappy in his job as a bank clerk and already interested in typography, replied and thence found his true métier.

22 *Typefaces for Books* (The British Library, 1990), p. 172.

23 *A Tally of Types*, p. 73.

24 S. H. Steinberg, *Five Hundred Years of Printing*, p. 169. In Stanley Morison's *On Type Designs* (Benn, 1962), p. 48, the figure is wrongly given as 2,204.

25 *An Introduction to the History of Printing Types* (Wace, 1961), pp. 61–3.

26 The switching may have been done spitefully. Relations between Morison and the works manager F. H. Pierpont were never good.
'Morison was perhaps rather disheartened with Monotype: neither Garamond, nor Baskerville, nor Poliphilus and Blado had been produced exactly as he wished. Fournier had suffered a worse disaster: as with Baskerville, two ver-sions had been produced, a "rough" and a "smooth"; while Morison was in America, there had been some doubt as to which version to pursue, and on 15

October, in the confusion after Duncan's death, the works decided to proceed with the one Morison did not prefer, the smooth. Matrices of 14pt and an 18pt italic were completed by March, but Morison had only just learnt what had happened. While he was away Burch and Pierpont argued, but it had gone too far for the "rough" Fournier, later christened Barbou, to be reinstated; on his return at the end of May he succeeded in rescuing the matrices of one size.' (Nicolas Barker, *Stanley Morison*, p. 177.)

Harold Duncan was the managing director (1900–24) who had employed Morison in 1923 and was his patron and supporter; William I. Burch was Duncan's successor – 'decisive but diplomatic – and respectful of Frank Pierpont's authority within his own empire at Salfords' (James Mosley, 'Eric Gill's Perpetua Type', *Fine Print*, vol. 8, no. 3 (July 1982), p. 93).

27 *A Tally of Types*, p. 80.

28 John Baskerville was buried, in accordance with the directions given in his will, in a conical building which he had converted from a windmill, in his garden at Easy Hill (his home near Birmingham). His will is quoted by Josiah Benton in *John Baskerville: Type-Founder and Printer, 1706–1775* (New York, The Typophiles, 1944), pp. 82–4:

'My further will & pleasure is and I Hearby Declare that the Device of Goods & Chattles as Above is upon this Express Condition that my Wife in Concert with my Ex^{ors} do Cause my Body to be Buried in a Conical Building in my own premises, Heartofore used as a mill which I have lately Raised Higher and painted and in a vault which I have prepared for It. This Doubtless to many may appear a Whim perhaps It is so – But is a whim for many years Resolve'd upon as I have a Hearty Contempt for all Superstition the Farce of a Consecreated Ground the Irish Barbarism of Sure and Certain Hopes &c. I also consider Revelation as It is call'd Exclusive of the Scraps of Morality casually Intermixt with It to be the most Impudent Abuse of Common Sense which Ever was Invented to Befool Mankind. I Expect some srewd Remark will be made on this my Declaration by the Ignorant & Bigotted who cannot Distinguish between Religion & Superstition and are Taught to Believe that morality (by which I understand all the Duties a man ows to God and his fellow Creatures) is not Sufficient to entitle him to Divine favour with professing to believe as they Call It Ceartain Absurd Doctrines & mysteries of which they have no more Conception than a Horse. This Morality Alone I profess to have been my Religion and the [Rule] of my Actions. to which I appeal how far my profession and practice have Been Consistant.'

And this was his epitaph:

Stranger.
Beneath this Cone in Unconscrated [*sic*] Ground
A Friend to the Liberties of Mankind Directed his Body be Inhum'd
May his Example Contribute to Emancipate thy Mind
From the Idle Fears of Superstition
And the Wicked Arts of Priesthood.

But he did not remain there, for the property was sold after his widow's death to John Ryland, Esq., who was living there when the house was attacked and burnt in the riots of 1791; the surrounding grounds were then converted to canal wharves by Thomas Gibson, an iron merchant, with a canal cut through, the old windmill demolished, but Baskerville's body beneath was 'undisturbed and apparently completely forgotten until the leaden coffin in which it was contained was accidentally discovered in December 1820' (Benjamin Walker, *The Resting Places of John Baskerville, the Thrice-Buried Printer* (City of Birmingham

School of Printing, 1944), p. 4). We are indebted to John Alfred Langford for including in the second volume of his *A Century of Birmingham Life* (Birmingham, E. C. Osborne, 1868) the text of 'Disinterment of Mr. Baskerville', from the *Aris's Birmingham Gazette* of 28th May 1821, which records that when the workmen discovered the coffin, 'it was however immediately covered up, and remained untouched until a few days since, when, the spot having been recently let for a wharf, it became necessary to remove the coffin, and it was accordingly disinterred, and deposited in Messrs. Gibson and Son's warehouse, where a few individuals were allowed to inspect it' (p. 358). 'The body was in a singular state of preservation, considering that it had been underground about 46 years. It was wrapt in a linen shroud... The skin on the face was dry and perfect. The eyes were gone, but the eyebrows, eyelashes, lips, and teeth remained. The skin on the abdomen and body generally was in the same state as that of the face. An exceedingly offensive effluvia, strongly resembling decayed cheese, arose from the body, and rendered it necessary to close the coffin in a short time...' It remained in the Gibson's warehouse in Cambridge Street for eight years until it was transferred to the shop of Job Marsten, a plumber and glazier. The coffin was again opened and viewed and the eighteen-years-old Thomas Underwood made a sketch of the corpse. Benjamin Walker says that the 'often repeated story that Marston made a public exhibition of the corpse, and that he charged a shilling a head for permission to view it . . . is not confirmed by any contemporary evidence. It is a fact, however, that many people did see it at the time . . .' And it was quite decayed by now. Thomas Underwood records that 'The body was much discomposed, but the teeth were perfect'; he believed that the 'effluvium' of the great man's corpse made people ill. ('Dr. Male and his daughter, who lived at the top of Newhall Street. . . . I believe they were laid up for some time with fever. A surgeon in Newhall Street . . . who tore a piece of shroud, which he incautiously put in his coat pocket, and died in a few days. The only ill effect upon myself, who was there upwards of an hour, was a distaste for food for several days.') The presence of the Baskerville corpse in Marsten's shop had become 'something of a public scandal' (Benjamin Walker, p. 7) and Marston, according to the account of his widow (published in the *Birmingham Weekly Post* of 22nd November 1879), applied to bury it at St Philip's church but permission was refused because of Mr Baskerville's apostasy. Upon learning of Mr Marsten's problem, 'Mr. Knott, a bookseller' (the quotation marks are used in Benjamin Walker's account), offered to place Mr Baskerville in his family vault in Christ Church, as 'he should consider it a great honour for Baskerville's remains to rest there', and this was done in the autumn of 1829. It was done by stealth – that is, with the help of a friend of Marston's, Mr Barker, a solicitor of eminence and a churchwarden of Christ Church, who arranged to carelessly leave the keys to the catacombs on the hall table at his house in New Street where Mr Marston might find them. John Baskerville's remains contained in his lead coffin were interred in vault no. 521 and rested there peacefully, no-one was to know, the subject having 'ceased to be of any public interest' (Walker, p. 8), until 1892 when Talbot Baines Reed, upon a suspicion that Mr Baskerville might be found in the Christ Church catacombs, 'induced Mr. Albert Taylor, one of the churchwardens, to make a careful examination of the registered persons who had bought vaults in the catacombs, and to compare it with the list of persons buried in them', and on 12th April 1893, upon the orders of the vicar, the Revd Canon Wilcox, Baskerville's lead coffin with his name in his own type 'soldered very irregularly' on to it, was removed from behind a brick wall and once again opened, examined and then replaced, the brick wall rebuilt and the slab put back. The church was demolished in 1899 and Mr Baskerville was removed to the Church of England cemetery in

Warstone Lane where he remains recumbently to this day. The inscription on the stone at Warstone Lane reads:

IN THESE CATACOMBS REST THE REMAINS OF

JOHN BASKERVILLE

THE FAMOUS PRINTER

HE DIED IN 1775, BUT THE PLACE OF HIS BURIAL WAS UNKNOWN UNTIL APRIL 12TH, 1893, WHEN THE OPENING OF THE UNREGISTERED CATACOMB NO. 521 DISCLOSED A COFFIN, WHICH ON FURTHER EXAMINATION WAS FOUND TO CONTAIN HIS BODY; THE REMAINS WERE LEFT INTACT, AND THE COFFIN WAS REPLACED IN THE CATACOMB AND PROPER ENTRY MADE IN THE BURIALS REGISTER BY THE VICAR.

29 Salvador de Madariaga, *Portrait of a Man Standing* (George Allen & Unwin, 1968), p. 57.

30 Édition de Kehl, Baden, 1783–90. Beaumarchais had bought the copyright from the publishers Pancoucke for 160,000 francs. There was a seventy-volume octavo set and a ninety-two volume duodecimo. A special set printed on parchment at the cost of 40,000 francs was dedicated to Empress Catherine II (Steinberg, pp. 192–4). 'I got ready everything which I was to take with me to Ceylon, which included ninety large volumes of the beautiful eighteenth-century edition of Voltaire printed in the Baskerville type and a wire-haired fox-terrier.' (Leonard Woolf, *Sowing* (The Hogarth Press, 1960), p. 220.)

31 Translated from Pierre Simon Fournier, *Manuel typographique*, vol. 2 (Paris, 1768), p. xxxix, by D. B. Updike, *Printing Types*, vol. 2 (Cambridge, Mass., Harvard University Press, 1937), p. 103.

32 *Printing Types*, vol. 2, p. 107.

33 ibid. p. 108.

34 Steinberg, *Five Hundred Years of Printing*, p. 173.

35 *Printing Types*, vol. 2, p. 115. Bruce Rogers, referring to this passage of Updike's, says: 'Baskerville was very fond of letter-spacing and most of his work is, in that respect, extremely ugly.' (*Paragraphs on Printing* (New York, William E. Rudge's Sons, 1943), p. 92.)

36 ibid. p. 116.

37 *A Tally of Types*, pp. 84–5.

38 The overseer at Kehl, J. B. Colas, made several criticisms of Baskerville's designs: 'his small capitals were condemned as being too small, several of his italic capitals were to be altered (including his characteristic *N* and *T*), and the alinement of the numerals 3 and 5 was to be changed' (John Dreyfus, 'The Baskerville Punches 1750–1950', *The Library*, fifth series, vol. 5, no. 1 (June 1950), pp. 36–7). The baseline alignment of the 3 and 5 was consistent with French reforms and a 30D roman cast by Deberny & Peignot with this alignment is shown on p. 64 of James Sutton's and Alan Bartram's *Atlas of Typeforms*; but the Linotype version, derived from similar founts cast by A. Bertrand in 1930 (the types were sold by them to Deberny & Peignot in 1936), features the reformed italic capitals and the italic figures but not the raised figures.

39 *The Work of Giovanni Mardersteig with 'Monotype' Faces* (Salfords, 1967), p. 6.

40 'Collins Fontana Type', *Signature*, no. 4 (November 1936), pp. 43–4.

41 *Methods of Book Design*, 2nd edn, p. 93.

42 *A Tally of Types*, pp. 87–8.

43 ibid. pp. 88, 89.

44 ibid. p. 89.

45 Bruce Rogers, *Paragraphs on Printing*, p. 186.

46 A letter to Harry Carter from Bruce Rogers is quoted in the notes to *A Tally of Types* (1973), p. 132: 'there were only two cases of each size and I bought the English size and set a few sample pages of Virgil's *Georgics*. Mr Mifflin saw them at an exhibition and wanted to know why they were not used. After some consideration I sold them back to Riverside and we began setting the *Rubaiyat* in it.'

47 Morison's letter to Updike of 2nd February 1925 is quoted in Nicolas Barker's *Stanley Morison* (Macmillan, 1972), p. 174: 'A prospectus by Mr. John Bell of the British Library, Strand, London, announcing the completion, under his direction by William Coleman and Richard Austin, of a set of types which he claims to be superior to all other letters founded in England. The prospectus is set in the same type as the specimen, roman, and italic, and the types are known to you as "Brimmer". The prospectus is dated May 1788.'

48 *The Making of Books*, p. 265.

49 *Methods of Book Design*, 3rd edn, p. 126.

50 Oliver Simon, *Printer and Playground* (Faber, 1956), pp. 45–6.

51 See Moran, *Stanley Morison*, p. 144.

52 J. B. Nichols, 'Memoir of William Bulmer, Esq.', *Gentleman's Magazine*, vol. 100, pt 2 (October 1830), p. 305.

53 Peter Isaac writes that William Martin 'appears to have learnt the art [of punch-cutting and typefounding] in the Birmingham foundry' ('William Bulmer', *The Library*, 5th series, vol. 13, no. 1 (March 1958), p. 38). Sir William Croft, in his lecture delivered at St Bride in 1955, said the same, but it appears he was more certain of it:
'Before incorporating Bulmer in the enterprise which became known as the Shakspeare Press, Nicol had already secured the services as a punch cutter of William Martin who was the brother of Robert Martin, Baskerville's apprentice and sucessor, and who had himself been trained in the foundry at Birmingham.' ('William Bulmer', *Bulmer Papers*, vol. 1, no. 2 (February 1964), p. 24.)

54 Nichols, p. 305.

55 *The Dramatic Works of Shakspeare*, with text revised by George Steevens and Isaac Reed, 9 vols with 180 engravings, Shakspeare Printing-Office, 1792–1802.

56 T. F. Dibdin, *Bibliographical Decameron*, vol. 2 (William Bulmer, 1817), p. 384.

57 *Poems by Goldsmith and Parnell* (Shakspeare Printing-Office, 1795), pp. v–viii.

58 'The earlier half of the nineteenth century was a low ebb of typography, though technically it was a period of great advance. New type faces appeared in greater numbers than ever, issuing from the foundries without distinction to recommend them or promise of useful service; and like a horde of locusts they overwhelmed the good things that had been in the land before them. The old faces had vanished before the novelty and conscious excellence of the early moderns; and now Baskerville, Bodoni, Didot, Bell, and the rest of them were cast into limbo by the crowd of nonentities they had fathered.' (Seán Jennett, *The Making of Books*, pp. 218–19.)
'But the golden age of Bulmer and Bensley was to prove all too brief. In their own lifetimes the seeds of decay were to swell and ripen and bear their dead-sea fruit: they were scarcely gone when the storm burst in good earnest. What followed was, in point of fact, a *dégringolade* as catastrophic as that of Lucifer though less edifying. The up-to-date type-specimen-books of the period show what a pitch of horror had now been reached. Complacently they exhibit obese blood-curdling, monstrosities, gnarled attenuated freaks, pretentious uncalligraphic "cursives", that remind one of the pickled contents of jars confined to the more private departments of scientific museums. Even apart from these dis-

play founts the staple fare was, if less blatantly, about as bad as it could be. Then came the reign of the steel engraving. In row upon row of *Caskets, Gems, Amulets, Landscape Annuals,* and *Literary Souvenirs,* it battened upon the shattered remains of what had once, at least in name, been typography, and we were well on the way to the subacid, desiccated, sterilized nonentities of type-faces which were to hold the field for the next fifty years.' (H. V. Marrot, *Bulmer and Bensley* (The Fleuron), 1926, pp. 5–6.)

59 See Walter Tracy, *Letters of Credit,* pp. 192–3.

60 D. H. Lawrence, 'Eric Gill's "Art Nonsense"', *The Book-Collector's Quarterly,* vol. 12 (October 1933), p. 1.

61 Coomaraswamy, *The Transformation of Art in Nature* (Constable, 1934), p. 64.

62 See James Mosely, 'Gill's R : a Tailpiece', *Monotype Recorder,* new series no. 8 (Autumn 1990), pp. 38–9.

63 *The Letter Forms and Type Designs of Eric Gill* (Eva Svensson, 1978), p. 48.

64 *Tally of Types,* p. 98.

65 10th June 1928 (Walter Shewring (ed.), *Letters of Eric Gill* (Cape, 1947), p. 232).

66 23rd June 1928 (quoted in Barker, p. 234).

67 See James Mosley, 'Eric Gill's Perpetua Type', *Fine Print,* vol. 8, no. 3 (July 1982), p. 93.

68 Quoted in Mosely, p. 94.

69 *Tally of Types,* p. 101.

70 ibid.

71 *The Letter Forms and Type Designs of Eric Gill,* p. 48.

72 The table shown in Appendix C of the second edition of Hugh Williamson's *Methods of Book Design* (Oxford, 1966) records Perpetua as the sixth most frequently appearing type (following Bembo, Baskerville, Times, Fournier and Imprint) from among the 823 books included in the National Book League's annual Exhibition of British Book Production from 1945 to 1955, but it is not found in any of the 831 books shown at the NBL exhibitions from 1956 to 1963 (no exhibition was held in 1958). In a review of the 1964 NBL Exhibition in the *Monotype Newsletter,* no. 74 (1964), on page 4, the authors remark : 'Since 1952 Perpetua has been going through a recession, perhaps as a reaction from being somewhat over-used in the immediate post-war years.'

73 Special characters and double letter matrices for Plantin italic (a curly ℛ, ligatured ct, st, in, as, is, us), Baskerville italic (gg, gy, ct, st, a set of long esses), Blado and other types are shown in the *Monotype Recorder,* vol. 39, no. 2 (Autumn 1950). Some of them were made at the request of Francis Meynell. A few of them are available for current digital types (Garamond italic, Fournier).

74 *The Letter Forms and Type Designs of Eric Gill,* pp. 55–6.

75 ibid. p. 55.

76 *Eric Gill : Further Thoughts by an Apprentice* (The Wynkyn de Worde Society, 1982), pp. 11–12.

77 Sebastian Carter, 'Eric Gill : the Man and His Letters', *Monotype Recorder,* new series no. 8 (Autumn 1990), p. 13. But the metal type was promoted for use on coated paper : 'The lack of strong contrast in the shading and the light, slab form of the serifs make it possible to print Joanna successfully on coated paper as well as on other paper surfaces.' (*'Monotype' Composition Faces* (Salfords, 1972), p. 44.)

78 *An Atlas of Typeforms* (Lund Humphries, 1968), p. 98.

79 S. L. Hartz, 'Van Krimpen', *Penrose Annual,* vol. 54 (1960), p. 29.

80 *'Monotype' Composition Faces* (Salfords, 1972), p. 42.

81 'Towards an Ideal Italic', *The Fleuron,* no. 5 (1926), p. 121.

82 *Letters of Credit,* p. 101.

83 ibid. p. 119.

84 *The Officina Bodoni*, trans. Hans Schmoller (Verona, 1980), p. 104.

85 'The Dante Type', *Fine Print*, vol. 11, no. 4 (October 1985), p. 221.

86 *Ein Leben den Büchern gewidmet* (Mainz, 1968), p. 20; translated by John Barr, *The Officina Bodoni* (The British Library, 1978), p. 58.

87 'The Dante Type', p. 221. The 'unit values' were fractions of the 18-unit em assigned to each Monotype character (e.g. the capital M being 18 units, lower-case y 9 units, the lower-case i 5 units).

88 ibid.

89 Linotype have just recently (in 2004) released the Pilgrim type for desktop users but still without ligatures, non-lining figures, small caps.

90 'The Juliana Type Design', *S. L. Hartz in de grafische wereld* (Brussels, Bibliotheek Albert I, 1969), p. 46.

91 The types were made in Didot sizes which were cast on the next-largest Anglo-American bodies by Monotype users in UK and USA (e.g. 9D on a 10-pt body, giving the appearance of a half-point leading owing to a discrepancy of 0·0051 in., the Didot being 0·0148 in., the English size 0·01383 in.). Types of continental origin (Walbaum, Dante, Lutetia, Romulus, Spectrum and Univers) were issued in Didot sizes as they were intended primarily for the continental market and while this wouldn't prove disadvantageous to most printers (if they possessed the requisite moulds), the types produced in Didot sizes were significantly 'psychologically handicapped' in the non-continental market (see the *Monotype Recorder*, vol. 44, no. 4 (1959), pp. 3–4). The *Monotype Newsletter*, no. 83 (March 1968) refers to Stempel display sizes of 14 to 60 Didot (p. 19).

92 Hans Schmoller, *Two Titans: Mardersteig and Tschichold* (New York, The Typophiles, 1990), p. 68.

93 'The ligatures ff, fi, and fl must not be used for all combinations of these letters, but only as follows. Set them where the letters belong together in the stem of a word: treffen, finden, flehen; set fl finally (Aufl.) and fi where i begins a suffix (häufig); note that fi then takes precedence over ff: pfäffish. Otherwise use the separate letters: auffällen, Schilfinsel, verwerflich (so too Auflage despite Aufl.), i.e. where the letters link elements in a compound, or at the junction of a prefix or of a suffix beginning with l. Note too that fl should be set separately in words that have related forms with -fel-: zweifle from zweifeln, Mufflon from Muffel. In foreign compounds set Offizier, Effluvium; but in the proper name Effi use ff. . . . Whenever there is any doubt, set separate letters. (Some German houses do not use ligatures in roman at all.)' (*Hart's Rules for Compositors and Readers*, 39th edn (Oxford, 1983), pp. 108–9.) This may partly explain the indifference to f-ligatures at H. Berthold and other German digital type manufacturers.

94 The Stempel specimen of 1966 shows an f and i joined by the f-bar but the stem of the f is not curved over the i and the i retains its dot. This was designed by Tschichold as an 'alternative' (it is shown in a drawing of 1965 reproduced on page 69 of Hans Schmoller's *Two Titans*) perhaps because of the designer's own dissatisfaction with the standard fi. A similar italic fi (retaining i-dot) featured in the original metal Linotype and Monotype character-sets.

95 Hermann Zapf says of Palatino: 'From the start, the roman, boldface and italic were designed for the composing machine'; and it had 'been conceived primarily for jobbing work' ('Autobiography in Type', *Motif*, vol. 3 (1959), p. 38). The 10-point 'pilot size' of the foundry type, cut by August Rosenberger, was used in Zapf's *Feder und Stichel* (*Pen and Graver*), printed by Stempel in 1949. The Linotype Palatino (designed as Aldus was for the duplexed matrix) was in its 10-point design quite more similar to the design of the present Aldus than the Lino-

type and Monotype digital Palatinos are. A version of Palatino which was adapted for photo-composition ('Linofilm' Palatino, 1962) proved quite more popular than the metal version outside of Germany and it seems part of the reason was that it was so freely copied – or *pirated*: indeed, more than any other typeface. 'The first large scale work set in Linotype Palatino was the festival publication for the 50th anniversary of the Gutenburg Gesellschaft in Mainz, in 1950' ('Autobiography in Type'). Aldus-Buchschrift, as it was called in Germany (it was originally called Leichte Palatino-Buchschrift), was introduced at the DRUPA exhibition in 1954; it was 'first used in No. 339 of the Insel-Bücherei, Hugo von Hofmannsthal's *Reden und Aufsätze* (*Speeches and Essays*)'; a specimen was shown in *Imprimatur*, vol. 12 (1954–5) and 9-point Aldus was used for the text of *Imprimatur*, new series, vol. 1 (1957). The *Linotype-Schriftenreigen* (Frankfurt am Main, 1962) shows a text-setting with a double-stroke hyphen (=) which was included in the standard character-set along with the single-stroke hyphen.

96 The *Motif* which featured Hermann Zapf's 'Autobiography' also contained a review of his type designs by Hans Schmoller who delivered the following 'criticisms of the Palatino-Aldus group': 'their somewhat squashed descenders, possibly forced upon the designer by the apparent need to conform to a German 'standard line' laid down with scant attention to the aesthetics of type design; the wilful omission of half of the final serif in roman h, n, and m, which gives them something slightly Chaplinesque; the excessively tall t in the Palatino roman and italic (as if he had realized this, Zapf corrected the error in Aldus); the lack of true parallels in roman W and w; the intrusion of calligraphic elements in roman X, x, and Y; and the different level of the cross-bar in italic *E* and *F*. Most of these are minor shortcomings, but they deny the types that final degree of harmony and "normality" which, in this country at least, are demanded from typefaces intended for general continuous reading.' ('Hermann Zapf, Type Designer', *Motif*, vol. 3 (1959), p. 50.) The 'country' demanding harmony and normality to which Mr Schmoller refers is Great Britain.

97 Georg Trump was director of the Meisterschule für Deutschlands Buchdrucker from 1934 to 1953, succeeding the school's founder Paul Renner (proponent of the 'new typography', designer of Futura) who was forced to resign when the Nazis came to power. I have seen many examples of Trump's graphic design, illustration, woodcuts, painting – all of which may be rightly called exquisite; most of which is a bit too German for my tastes – and I regard him as an artist of remarkable sensibility. The best biography of Trump in English, short as it is, is Sebastian Carter's in his *Twentieth Century Type Designers*, pp. 110–15. 'Renner, anxious that the directorship should not go to a Nazi appointee, persuaded Trump to take it on, and Trump thereby undertook the diplomatic and administrative burden of steering the school through the difficult years which followed' (p. 111). Trump was called up and served as a company comander throughout World War II; he was wounded in the stomach towards the end of the war and because of this wound resigned from his post at the Meisterschule in 1953. We are considering the merits of types and typography in this book but one must note a certain uneasiness about including the work of the director of the institution which published the pro-Nazi document, *Grafische Berufsschule* in 1935 (shown on page 162 of the first edition of Robin Kinross's *Modern Typography*), and how many other pro-Nazi documents one doesn't know.

98 Many of Trump's designs show the influence of Ernst Schneidler under whom he studied at the Kunstgewebeschule at Stuttgart in 1919–23. Compare the shapes of his capital C, E, F, G, R in Trump-Mediäval to those of Schneidler Old Style.

Bibliography

Except where noted, the books and periodicals listed here were published in London; *Oxford University Press* and *Cambridge University Press* are called *Oxford* and *Cambridge*. *Penrose Annuals* were published by Lund Humphries. When it's of interest, the date of first edition, in brackets, follows the date of the edition I have used.

(Adobe InDesign) 'In Depth: Text and Typography', San Jose, California, Adobe Systems Inc., 2002. Available online as a PDF document.

Barker, Nicolas, *Stanley Morison*, Macmillan, 1972.

'Printing's Second Revolution', *Times Literary Supplement*, no. 3744, 7th December 1973, pp. 1491–2.

Barr, John, *The Officina Bodoni*, The British Library, 1978.

Bartram, Alan, 'The grid: an aid or an end?', *Penrose Annual*, vol. 63 (1970), pp. 169–80.

Making Books: Design in British Publishing Since 1945, The British Library, 1999.

Creating the Printed Page, BAS Printers/The British Library, 2000.

Beaujon, Paul (Beatrice Warde), 'The "Garamond" Types: sixteenth and seventeenth century sources considered', *The Fleuron*, vol. 5 (1926), pp. 131–79.

Bennett, William, *John Baskerville, the Birmingham Printer*, 2 vols, City of Birmingham School of Printing, 1937.

Benton, Josiah, *John Baskerville: Type-Founder and Printer, 1706–1775*, New York, The Typophiles, 1944 (1914).

Berry, W. Turner, and A. F. Johnson, *Catalogue of Specimens of Printing Types by English and Scottish Founders, 1665–1830*, Oxford, 1935. Introduction by Stanley Morison.

Biggs, John R., *Use of Type*, Blandford, 1954.

An Approach to Type, 2nd edn, Blandford, 1961.

Bluhm, Andrew, *Photosetting*, Pergamon Press, 1968.

Boag, Andrew, 'Monotype and photosetting', JPHS (*Journal of the Printing Historical Society*), new series 2 (Winter 2000), pp. 57–77.

Boag, Andrew, and Lawrence W. Wallis (eds), *One Hundred Years of Typemaking 1897–1997*, *Monotype Recorder*, new series no. 10 (1997).

Bringhurst, Robert, *The Elements of Typographic Style*, 2nd edn, Point Roberts, Washington, Hartley & Marks, 1996.

Burbidge, P. G., *Notes and References*, Cambridge, 1952.

Prelims and End-pages, Cambridge, 1963.

Burchfield, R. W. (ed.), *Fowler's Modern English Usage*, 3rd edn, Oxford, 1996.

Burt, Sir Cyril, *A Psychological Study of Typography*, Cambridge, 1959.

Butcher, Judith, *Copy-Editing*, 2nd edn, Cambridge, 1989.

Carey, G. V., *Making an Index*, Cambridge, 1951.

Punctuation, Cambridge, 1957.

Mind the Stop, Harmondsworth, Penguin, 1971.

Carter, Harry, 'Collins Fontana Type', *Signature*, no. 4 (November 1936), pp. 42–6.

'Monotype Van Dijck and Christoffel Van Dyck', *Signature*, no. 6 (July 1937), pp. 45–9.

'Optical Scale in Typefounding', *Typography*, no. 4 (1937), pp. 2–6.

A View of Early Typography, Oxford, 1969.

Carter, Sebastian, *Twentieth Century Type Designers*, Trefoil, 1987.

Carter, Sebastian, John Dreyfus, *et al.*, *Eric Gill: the Continuing Tradition*, *Monotype Recorder*, new series no. 8 (Autumn 1990).

Carter, Will, 'Monotype Spectrum', *Penrose Annual*, vol. 49 (1955), pp. 54–5.

Chambers English Dictionary, 7th edn, Edinburgh, W. & R. Chambers, 1988.

Chicago Manual of Style, The, 15th edn, University of Chicago Press, 2003.

Cinamon, Gerald (ed.), *et al.*, *The Monotype Recorder*, new series no. 6 (April 1987). Hans Schmoller number.

Clapperton, Robert Henderson, *Modern Paper-Making*, Blackwell, 1952.

(Clowes), *Book Types from Clowes*, 1965.

Collins, F. Howard, *Collins Authors and Printers Dictionary*, revised by Stanley Beale, 11th edn, Oxford, 1973.

(Cowells), *House Rules, for the Guidance of Compositors and Readers and our Customers*, Ipswich, 1952.

(Cox & Wyman), *Types at Your Service*, 1962.

Croft, Sir William, 'William Bulmer', *Bulmer Papers*, vol. 1, no. 2 (February 1964), pp. 13–29. Based on the St Bride lecture delivered in 1955.

Crutchley, Brooke, *To Be a Printer*, The Bodley Head, 1980.

Day, Kenneth, *Book Typography 1815–1965 in Europe and the United States of America*, Ernest Benn, 1966.

Dooijes, Dick, *Mijn Leven met Letters*, Amsterdam, De Buitenkant, 1991.

Dowding, Geoffrey, *Finer Points in the Spacing and Arrangement of Type*, Wace, 1954.

Factors in the Choice of Type Faces, Wace, 1957.

An Introduction to the History of Printing Types, Wace, 1961.

Dreyfus, John, 'The Baskerville Punches, 1750–1950', *The Library*, fifth series, vol. 5, no. 1 (June 1950), pp. 26–48.

The Work of Jan van Krimpen, Sylvan Press, 1952.

'Spectrum: Designed by Jan van Krimpen', *Penrose Annual*, vol. 48 (1954), pp. 47–53.

The Work of Giovanni Mardersteig, Salfords, Monotype, 1967.

'Sabon: the first "harmonized" type', *Penrose Annual*, vol. 61 (1968), pp. 63–76.

'The Impact of Stanley Morison', *Penrose Annual*, vol. 62 (1969), pp. 94–111.

'Beatrice Warde: the First Lady of typography', *Penrose Annual*, vol. 63 (1970), pp. 71–6.

'The Evolution of *Times* New Roman', *Penrose Annual*, vol. 66 (1973), pp. 165–74.

'The Dante Type', *Fine Print*, vol. 11, no. 4 (October 1985), pp. 219–21.

Dwiggins, W. A., *Caledonia: a New Printing Type Designed for Mergenthaler Linotype Company*, Brooklyn, Mergenthaler Linotype, 1939.

Ede, Charles (ed.), *The Art of the Book*, Studio, 1951.

Enschedé, B. F., *et al.*, *S. L. Hartz in de grafische wereld*, Brussels, Bibliotheek Albert I, 1969.

Epelboim, Julie, James R. Booth and Robert M. Steinman, 'Much ado about nothing: the place of space in text', *Vision Research*, vol. 36, no. 3 (1996), pp. 465–70.

Farleigh, John (ed.), *Fifteen Craftsmen and Their Crafts*, Sylvan Press, 1945.

Gill, Eric, *An Essay on Typography*, 2nd edn, Sheed & Ward, 1936; re-set, 1954; reprinted with an introduction, Lund Humphries, 1988.

(Gill, Eric), *Monotype Recorder*, vol. 41, no. 3 (1959). ('Commemorating an Exhibition of Lettering and Type Design by Eric Gill. Held at Monotype House, October 1958.')

Gowers, Sir Ernest, *The Complete Plain Words*, Penguin, 1962.

Hansard, T. C., *Typographia*, Baldwin, Cradock & Joy, 1825.

Harling, Robert, 'Eric Gill's Pilgrim (né Bunyan) Type', *Penrose Annual*, vol. 47 (1953), pp. 53–5.

  The Letter Forms and Type Designs of Eric Gill, Eva Svensson, 1978.

Hart's Rules for Compositors and Readers, 39th edn, Oxford, 1983.

Hartz, S. L., 'An approach to type designing' *Penrose Annual*, vol. 52 (1958), pp. 39–42.

  'Van Krimpen', *Penrose Annual*, vol. 54 (1960), pp. 28–30.

(Hazell, Watson & Viney), *Printing Panorama*, Hazell, Watson & Viney and Sun Printers Limited, 1951.

Heiderhoff, Horst, 'The Discovery of a Type Designer: Miklós Kis', *Fine Print*, vol. 10, no. 1 (January 1984), pp. 25–30.

Hendel, Richard, *On Book Design*, New Haven, Yale University Press, 1998.

Hersch, Roger (ed.), *Visual and Technical Aspects of Type*, Cambridge, 1993.

Hewitt, R. A., *Style for Print and Proof-Correcting*, Blandford, 1957.

Hlavsa, Oldřich, *A Book of Type and Design*, trans. Sylvia Fink, Peter Neville, 1960.

HMSO, *Rules for Authors and Printers* (H.M. Stationery Office Guide, part 3), 1935.

Hostettler, Rudolf, *A Selection of Types*, St Gall, Zollikofer, 1949.

Hurst, C. A., and F. R. Lawrence, *Letterpress: Composition and Machine-work*, Ernest Benn, 1963.

Hutchings, R. S., *The Western Heritage of Type Design*, Cory, Adams & Mackay, 1963.

Hutchins, Michael, *Typographics*, Studio Vista, 1969.

Hyder, Darrell, 'Swiss typography today', *Penrose Annual*, vol. 63 (1970), pp. 117–25.

Isaac, Peter G. C., 'William Bulmer', *The Library*, fifth series, vol. 13, no. 1 (March 1958), pp. 37–50.

  William Bulmer, Bain & Williams, 1993.

Jackson, Holbrook, *The Printing of Books*, Cassell, 1938.

Jarrett, James, *Printing Style for Authors, Compositors and Readers*, George Allen & Unwin, 1960.

Jaspert, W. Pincus, W. Turner Berry and A. F. Johnson, *The Encyclopaedia of Typefaces*, rev. edn, Blandford, 1983 (1953, 1970).

Jenkins, Nicolas, 'Redesign Book Design', *Penrose Annual*, vol. 63 (1970), pp. 159–67.

Jennett, Seán, *The Making of Books*, Faber, 1951.

Johnson, A. F., 'Romulus', *Signature*, no. 13 (January 1940), pp. 38–9.

  Type Designs: Their History and Development, 3rd edn, André Deutsch, 1966.

Jones, Linda Lloyd, and Jeremy Aynsley, *Fifty Penguin Years*, Penguin, 1985.

Jury, David, *About Face: Reviving the Rules of Typography*, RotoVision, 2000.

Kindersley, David, 'Optical letter spacing', *Penrose Annual*, vol. 62 (1969), pp. 167–76.

  Optical Letter Spacing for the New Printing Systems, Lund Humphries, 1976.

  Eric Gill: Further Thoughts by an Apprentice, Wynkyn de Worde Society, 1982.

Kinross, Robin, 'What is a Typeface?', *Baseline*, no. 7 (1986), pp. 14–18.

  Modern typography: an essay in critical history, Hyphen, 1992.

  Unjustified texts, Hyphen, 2002.

Krimpen, Jan van, *On Designing and Devising Type*, Haarlem, Tjeen Willink, 1957.

Kvern, Olav Martin, and David Blatner, *Real World Adobe InDesign 2*, Berkeley, California, Peachpit Press, 2003.

Lang, P. H., 'Swelled Rules and Typographic Flourishes', *Signature*, no. 9 (July 1938), pp. 43–52.

Langford, John Alfred, *A Century of Birmingham Life: or, A Chronicle of Local Events, from 1741 to 1841*, vol. 2, Birmingham, E. C. Osborne, 1868.

Lewis, Clive, and Peter Walker, 'Typographic influences on reading', *British Journal of Psychology*, vol. 80, no. 2 (1989), pp. 241–57.

Lewis, John, *Typography: Basic Principles*, Studio, 1963.
Typography: Design and Practice, Barrie & Jenkins, 1978.

Lewis, John, and John Brinkley, *Graphic Design*, Routledge and Kegan Paul, 1954.

(Linotype GmbH), *Linotype-Schriftenreigen*, Frankfurt am Main, 1962.

(Linotype & Machinery Ltd), *Linotype type faces and matrix information*, 1969.

(Lund Humphries), *Lund Humphries Desk Book*, 5th edn, 1971.

MacCarthy, Fiona, *Eric Gill*, Faber, 1989.

McIntosh, Ronald, *Hyphenation*, Bradford, Computer Hyphenation, 1990; html version at www.hyphenologist.co.uk/book/BOOK-ED3.HTM.

(Mackays of Chatham), *Type for Books: a Designer's Manual*, The Bodley Head, 1976 (1959).

McLean, Ruari, *Modern Book Design*, Longmans, 1951.
Modern Book Design from William Morris to the Present Day, Faber, 1958.
'Jan Tschichold', *Penrose Annual*, vol. 63 (1970), pp. 89–105.
Jan Tschichold: Typographer, Lund Humphries, 1976.
The Thames and Hudson Manual of Typography, Thames and Hudson, 1980.
True to Type, New Castle, Delaware, Oak Knoll/London, Werner Shaw, 2000.

McLean, Ruari (ed.), *Typographers on Type*, Lund Humphries, 1995.

Mardersteig, Giovanni, *Ein Leben den Büchern gewidmet*, Mainz, Verlag der Gutenberg-Gesellschaft, 1968.
The Officina Bodoni: an Account of the Work of a Hand Press 1923–1977, ed. and trans. Hans Schmoller, The Bodley Head, 1980.

Marrot, H. V., *William Bulmer, Thomas Bensley: a Study in Transition*, The Fleuron, 1926.

Meynell, Sir Francis, *English Printed Books*, Collins, 1946.
My Lives, The Bodley Head, 1971.

Middendorp, Jan, *Dutch Typography*, Rotterdam, 010 Publishers, 2004.

(Monotype Ltd), *Monotype Recorder*, vol. 41, no. 4 (1959). (Walbaum types.)
Monotype Recorder, vol. 42, no. 2 (Spring 1961). (Monophoto filmsetters.)
Monotype Newsletter, no. 72 (February 1964). (Word division.)
Monotype Newsletter, no. 73 (June 1964). (Capitalisation; Apollo specimens.)
Monotype Newsletter, no. 83 (March 1968). (Edward Young on book typography.)
Monotype Newsletter, no. 84 (September 1968). (Justified and fixed word-spacing.)
Monotype Newsletter, no. 88 (February 1971). (On dashes.)
Specimen Book of 'Monophoto' Filmsetter Faces (1960s).
'Monotype' Composition Faces, 1972.
Lasercomp Typeface Index, 1987.
Dante (type specimen), 1992.

Moran, James, *Stanley Morison 1889–1967*, *The Monotype Recorder*, vol. 43, no. 3 (Autumn 1968).
Stanley Morison, Lund Humphries, 1971.

Cox & Wyman Ltd: a Company History, Cox & Wyman, 1977.

Clays of Bungay, Richard Clay, 1984.

Morison, Stanley, 'Towards an Ideal Italic', *The Fleuron*, no. 5 (1926), pp. 93–129.

    On Type Designs of the Past and Present, rev. edn, Ernest Benn, 1962 (The Fleuron, 1926).

    First Principles of Typography, Cambridge, 1951 (1936).

    John Bell 1745–1831, Cambridge, 1930.

    Tact in Typographical Design, Cambridge, Rampant Lions Press, 1962. (Extract from the introduction to *The Typographic Book*, Ernest Benn, 1963.)

    A Tally of Types, Cambridge, 1973 (1953).

Morison, Stanley, and Kenneth Day, *The Typographic Book*, Benn, 1963.

Mosley, James, 'Eric Gill's Perpetua Type', *Fine Print*, vol. 8, no. 3 (July 1982), pp. 90–5.

Newdigate, Bernard H., 'Book Production Notes' (on Linotype Baskerville and Georgian), *The London Mercury*, vol. 25, no. 1 (November 1931), p. 103.

    The Art of the Book, Studio, 1938.

(Nichols, J. B.), 'Memoir of William Bulmer, Esq.', *Gentleman's Magazine*, vol. 100, pt 2 (October 1830), pp. 305–10.

Owens, L. T., *J. H. Mason: Scholar-Printer*, Frederick Muller, 1976.

Pardoe, F. E., *John Baskerville of Birmingham*, Frederick Muller, 1975.

Partridge, Eric, *You Have a Point There*, Hamish Hamilton, 1964 (1953).

(Penguin Books), *The Penguin Story*, Harmondsworth, Penguin, 1956.

    Penguin's Progress 1935–1960, Harmondsworth, Penguin, 1960.

    Editor's Manual of Penguin House Style, Harmondsworth, Penguin, 1973 (1967).

Pickering, Charles, *Bookwork and Imposition*, Pitman, 1948.

Plomer, Henry R., *A Short History of English Printing, 1476–1898*, Kegan Paul, Trench, Trübner, 1900.

Rayner, John, *Wood Engravings by Thomas Bewick*, Penguin, 1947.

Reed, Talbot Baines, *A History of the Old English Letter Foundries*, Elliot Stock, 1887; revised and enlarged edn by A. F. Johnson, Faber & Faber, 1952.

Rees, Herbert, *Rules of Printed English*, Darton, Longman & Todd, 1970.

René-Martin, Linda, 'Variations on the typographer', *Penrose Annual*, vol. 56 (1962), pp. 24–30.

Ritter, R. M., *The Oxford Guide to Style*, Oxford, 2002.

Rogers, Bruce, *Report on the Typography of the Cambridge University Press Prepared in 1917 at the Request of the Syndics*, Cambridge, 1950.

    Paragraphs on Printing, New York, William E. Rudge's Sons, 1943; reprinted New York, Dover, 1979.

    The Centaur Types, Chicago, October House, 1949.

Roberts, Raymond, *Typographic Design*, Ernest Benn, 1966.

Rogerson, Ian, *George W. Jones: Master of Master Printers 1860–1942*, Manchester Metropolitan University Library, 1993.

Ryder, John, *The Case for Legibility*, The Bodley Head, 1979.

Schmoller, Hans, 'Hermann Zapf, Type Designer', *Motif*, vol. 3 (1959), pp. 49–50.

    Two Titans: Mardersteig and Tschichold, New York, The Typophiles, 1990.

(Seybold), *Seybold Report on Desktop Publishing*, vol. 4, no. 10 (June 1990), pp. 3–23.

Simon, Herbert, *Song and Words: a History of the Curwen Press*, George Allen & Unwin, 1973.

Simon, Oliver, *Introduction to Typography*, Faber, 1945; and Harmondsworth, Penguin, 1954.

    Printer and Playground, Faber, 1956.

Smeijers, Fred, *Counterpunch*, Hyphen, 1996.

Spencer, Herbert, 'The responsibilities of the design profession', *Penrose Annual*, vol. 57 (1964), pp. 18–23.

    The Visible Word, 2nd edn, Royal College of Art, 1969.

Steinberg, S. H., *Five Hundred Years of Printing*, 2nd edn, Penguin, 1966.

(Stephenson Blake), *Printing Types*, Sheffield, 1969.

Sutton, James, and Alan Bartram, *An Atlas of Typeforms*, Lund Humphries, 1968.

    Typefaces for Books, The British Library, 1990.

Tarling, Alan, *Will Carter, Printer*, The Galahad Press, 1968.

Thorpe, Joseph, *B. H. Newdigate*, Basil Blackwell, 1950.

Timperley, C. H, *Dictionary of Printers and Printing*, H. Johnson, 1839.

Tracy, Walter, *Letters of Credit*, Gordon Fraser, 1986.

    The Typographic Scene, Gordon Fraser, 1988.

Trevitt, John, *Book Design*, Cambridge, 1980.

Trump, Georg, *Vita Activa*, Munich, Typographische Gesellschaft, 1967.

Tschichold, Jan, 'Clay in the Potter's Hand . . .', *Penrose Annual*, vol. 43 (1949), pp. 21–2.

    I bogens tjeneste, Copenhagen, Forening for Boghaandværk, 1951 (*Designing Books*, New York, Wittenborn Schultz, 1951).

(Tschichold, Jan), *Leben und Werk des Typographen Jan Tschichold*, with notes by Werner Klemke, Dresden, VEB, 1977.

Updike, D. B., *Printing Types*, 2nd edn, 2 vols, Cambridge, Massachusetts, Harvard University Press, 1937; reprinted Oxford, 1962.

Walker, Benjamin, *The Resting Places of John Baskerville, the Thrice-Buried Printer*, City of Birmingham School of Printing, 1944.

Wallis, Lawrence, 'Filmsetting in Focus', *The Monotype Recorder*, vol. 43, no. 2 (Summer 1965).

    Electronic Typesetting: A Quarter Century of Electronic Upheaval, Paradigm, 1984.

    Taking Bearings in the New Technology, Wynkyn de Worde Society, 1988.

    Typomania, Upton-upon-Severn, Severnside, 1993.

Waite, Maurice (ed.), *The Oxford Spelling Dictionary*, Oxford, 2000.

(Warde, Beatrice), *The Monotype Recorder*, vol. 44, no. 1 (1970).

Wardrop, James, 'Mr. Watman, Papermaker', *Signature*, no. 9 (July 1938), pp. 1–18.

Western Printing Services Ltd, *The Western Type Book*, foreword by Hans Schmoller, Hamish Hamilton, 1960.

Williamson, Hugh, *Methods of Book Design*, 2nd edn, Oxford, 1966.

    Methods of Book Design, 3rd edn, New Haven, Yale University Press, 1983.

    Photocomposition at the Alden Press, Oxford, The Bodley Head, 1981.

Zachrisson, Bror, *Studies in the Legibility of Printed Text*, Stockholm, Almquist & Wiksell, 1965.

Zapf, Hermann, 'Autobiography in Type', *Motif*, vol. 3 (1959), pp. 33–49.

    Typographische Variationen, Frankfurt am Main, D. Stempel AG, 1963.

    Hermann Zapf and His Design Philosophy, Chicago, Society of Typographic Arts, 1987.

    'About micro-typography and the *hz*-program', *Electronic Publishing*, vol. 6, no. 3 (September 1993), pp. 283–8.

Index